RED, WHITE, OR YELLOW?

RED, WHITE, OR YELLOW?

The Media and the Military at War in Iraq

CHARLES JONES

STACKPOLE
BOOKS

Published by
STACKPOLE BOOKS
5067 Ritter Road
Mechanicsburg, PA 17055
www.stackpolebooks.com

Printed in the United States of America

10   9   8   7   6   5   4   3   2   1

FIRST EDITION

Library of Congress Cataloging-in-Publication Data

Jones, Charles, 1952–
    Red, white, or yellow? : the media and the military at war in Iraq / Charles Jones. — 1st ed.
        p. cm.
    Includes bibliographical references and index.
    ISBN 978-0-8117-0402-1
    1. Iraq War, 2003—Mass media and the war. I. Title.

DS79.76.J66 2008
070.4'495670443—dc22

                                                    2008005461

Table of Contents

Introduction

Covering war brings periods of boredom, confusion, and then—sharp as a rifle's crack—intense fear mixed with horror and sorrow. For many reporters and photographers, covering Iraq has added one more layer of uncertainty: clashes with the U.S. military, and sometimes the American public, over reporting such a politically charged conflict.

New York Times Baghdad correspondent Damien Cave had one overarching goal when he embedded with a U.S. Army Stryker platoon in early 2007: to report on the early days of the much-vaunted "surge" of American forces under Gen. David Petraeus. After witnessing from only a few feet away the tragic death of a beloved platoon leader, Cave exercised the same sound journalistic principles as the long line of talented war reporters before him, from Ernie Pyle to Joe Galloway to David Halberstam. "Our main concern was staying true to the substance and feel of what happened," he told me, to convey "the realities of war and the courage and emotions felt by those who fight."

Unlike his predecessors, though, Cave performed extra duty for the *Times*. Along with his wife, Diana Oliva Cave, he prepared a video of the events that transpired on Haifa Street in Baghdad. The video, which ran on the newspaper's website, added another dimension to his print coverage. But it also created an unexpected backlash in the States. When the sergeant's family in southern Texas saw the poignant footage of their wounded warrior, they were outraged and complained to their congressman and the army. Like so many news stories today—from presidential candidates to celebrity starlets to star athletes—the news-gathering process itself became news. The story of Damien Cave and his near-expulsion from Iraq fills an entire chapter of this book because it provides a case study of the difficulties of covering war in the twenty-first century.

Reporting on any combat in the era of 24/7 media, with a growing array of Internet-connected news outlets, has created a volatile situation between the media and the military. The invasion of Iraq and its messy, ill-planned aftermath left a minefield of unexplored terrain for the military's public-affairs specialists who must balance the public's right to know—a staple of American democracy—with the military's need for operational security.

Initially, I explored these issues from a safe distance, interviewing veteran correspondents such as Rick Atkinson of the *Washington Post*, Jamie McIntyre of CNN, and Jim Lehrer of PBS's *NewsHour* among them. However, I realized that only by venturing into Iraq would I get any sense of the actual situation on the ground. My time with the U.S. Marines at Camp Fallujah and the insights of the top public-relations officer there, Maj. Jeff Pool, proved invaluable in better understanding what some call the art of "perception warfare" and others dismiss as mere propaganda. Even the skeptics—understandably angry over the botched planning early in the war—should admit that the First Amendment needs to be honored as much as possible on the battlefield.

Even critics of the military and the government should appreciate the painstaking work of officers and enlisted men and women like Pool who try to find the right balance to inform the American public while not serving as dupes for enemy propagandists. It's instructive to consider the four rules that Pool shared with me one night at Camp Fallujah:

1. Tell the truth.
2. Don't be the enemy's public affairs officer.
3. Don't get anyone killed or fired.
4. No P.R. stunts.

Honesty is the underlying premise of these rules. During my visit in mid-2007, the marines were seeing some signs of success in western Iraq's Anbar Province, where they had forged an alliance with the Sunni sheiks. Yet there was an air of doubt, at times even pessimism, about the ultimate outcome of the costly intervention in the Mesopotamian quicksand. Most observers doubted that the U.S. could ever leave Iraq without leaving behind a bloodbath. But was Sen. John McCain's prediction of a century in Iraq the only option?

"It's already agreed we lost," Major Pool said of the media's consensus. "Now the question is: How can we lose gracefully? How can we lose *less*?"

This ambiguity put him and other public-affairs specialists in a tight spot. "How can you combat against that and *not* be the propagandist?" And how could they provide access to the fighting while still honoring the wishes of grieving families back home? Early in the war, Donald Rumsfeld had issued an edict blacking out coverage of the return of the flag-draped coffins of the increasing number of war dead. But as Rick Atkinson wrote after the 2003 invasion, "Every soldier's death is a public event." Yet doesn't the soldier—and his or her family—have an inherent right to privacy?

These were tough questions for tough people inside and outside the media, with no simple answers or clear-cut solutions. The next controversy was probably the click of a camera or the sending of an e-mail away. You'll meet a young Associated Press reporter, Lauren Frayer, who felt frustrated that her peers back home never read the newspapers and seemed to have lost their collective minds in a world of pop-culture news about the likes of Anna Nicole Smith and Paris Hilton. And you'll meet *Time* columnist Joe Klein, who graciously took time out with me in a Baghdad hallway to explain his passionate interest in the war's outcome.

What began for me as a cool examination of a distant war soon became a close encounter with the media, the military, and some of the Iraqis who were trying to pull their land out of its endless cycle of violence. My hope is that what I have recorded here will help shed light on their struggles—and the struggles of everyone working toward a world where peace, not war, is breaking news.

PROVINCES OF IRAQ

Chapter One

WAR?
WHAT WAR?

S itting in the chow hall at Camp Fallujah, Maj. Gen. Walter E. Gaskin glanced up from dinner and wearily shook his head at the news blaring out of the big-screen TV. It didn't matter whether it was Fox News or CNN, the two main networks that were kept on at military bases around Iraq. The headline story in June 2007 was still the same: Paris Hilton.

This bothered Gaskin, commanding general of the 35,000-strong II Marine Expeditionary Force (II MEF), charged with patrolling Anbar Province in northwest Iraq. Anbar, the size of North Carolina, appeared to be calming down after gaining a reputation as a hotbed of the Al Qaeda–led insurgency of 2004–06 in the province's largest cities—Fallujah, Ramadi, and Haditha. But by mid-2007, American commanders such as Gaskin were claiming a measure of military and political and stability in the largest of Iraq's eighteen provinces.

By arming the tribes that exerted the most control over the 1.2 million Arab Sunnis along the green belt of the Euphrates River, American military and State Department officials said they achieved a precipitous drop in hostilities and a resulting rise in confidence. Rather than dwell on the past, Gaskin and others predicted a future where peace was more than a mirage on the desert horizon.

The "Anbar model," as it had become known, led to the formation of new coalitions with Sunni groups that once fought shoulder-to-shoulder with foreign fighters from Syria, Jordan, Egypt, Chechnya, and Saudi Arabia in some of the bloodiest house-to-house fighting of the war. The policy of arming such recent foes was controversial—because the possibility always existed that they could turn against the Americans or the fragile Iraqi government led by the Shiites, long the doormat of the Sunni-dominated regime of deposed dictator Saddam Hussein. The same strategy had backfired in Afghanistan when CIA-armed freedom fighters in Afghanistan later turned their surface-to-air missiles on American planes after ridding their country of Soviet forces.

But over a dinner of fried chicken and mashed potatoes, Gaskin, a gregarious general known for chatting away the night with his troops in Camp Fallujah's mess hall, exhibited a kind of all-American optimism worthy of Ronald Reagan.

The message that turned around the Anbar sheiks and other key leaders, he said, was getting across to them that foreign "fighters killed [their] kids" and ruined their cities, where the sheiks formed the Arab equivalent of the Chamber of Commerce. After all that destruction, Gaskin said the Americans could justifiably say to the Sunni leaders, "Let Al Qaeda explain it."

The Americans had backed their words with action, he said, by training Anbar's men to defend themselves and avoid a repeat of the carnage that had killed their friends and family, sacked their businesses, and left their towns and cities in a shambles.

"That's where we are now," Gaskin said. Yet TV news was generally neglecting these developments, favoring the vapid saga of Paris Hilton getting in and out of jail. The starlet's image flickered on the screen, providing an unlikely backdrop as the general continued his sober assessment of the situation: "We have to work with the government and the military."

What about all the mistakes the Bush administration made in the wake of the 2003 invasion, from sending home the Iraqi Army to purging the government of Baathists—two acts that many military analysts agreed had sewn the seeds of the ongoing insurgency? "It doesn't matter how we got here," Gaskin replied earnestly. "It does matter that we're here. Pulling out before we're done only complicates things."

It had been four years since President Bush appeared on television from the White House to announce the invasion of Iraq. With American flags and family photos in the background, Bush kept his cards close to his vest, saying only that the "early stages" of the military campaign had begun. Later, it was reported that the president approved the launch of two F-117 stealth fighters, armed with a pair of 2,000-pound bunker buster bombs, to kill Saddam Hussein at Dora Farm, a family complex southeast of Baghdad on the banks of the Tigris River. The day before, a CIA operative had reported that Saddam was at the complex that bore the code name "slaughterhouse."

Staring earnestly into the camera, Bush informed America—and presumably Saddam, if he were watching from the safety of a fortified bunker—that he had launched "a campaign on the harsh terrain of a nation as large as California." This "could be longer and more difficult than some predict."

The preemptive attack of March 19, 2003, missed Saddam, but the president's prediction was on target. After the "shock and awe" air attacks on Iraq and the speedy, successful ground campaign by the U.S. Army and Marines, many of the dire predictions of the war's handful of vocal critics had come true. By mid-2007, some 3,600 Americans had died in Iraq, with tens of thousands more Iraqi soldiers, insurgents, and civilians perishing. Despite an additional 30,000 troops as part of the 2007 "surge" strategy to root out insurgents, sectarian strife continued to kill dozens of men, women, and children daily.

Yet if America did pull out its massive force—as a growing number of Democrats and even some Republicans were advocating back in Washington—General Gaskin said the U.S. would probably have to return to the "cradle of civilization" someday because of its strategic importance. "Why not finish it while we're here?" he asked.

It was the most pressing question of our time, yet on this summer night in Fallujah, I had the top commander in Anbar all to myself for dinner. At the time, I was one of only four embedded reporters in the province and thirty-nine in the entire country. I was told by Marine public affairs that there were only nine embeds with military units in Iraq during 2006. (These numbers exclude the dozens of reporters, editors, and other employees of several large American newspapers, wire services, or TV networks in Baghdad who work independently and are not embedded with the military). Even with the Baghdad contingent, the media's presence was paltry compared to the heady days of 2003 when more than 700 American journalists took up the Defense Department's offer to join American forces for the late-March invasion.

Gaskin, like many military commanders, was aware of the declining interest in the daily business of fighting and dying in Iraq. Glancing up at the big screen TV—a staple of the military's dining, fitness, and leisure facilities—he observed, "It amazes me how much coverage Anna Nicole [Smith] and Paris Hilton get." Months before, the lurid saga of Smith, the drug-addled sex kitten with eye-popping measurements, dominated the 24/7 cable news cycle. Now a rich waif named Paris was getting the celebrity treatment, Gaskin noted in disgust, "All because she wouldn't abide by the law."

Gaskin is one of America's top African-American military leaders, commanding a force of more than 35,000 Marines, soldiers, sailors, and airmen in what was known as Multinational Forces-West Iraq. His military career began with a Naval ROTC scholarship at a small college in Georgia. Given his blue-collar roots, the amiable general had a hard time comprehending his fellow countrymen's interest in starlets over soldiers.

"You gotta be joking, as far as the priorities of the nation go," he said. "These young men and women joined their military when the country was at war . . . to protect a way of life." He glanced around the room, filled mostly with young men and women who worked each day patrolling Anbar and training Iraq's police and military forces.

It was a shame, he said, that there was such scant coverage of the Anbar successes, and so little interest in the nuts and bolts of the story, the military's cooperation with local and regional officials to restore electricity, water, telephones, and transportation. "That's part of the story that's missing."

The general's lament was reflected in media studies conducted later that summer. "Press coverage of the war in Iraq declined markedly" between April and June 2007, according to the Washington-based Project for Excellence in Journalism. The three major issues of the war—the policy debate over the troop levels and funding in Congress, events in Iraq, and the impact on the U.S. home front—"filled 15 percent of the total news hole in the quarter, a drop of roughly a third from the first three months of the year, when it filled 22 percent," the study found, based on a broad weekly cross-section of American news media.[1]

"Americans aren't connected to this war," ABC correspondent Martha Raddatz told the Washington Post in late 2007. "The only people really paying the price are service members and their families. That's why I feel so strongly about telling their stories."[2]

Why the drop-off in interest in a war that reporters once rushed to cover? Did Americans really care more about vapid starlets than about their own sons and daughters at war? Was it a failure of the Bush administration in selling the importance of the story? Or was the media itself to blame for backing off the biggest story of the day?

Several days before meeting General Gaskin, I posed these questions to a star journalist I recognized at the Combined Press Information Center at the U.S. military command in Baghdad: Joe Klein, the Time magazine columnist and a regular on Washington talk shows.

As Klein and I waited to get our press credentials—complete with biometric eye scans—he gave me the Reader's Digest version of how he came to be in a hallway filled with sleepy journalists and cheerful public affairs personnel.

"I'm not a war correspondent, obviously. I'm a political columnist," said the once-anonymous author of *Primary Colors*, the satirical novel based on Bill Clinton's 1992 presidential campaign. "My story was I was in retirement. I had left the *New Yorker* after the 2000 campaign, which I thought was going to be the peak of my career. I was going to write a couple of elegant *New Yorker* stories a year. Then September 11th happened, and nine of my neighbors in the small town I live in in New York didn't come home."

Klein somberly explained how he'd decided it was time to learn about Islam and "to learn about the U.S. military in a way I never had before, and about [U.S.] intelligence."

So he came out of early retirement and started writing a column about world and political affairs for *Time*. And like General Gaskin, Klein said he'd noticed that his intense interest in the war and America's overall security situation was not shared by many of his countrymen. Reflecting back to 2001, he said, "From that moment to this, it has been a downward grade in public awareness of this story, while my level has remained where it is, and has actually increased as I've gotten to know the military and gotten to know the intelligence community, and really studied, and drilled down on this region."

Klein's hands fluttered like the wings of a dying bird as he described the declining arc of America's interest in its global situation, contrasted with his own ascent into the story. It was only eight o'clock in the morning, but he was in high gear.

Why the public apathy?

"Lack of leadership," he replied, "at the presidential level. You talk to any of the folks out here, and the second or third thing they'll tell you is the disconnect between what they're doing and where the country is. The comparison I like to make is my parents always told me about Franklin Roosevelt. Right after Pearl Harbor, Roosevelt told everybody to go out and buy maps of the world and boxes of pins. He became the national geography teacher. Our parents knew global geography a lot better than we do.

"Bush had a responsibility to do something similar, if he actually thought we were in a war, if he actually thought it was a long-term war against the forces of Islamic radicalism, which I truly believe. He had a truly educational function. But instead of actually educating us, he spun. The top priority inside the White House, infuriatingly to me, has been spinning the war, rather than fighting it—much less winning it."

With mortar attacks on the once-impregnable Green Zone on the rise, I asked Klein if he thought Baghdad in 2007 was similar to Saigon in 1975. Was it on the verge of falling? Or was it more like Korea in the 1950s, with America poised for a long-term occupation to prop up a wobbly government?

"I think it's something different than those two places," he said. "And it has really pissed me off that the Bush Administration has used those places as an example." In Vietnam and Korea, he continued, "you had homogeneity. Here you don't. Here what you have is a country which is not a country. What you have is something which was cobbled together in Cairo in 1921. So the analogies are not appropriate. We haven't seen this before. People I know in [U.S.] intelligence, one guy said to me, 'This really makes your brain hurt.'

"I've spent every day for the last four years thinking and reporting about this, and my constant question is how do we get from here to there? I've asked everybody," he said, including the U.S. commander, Gen. David Petraeus, whom Klein was set to visit. The general's public affairs team lingered nearby in the hallway, waiting for the right moment to interrupt Klein and spirit him away from me.

"Not a single person is able to say how we get from here to there," he said. But even though there was much doubt and confusion even at the highest level of the military, he said he would keep following the story. "My heart goes out to these folks [the military] because they're about the only people in our country who are taking this seriously."

When the Paris Hilton headlines were pointed out to him, Klein nodded and sighed. "I don't think we're taking [the war] seriously enough. I think all publications and networks are seeing the same kind of marketing surveys" showing Americans had grown tired of war news. "Advertisers don't want to have their ads on pages next to it," he said. "We've gotten really lazy as a country. I named a character in *Primary Colors* after this. Orlando Ortzio, the governor of New York. Machiavelli said *ortzio* is the greatest enemy of the republic. *Ortzio* is Italian for 'indolence.'"

One of Petraeus's senior staff members arrived to lead Klein away. Before he left, Klein called covering Iraq "the most frustrating and rewarding experience of my life as a journalist."

Unlike many of his colleagues in the American media, though, Klein had come back for more.

Chapter Two

BRIGHT
SHINING WAR

After Rex Bowman saw the Twin Towers fall, he knew it was time to renew his passport. He was far from New York City, laboring in a one-man news bureau in southwest Virginia, with about as much chance of traveling abroad as he had of covering the Super Bowl. But something in Bowman's bones told him to start preparing for war.

"I went out and got my passport after 9/11," recalled the slight, self-effacing Virginian with a salt-and-pepper goatee. "I knew a war was coming. I knew we'd go to Afghanistan."

At forty-two, Bowman may have lacked combat experience, but he did know a few things about the military. In the 1980s, he worked in U.S. Air Force intelligence, including a two-year stint in Berlin as a Russian linguist and occasionally as a courier delivering top-secret documents before the end of the Cold War. He met his future wife, Jennifer, in Germany and followed her when she took a job at the National Security Agency near Washington, DC. After leaving the air force, he worked for the *Washington Times* but eventually returned to his favorite part of the country, the Blue Ridge Mountains and the comfortable city of Roanoke, Virginia.

One veteran journalist who never shied away from questioning authority was Rick Atkinson, the Pulitzer Prize–winning reporter and historian. The son of a career army officer, Atkinson won an appointment to the U.S. Military Academy when he graduated from high school in 1970. But he did an about-face from West Point because of the changing times; the Vietnam War and the post-Woodstock culture took him down a different career path than his father.

Yet even in the heights of early 1970s revelry, Atkinson remained a precocious scholarship student at East Carolina University, tearing through the prose and poetry of Faulkner, Fitzgerald, Bellow, Vonnegut, Stevens, Yeats, and Joyce. After earning a master's degree in English at the University of Chicago, Atkinson set out to earn a living by his pen. He spent a year at an obscure small newspaper in Pittsburg, Kansas, then was snatched up by the *Kansas City Star*. He quickly distinguished himself as an aggressive reporter who could write with the panache and keen eye for detail of the *Star*'s most famous alumnus, Ernest Hemingway.

Atkinson's literate style of reporting crested early in 1981 when he covered the reunion of West Point graduates of the Class of 1966—the class that had lost the most men (thirty) in Southeast Asia. The Pulitzer committee cited his multipart series when it awarded Atkinson its 1982 prize for national reporting. Later he would expand the newspaper series into his critically acclaimed book *The Long Gray Line: The American Journey of West Point's Class of 1966*.

The might-have-been West Pointer then marched over to the *Washington Post* and became a Pentagon and war correspondent, covering the first Gulf War (chronicled in his second book, *Crusade*) and the debacle in Somalia, and writing news and features about the military and soldiers around the world.

But by the time George W. Bush's administration began its secret preparations to invade Iraq, Atkinson had left the *Post* to work full time on a trilogy about World War II. In December 2002, he received a call from the newspaper's publisher, Donald Graham, asking him to return to the *Post* on assignment to beef up the paper's military reporting. The timing was fortuitous: he had just finished the first book of his trilogy,

An Army at Dawn, and a break from the solitary world of authorship held a certain appeal.

His trip to Baghdad started inauspiciously enough in the parking lot of a Shoney's restaurant in Hopkinsville, Kentucky, where he joined about sixty other journalists on chartered buses bound for nearby Fort Campbell, home of the 101st Airborne Division.

Earlier, he had received a seven-page document listing the ground rules for the estimated 777 reporters and photographers joining army, navy, air force, and marine units under a Defense Department plan that had been worked out with news organizations. The rules were meant to avoid the pain, agony, and criticism that followed the tightly controlled press policies of the first Gulf War more than a decade before.

More often than not, Gulf War I was an exercise in government censorship and image management—what *Wall Street Journal* correspondent John J. Fialka called "a finely orchestrated burst of high-tech violence where smart bombs landed precisely on the cross hairs." The rescue of Kuwait from Saddam's marauders marked the first time the major television networks—taking CNN's lead—created martial theme music and displayed glitzy, star-spangled logos. America's last war of the twentieth century became a branded product, like Air Jordans, Starbucks, or Apple computers.

But for journalists desperately trying to file stories or photos 7,000 miles away from their home bases, the Gulf War presented a gauntlet of frustration as reporters were "escorted away from most of the violence because the bodies of the dead chopped up by artillery, pulverized by B-52 raids, or lacerated by friendly fire don't play well, politically," Fialka wrote.[2] Ironically, the army's reluctance to allow real-time combat reporting in Gulf War I—fueled by lingering resentments over Vietnam coverage—led to a flurry of great press for the Marine Corps, which cranked its well-oiled publicity machine into high gear.

CNN's Christiane Amanpour later argued that such military gag orders should never be repeated or tolerated. "The Pentagon and the Western military establishment simply did not want reporters fouling up their war," she said of the first Gulf War. "For [many of] them Vietnam bad, the media is against us—us versus them." For a time, Jones admitted, he shared such knuckle-dragging attitudes.

But as he worked for the marines in Congress and at the Pentagon, his thinking began to shift. "I started to understand the relationship between the branches of government, and the role the media has is very central in keeping" leaders accountable, he said. Over time, Jones developed three principles in working with the press: first, tell the truth; second, it's okay to say, "I don't know"; and third, never duck an issue. The general had another saying that could apply to any sector in life, business, education, or politics: "Bad news doesn't get better with age."

The marines, as they showed in the Gulf War, are known for their press acumen—and, some say, manipulation. Military writer Ralph Peters told me, "The marines are generally prompt, forthcoming, and impressive; the army is gun-shy, clumsy, and naive; the air force lies without the least scruple, which sometimes works but sometimes backfires; and the navy just invites journalists to visit a carrier."

As Rick Atkinson pondered the best way to cover the army's 101st Airborne Division in Iraq, he knew from experience that he should get to know its commanders ahead of time so that they might trust him when the shooting started. The month before reporting to Fort Campbell with the media horde, he accompanied the 101st on some night helicopter operations and also spent time catching up with the commander of the 17,000-strong division, Maj. Gen. David Petraeus.

He first met the general in the early 1990s, when Petraeus was a major working in the Pentagon drafting speeches for the army chief of staff. Atkinson would chronicle the general's ultracompetitive, type-A tendencies, which had become legendary even before the man nicknamed "Peaches" graduated near the top of the West Point Class of 1974—the same year, incidentally, that Atkinson would have graduated had he taken a different path in life.

Petraeus became known as a legendary athlete who even at fifty years of age could outrun officers half his age. The general's legend grew in 1991 during a training exercise when a rifleman with live ammunition tripped and fell, accidentally firing a round that hit Petraeus in the chest. He never saw the muzzle flash. Petraeus survived the gunshot wound and barely made a sound when a tube was jammed into him.

Atkinson, for his part, had no intentions of trying to prove his toughness in the looming war in Mesopotamia. "I was too old to go with a rifle company," he told me. "It's not what I wanted to see." By attaching himself to Petraeus's command group, he hoped to have a "vantage point where I could look down" on the seven brigades, but also be able to look up at the command structure that would order the 101st and other large units into Iraq.

Despite all of his preparations, the veteran reporter was blindsided by the army, which invited another reporter to tag along with Petraeus. Jim Dwyer, a Pulitzer-winning writer for the *New York Times*, was brought in by "the wily army," which "wanted to keep me honest," Atkinson remarked.

Though he quickly befriended Dwyer, Atkinson said his hopes of avoiding daily deadlines were dashed by having the *Post*'s main competition traveling with him. Now he would be forced to produce daily dispatches to avoid getting scooped.

Petraeus became known as a legendary athlete who even at fifty years of age could outrun officers half his age. The general's legend grew in 1991 during a training exercise when a rifleman with live ammunition tripped and fell, accidentally firing a round that hit Petraeus in the chest. He never saw the muzzle flash. Petraeus survived the gunshot wound and barely made a sound when a tube was jammed into him.

Atkinson, for his part, had no intentions of trying to prove his toughness in the looming war in Mesopotamia. "I was too old to go with a rifle company," he told me. "It's not what I wanted to see." By attaching himself to Petraeus's command group, he hoped to have a "vantage point where I could look down" on the seven brigades, but also be able to look up at the command structure that would order the 101st and other large units into Iraq.

Despite all of his preparations, the veteran reporter was blindsided by the army, which invited another reporter to tag along with Petraeus. Jim Dwyer, a Pulitzer-winning writer for the *New York Times*, was brought in by "the wily army," which "wanted to keep me honest," Atkinson remarked.

Though he quickly befriended Dwyer, Atkinson said his hopes of avoiding daily deadlines were dashed by having the *Post*'s main competition traveling with him. Now he would be forced to produce daily dispatches to avoid getting scooped.

Chapter Three

ON THE
WAR WAGON

By early March 2003, the Bush administration was completing a sophisticated public relations campaign that managed to whip most Americans into a kind of war fever.

The opening rhetorical shots had been fired more than a year before during the 2002 State of the Union Address as Bush branded three countries—North Korea, Iran, and Iraq—as part of an "axis of evil" threatening the very existence of the free world. The tough talk was meant to draw historical parallels with the Axis powers of World War II—Germany, Italy, and Japan—that the U.S., Great Britain, the Soviet Union, and other allies defeated and to tap into the deep reservoir of patriotism that still remained after the 9/11 attacks.

Some 52 million Americans watched Bush's primetime performance on Tuesday, January 29, 2002, the largest audience for a State of the Union address since Bill Clinton's 1998 address during the peak of the Monica Lewinsky sex scandal.[1] At the time, Bush's approval rating as a "strong leader" stood at 66 percent. Though Bush lost the popular vote in 2000, the flag-waving crusade of Bush and his advisors—Vice President Dick Cheney, Secretary of State Colin Powell, Secretary of

Defense Donald Rumsfeld, and National Security Advisor Condoleezza Rice—won over many Democrats who probably never expected to be on the same side of the political fence as the plainspoken Republican from Texas.

As Hamid Karzai, the recently installed interim leader of Afghanistan, gazed down from the upstairs gallery, both sides of the aisle in Congress cheered Bush like a conquering hero. The administration's goal, Bush said, was "to prevent regimes that sponsor terror from threatening America or our friends and allies with weapons of mass destruction. Some of these regimes have been pretty quiet since September the 11th. But we know their true nature. North Korea is a regime arming with missiles and weapons of mass destruction, while starving its citizens." Moving on to the second part of his unholy trinity, Bush said, "Iran aggressively pursues these weapons and exports terror, while an unelected few repress the Iranian people's hope for freedom."

He saved what he viewed as the worst offender for last. "Iraq continues to flaunt its hostility toward America and to support terror. The Iraqi regime has plotted to develop anthrax, and nerve gas, and nuclear weapons for over a decade. This is a regime that has already used poison gas to murder thousands of its own citizens—leaving the bodies of mothers huddled over their dead children. This is a regime that agreed to international inspections—then kicked out the inspectors. This is a regime that has something to hide from the civilized world.

"States like these," Bush warned in his gravest tone, "and their terrorist allies, constitute an axis of evil, arming to threaten the peace of the world. By seeking weapons of mass destruction, these regimes pose a grave and growing danger. They could provide these arms to terrorists, giving them the means to match their hatred. They could attack our allies or attempt to blackmail the United States. In any of these cases, the price of indifference would be catastrophic."

Later in the speech, Bush vowed that he would "not wait on events while dangers gather."

The Bush administration spent the rest of the year backing up what became known as his "axis of evil" speech. Yet in this hyper-patriotic environment, most reporters failed to test the administration's dooms-day claims that Saddam Hussein had hidden weapons of mass destruction in his desert palaces and bunkers—and that Tel Aviv and even London were potential targets. During press conferences in late 2001 and early 2002, Bush was more likely to be asked about the location of Osama bin Laden, the situation in Afghanistan, or the collapse of Enron than about Iraq.

The media's less-than-stellar, sometimes docile, performance continued throughout 2002 and much of 2003, at least until the invasion. On March 6, 2003, two weeks before Bush ordered the war to start, he held a press conference at the White House during which he chose the questioners. The press corps acquiesced.

"Mr. President," one reporter asked, "how is your faith guiding you?"

Washington Post media critic Howard Kurtz later called such coverage a "sham," and Bill Moyers of PBS pointed out in his ninety-minute report, "Buying the War," that Bush invoked 9/11 and Al Qaeda at least a dozen times during the pre-invasion press conference. "The press has yet to come to terms with its role in enabling the Bush administration to go to war on false pretenses," Moyers said.

Bush's "axis of evil" speech had another, unintended link to World War II, the propaganda machine created by Adolf Hitler's spinmeister, Joseph Goebbels. "The conquest of the masses" was possible only by spreading propaganda "to prepare the ground psychologically for political action and military aggression," one Nazi officer said during the war crimes trials in Nuremberg after World War II.[2]

In the United States, the seeds of the media's acquiescence in 2003 were sewn less than two years before with the Al Qaeda–led attacks on New York and Washington. "The press operates out of New York City much more than Washington," Larry Sabato, the University of Virginia government professor and political pundit, told me. "That's why 9/11 was powerful." Most members of the media knew someone affected by or killed on 9/11 or reported on it themselves, Sabato said.

NBC military correspondent, Jim Miklaszewski, candidly admitted to such personal outrage when he saw the Pentagon in flames. As he stood looking at the gaping hole in the side of the massive building, Miklaszewski said, "My personal thought was, 'We've got to get those bastards.' And I think that's what everybody thought that day."[3]

Sabato, who regularly talks with major TV and print journalists, recalled the lingering impact of the 9/11 attacks on the collective psyche of the news media. He thinks it was on a par with the emotional wallop packed by the 1963 assassination of President John F. Kennedy, shaking the foundation of America's sense of security and knocking down the walls of journalistic objectivity. "I've been told almost all of the major figures broke down off the air [while covering 9/11]. It was so personal," Sabato said. "They realized this group of people wanted to kill them." CBS news anchor Dan Rather, for example, wept on David Letterman's late-night show after the attacks.

"The effect of that was just to dampen the natural critical instinct of the press. They are, after all, human beings," Sabato said, though he added with a laugh that some cynics might not agree. "You almost felt unpatriotic not to support the war. I think there were quite a few people with some doubts, but they chose to stay quiet." There was something else at play as well, the government and politics professor said: "The groupthink that exists in the press. The press likes to think of itself as anti-establishment and contrarian. Nothing could be farther from the truth."

A few lone wolves in the media pack did challenge Bush's insinuations about WMDs and the alleged links between bin Laden and Saddam Hussein. Warren Stroebel and Jonathan Landay, reporters with the Knight Ridder/McClatchey bureau in Washington, and Charles J. Hanley of the Associated Press, were among some of the earliest skeptics about the Bush administration's WMD fixation. They went out on a limb and reportedly lost a good deal over sleep over it.

But as Moyers noted in his PBS documentary, such digging and skeptical reporting never found a national audience because it didn't appear in the *New York Times* and *Washington Post*, the two papers that set the agenda for national news programs on TV. Walter Pincus of the *Washington Post* told Moyers about the culture of conformity that crept into the major papers, since reporters "do worry about sort of getting out ahead of something."

Such navel-gazing never took place before the invasion, and such introspection was impossible for reporters like Bowman and Atkinson, who had more immediate problems to solve before covering the war. They had to solve practical questions such as finding the right gear for the desert or booking the best flight to Kuwait City to meet marine or army units getting ready for the invasion.

Bowman's persistence with his editors in Richmond had paid off. He got the nod when the *Times-Dispatch* decided to send a reporter to join a marine unit staging with the American forces in Kuwait. "I didn't know how to go about it," Bowman admitted later when asked how he got ready for his long journey to the east. He started by doing basic reporting. He picked up the phone and called the Kuwait consulate in Washington.

Much to Bowman's delight, he was transferred to an embassy official whose father had once worked as an intern at the Richmond newspaper. The friendly Kuwaiti helped Bowman determine what shots to get and offered pointers on packing for the desert. "I went down to the army-navy surplus store in Salem and bought a used protective vest for $45 and a helmet for $20."

How did he talk to his family about his imminent departure to a war zone? "The kids had no say in it, but my wife knew it was something I always wanted to do. She was terrified of the prospect, but thought I'd hold it against her" if she tried to stop him from going.

Bowman tapped into a native optimism as he prepared to go, even with the potential of entering a chemical or biological war zone, at least as portrayed by the White House. "I go through life thinking nothing bad is going to happen to me," he said.

Suitably inoculated and armed with a satellite phone and laptop computer, Bowman kissed his wife and kids good-bye in Roanoke and headed off to war—to embed with the 1st Battalion, 4th Regiment, of the 1st Marine Division.

Did he have any qualms about the new embedding system that required him to sign a set of rules restricting what he could write based on the "operational security" of the American forces—a determination that would be made by military commanders on the ground? "Not at all," he replied. "I was surprised when I came back and discovered there'd been a debate about whether the embeds had been co-opted." Bowman listed three reasons for his pro-embed stance:

First, reporters were used to staying objective and not taking sides about news events they cover. "We're good enough journalists that we could write about our own mother's murder indictment," Bowman said. "It never dawned on me not to write anything [critical] about the people I was traveling with. I can't believe any reporter could be co-opted," he said, adding, "Maybe it's a naive faith in my profession."

Second, even though embedded reporters were limited in what they could see and write about—that is, they saw the war strictly from the perspective of the unit they were accompanying—the larger papers still write the "big-picture stories," Bowman said. Embedded reporters play a different role, providing "micro-pictures" that are augmented by the larger media "macro-pictures." Most papers, including his own, balanced the small and big pictures of the war, he said.

Third, Bowman asserted, "The alternative to embedding is so much worse that you had to be a proponent for it. . . . We're forgetting the Gulf War and what happened" in 1991, when news was censored and journalists had scant access to the troops doing the fighting.

After a fourteen-hour flight to Kuwait City, Bowman continued his makeshift preparations for covering combat. After arriving in the desert kingdom, Bowman realized that he'd neglected to bring a key item for surviving its cool desert nights: a sleeping bag. Along with Evan Wright, a colorful freelance writer covering the war for *Rolling Stone*, Bowman found a department store and bought a fleece sleeping bag for $10.

"It was like a toy compared to the high-dollar sleeping bags the marines were carrying around," he wryly observed. "It couldn't have been worse if I had a Snoopy and Peanuts Gang bag."

At Camp Anaconda, a staging area outside Kuwait City, about thirty miles south of the Iraqi border, Bowman met the roughly 200 men of Charlie Company, including their commander, Capt. Brian Collins, a 1994 graduate of the Virginia Military Institute. "I was surprised about the liberal arts educations of the marine officers," Bowman recalled.

Calling his company's lieutenants and sergeants to meet the reporter from back in Virginia, Collins told them, "We're going to trust him to do his job as well as we do ours." Feel free to talk to him, Collins said, but if you do, "Know that it could end up in a story." It was a key moment "that opened doors," Bowman said. "Over the next six weeks, I could go up to any lieutenant, or any marine for that matter, and ask them what was going on."

Also in March 2003, Rick Atkinson rejoined General Petraeus and the 101st Airborne Division at Camp New Jersey, a staging area for American troops in north-central Kuwait. Driving up the six-lane Route 80, he recalled the last time he'd seen this remote road, dubbed the Highway of Death, where Saddam's troops had fled Kuwait City in 1991 and were trapped and mowed down by American warplanes. He'd last seen the highway twelve years earlier, at the end of the first Gulf War, when he saw a landscape filled with burned-out vehicles and the loot left behind by the fleeing Iraqi Army. Now the place looked positively sterile. On the verge of this second war with Iraq—this time with the intent to thrust a dagger, or at least a cruise missile, into the heart of Saddam Hussein—the chief worry was that the Iraqi dictator would unleash clouds of sarin gas, botulinum toxin, or mustard gas. Reporters had spent plenty of time pondering the possible effects of this science-fiction scenario. The waiting reporters debated whether or not they would get "slimed."

The signal for a gas attack would be three honks of a horn, an army sergeant warned, or someone yelling, "Gas! Gas! Gas!" They would know a gas attack was underway when they saw someone else putting on a gas mask. Atkinson remembered Wilfred Owen and his poem "Dulce et Decorum Est": "Gas! Gas! Quick, boys!—An ecstasy of fumbling." He had serious doubts that he could meet the army's nine-second standard for getting his gas mask out of the case and strapped on his face.

Whatever his shortcomings in the equipment realm, Atkinson had a laserlike focus on the mission at hand: Stay close to Petraeus, whom he called "intense, good-humored, and driven," but not to the point of alienating him. "I did not want to make Petraeus's burden heavier by making him feel that every comment and gesture was under scrutiny," he later wrote. "Having a reporter at his elbow, and sixty in the division, made the 101st something of a fishbowl. But I sensed that he liked having someone to talk to outside the chain of command. Even amid seventeen thousand soldiers, a division commander can feel isolated and alone."[4]

The reporter and the general seemed to have a good working relationship—one that would be severely tested once the bullets and bombs started flying and the stories from the field scored direct hits back home.

Chapter Four

RED, WHITE, OR YELLOW?

As the media mobilized for war, military public-affairs specialists scrambled to meet the demands of the mission ahead. Like their civilian counterparts, the public-affairs officers (PAOs) often had to make things up as they went along.

"I got a phone call after Christmas 2002, that we might float around the Gulf" near Kuwait, recalled Capt. Kelly Frushour, a twenty-seven-year-old PAO with the 2nd Marine Expeditionary Brigade in Camp Lejeune, North Carolina. "We didn't get our deployment order until four days before we left in early January."

She joined about 7,000 marines on seven ships leaving from the naval base at Norfolk, Virginia, and wondered what lay ahead halfway around the world. "I knew the DOD [Department of Defense] was going to embed reporters, and it was my job to inform the commanders of that so they could prepare for the additional bodies. Battalions were to receive four bodies, and squadrons would receive two." Though it may sound clinical, she explained, the terminology had a clarifying purpose. "I say 'bodies' because if one news organization sent a reporter and a cameraman and a sound guy, that was three bodies. It wasn't three news organizations. It was three actual people."

Whatever you called them, the added bodies would not be universally welcomed by battalion or company commanders getting ready for this great unknown expedition into an armed-to-the-teeth police state with a history of using chemical weapons. Not everyone would react in the enlightened fashion of Captain Collins of the marines or General Petraeus of the army.

"I remember telling one commander that he was going to have a media embedded with him," Frushour recalled. "He said, 'No, I'm not going to do that.'" Though she was outranked by the lieutenant colonel, Frushour held her ground. "Sir," she recalled telling him, "I am not *asking* you to embed the media. I am letting you know that it *is* going to happen. DOD has mandated it. Every battalion has to do this."

The lieutenant colonel eventually cooperated, but Frushour knew there would be more challenges to come. Though she knew the overall concept of embedding reporters, the actual orders had not yet come by the time the marines sailed out of Norfolk. There were countless unanswered questions about how this would actually work, such as how TV crews would get around and how some reporters would be treated. As they steamed across the Atlantic, she discovered one reporter from the Norfolk newspaper already embedded with the navy. Would he be allowed to extend his embed orders and slip into Kuwait with the marines?

No one was answering these and countless other questions that kept cropping up before they even tied up the ships in Kuwait. "All of the reporters wanted to go with ground combat units [because] they were the ones kicking in the doors. But you didn't want to have competing media in the same units."

As a female marine, she often was asked to deal with issues surrounding assigning female journalists to the corps' combat units. When one marine commander learned he was going to have a woman reporter, he strenuously objected. "No, I'm not going to do that," he told

Frushour. "I'll keep her with the headquarters element. That way she won't have to deal with us."

Frushour sighed, and said she'd try to sell it to the veteran journalist, Sue Lackey. Perhaps the marine commander didn't realize that her publication, *Jane's Defense Weekly*, was not a fashion magazine. "She didn't buy it for a second," Frushour recalled. "She said because I'm a woman, I'm being discriminated against." Lackey, who was called "Big Red," got her way. "She treated them like a mom and spoke fluent Arabic. They ended up using her to do translation." The marines wound up marveling at Lackey's connections and contacts throughout Iraq. (Lackey has since left *Jane's Defense Weekly* and could not be reached for comment.)

Such conflicts with Frushour's superiors often proved to be a thankless task. The commander threatened to get her fired over her advocacy for the experienced defense correspondent. It blew over, but not before Lackey chewed out the battalion commander.

By March 15, 2003, Bowman was ensconced with the 1st Battalion of the 4th Regiment of the Marine Corps' 1st Division. True to his battle plan, he eschewed the big-picture stories to try to capture something of the interests, foibles, and passions of the average nineteen- or twenty-year-old marine. "Is Jennifer Lopez dead? Did President Bush storm out of a United Nations session after giving world leaders a piece of his mind? Some Marines here say yes to both questions," he wrote in the March 15, 2003, *Richmond Times-Dispatch*.

Bowman described the way rumors added "spice to a routine that has otherwise grown wearisome. Every day the Marines stay busy mastering the details of their deadly craft. They rehearse assault, clean weapons, repair their vehicles and communications gear, practice first aid, exercise and eat the unpopular food rations called MREs—meals ready to eat."

After hours of trying to fight the inevitable boredom in the harsh desert environment, he wrote, "They crawl into their sleeping bags at night and the wind fills their tents with so much sand they have to wear bandannas and scarves over their mouths to sleep. When they wake in the morning, they have to clear gunk from their eyes and grit from their noses, then wipe the dust from their faces. During the day, they search for a spot of shade beside a tent to escape the blazing heat."

As bad as the heat, sand, and ennui were, many marines said there could be something worse: the idea that they might be ordered home. "It would probably drive me crazy if they delayed everything another two weeks," said PFC Joshua Clatterbuck of Culpeper, Virginia.

Captain Collins was working Charlie Company hard during this waiting time. "Collins is a gregarious man, loud, profane and frequently funny," Bowman wrote. "And always demanding. Several days ago, he led his men out to the desert to practice storming an imaginary enemy position. Halting the convoy of armored vehicles and 7-ton trucks at the foot of a dune, Collins ordered one platoon to lay down a suppressing fire to keep the enemy's heads down while an engineering unit moved in to clear any mine fields. Collins then ordered another platoon to charge through the breach created by the engineers. Collins didn't like what he saw. He made them do it over. Again and again."

On March 19, 2003, U.S. Special Forces crossed the border into western Iraq to take out Scud missiles, and in a dramatic last-minute decision, the president sent F-117A Nighthawks, the air force's first stealth fighter, to bomb Dora Farm, a complex southeast of Baghdad on the bank of the Tigris River, known to be a retreat for Saddam's wife. Bush hoped to take out at least one "axis of evil" before the ground combat even began. The bunker-buster bombs hit their target, but Saddam, who possessed an uncanny knack for evasion and escape, survived.

For Charlie Company, the day of battle had come. Collins called his men together to brace them for the unknown and, in a ritual as old as David and Goliath, gird them for battle while seven-ton trucks roared by and transport helicopters thumped overhead. Bowman described the scene:

With his helmeted men gathered around him in the hot sands of Kuwait, Collins told them their hour will soon be at hand. He told them they will be afraid. He told them they will win anyway. As Collins spoke, the boom of cannons sounded to the north. . . . The thunderous noise lent gravity to a speech already far more grave than anything a president could have said to the sun-chapped Marines.

Collins' words to his men might have sounded corny in a John Wayne movie. But, assuming war is imminent and knowing they are the ones being asked to risk their short lives, Collins' men hung on his every sentence.

He told them now is the moment that will define their lives. Collins said, "You need to take a hard look to your left and to your right, look at the Marines around you. . . . Even if you don't know their names, I guarantee you their faces will be etched in your memory forever."

The following day, the 183,000-strong U.S., British, and coalition forces began the 250-mile march to Baghdad. Bowman crammed inside an armored assault vehicle, otherwise known as an AAV or amtrac. It was bad enough that they were butt-to-butt, elbow-to-elbow. Adding to the discomfort were the chemical protection suits, which were hot and unwieldy.

"I was crammed in with sixteen guys, and we rode for thirty-one hours without a stop," Bowman told me. "It nearly killed me. It was the only time in the war I thought I may have made a mistake by embedding." As the hours and miles mounted, Bowman realized that at age forty-two, he was twice as old as most of the marines. He started to doubt his decision to cover the war, thinking, "Maybe I'm not able to sit on a hard bench for thirty-one hours with gear hitting me in the head."

As the invasion unfolded, hundreds of other journalists faced the same pain—and dangers—of the long claustrophobic confinement. NBC correspondent David Bloom, thirty-nine years old, died on April 6, 2003, from a pulmonary embolism—a blood clot that moved from the leg to the lung—caused by a condition called deep-vein thrombosis. The combination of several long flights between New York and Kuwait before the war, a genetic predisposition to clots, and, finally, the ill effects of dehydration and crouching in a cramped tank for hours on end caused Bloom's untimely death, according to news accounts.

Bowman, his doubts and sore butt notwithstanding, survived. But it was a close call. By the time Charlie Company halted its dash across the desert, Bowman recalled, he was ready to crack. "When they opened the door, I might have snapped and gone crazy." He thought his reaction was unique, but then he overheard marines remarking about how they too felt close to reaching their breaking points.

After more than a day in transit, they still had not come under fire. The battalion had taken a few prisoners along the way—Iraqi gunners fleeing defensive positions along the border with Kuwait. Bowman, suffering inside the amtrac, didn't get to see the captures and only heard about it later.

The marines were somewhere in southern Iraq, but otherwise, the Richmond reporter was clueless about his exact location. He had purchased a map at Barnes & Noble back home, and though it came in handy later, it wasn't much use at this point in the grueling trip. The only link to the other units was a laptop computer equipped with computer software, blue force tracker, showing the location of each American unit. "Every unit had a blue dot, and we could watch those dots flowing north," Bowman said.

The laptop provided a surreal sight, sort of like watching blue viruses invading the body of Iraq. Watching the entire U.S. invasion force on the move, Bowman realized he could easily write a big-picture story about the location of the units. All it would have taken would have been a quote from a senior officer describing the progress of the operation. But he wasn't here to paint on a big canvas. Leave that to the *Times* or *Post*. Bowman knew his job was to chronicle what was happening to the good men of Charlie Company—though after being holed up like a mushroom for more than a day, there wasn't much to say, unless he decided to write about the science experiment that was probably growing inside the protective suit that he still wore without a change of clothes beneath.

There was one dispatch he wanted to post, however. When he emerged into the sunlight, Bowman set up his solar-powered satellite phone and tapped out a brief story on his laptop which said, We made it. We are in Iraq. "I filed something more or less to let the editors know I was alive. It had no news value. It was one of the kinds of stories I didn't want to file, but I felt I had to let my editors and my wife know I was alive." At that point, he didn't know whether the U.S. was taking battle casualties or not.

The next day, south of Nasiriyah, a key crossroads city in southeastern Iraq on the Euphrates River, Charlie Company was stuck in the rear of the convoy, and the men were getting grumpy. Their temporary boredom didn't last long, though. As Bowman wrote later in the *Times-Dispatch*, "Assailants in a small convoy had tried to crash through a checkpoint of the Marines' advance column. The Marines blasted the convoy to pieces. Six women and three children in the vehicles with the gun-toting attackers were injured." Lt. Col. John Mayer, the 1st Battalion's commander, told him, "The bastards are using women and children as human shields to infiltrate."

While duly reporting any attacks, Bowman kept painting his Pyle-like portraits of men at war. "If the 1st Battalion is any standard, the average Marine in Iraq is 19 or 20 years old. He's got a girlfriend back home or maybe a wife. Maybe even a child. He came to the Corps right out of high school, or maybe after a semester or two of college. He doesn't plan to stay in the Marines forever, just long enough to save money for college or until he figures out what he wants to do with his life."

Many young men and women enlisted just after 9/11 out of a sense of duty or patriotism. Now, though, the gritty reality of war was sinking in for these marines in Iraq, just as surely as it had for American GIs decades before.

"At this point in the campaign," Bowman continued, "The average Marine also stinks. His clothes are caked in mud and dust and he's wearing the same underwear he put on nine days ago. His feet are in sad shape from wearing the same socks every day and sleeping with his boots on most nights. His butt is sore from sitting entire days on the hard benches of the assault vehicles. His lips are chapped, cracked and bloody. He now knows the value of Chapstick."

Bowman documented the "dismal flavor of the military rations." Meals Ready to Eat, or MREs, had been renamed "Meals Rejected by the Enemy." A tiny bottle of Tabasco sauce, he noted, was the key to putting some life into the bland foodstuffs. The comforts of home, from Krispy Kreme donuts to a "soft couch that doesn't benumb his butt," were duly noted. "And speaking of butts," Bowman concluded in his March 28, 2003, dispatch, the young Marine "doesn't know much about the finer points of geopolitics and international diplomacy, but the average Marine wouldn't mind personally putting his boot in Saddam Hussein's backside. He likes to enjoy a day of rest from the war, but he also wants to get it on and get it over with. And he firmly believes the road home takes a dangerous but inevitable turn through Baghdad."

As Bowman wrote for the folks back home, Rick Atkinson did the same, albeit with the sure knowledge that among the people reading his paper, the *Washington Post*, were Congress, the Defense Department, and perhaps even President Bush. The high-level stakes of his coverage became obvious when Atkinson sounded one of the first alarms about the wisdom of Tommy Franks's speed-dial invasion plan, which Bush had encouraged and Rumsfeld called "shock and awe."

But for the troops on the ground and commanders like Petraeus, any feelings of awe wore off as quickly as the novelty of wearing a bulky chemical protection suit. The 101st Airborne made its way to Baghdad, slogging through the wind and mud and talc that made breathing difficult. The weather grounded helicopters and slowed their progress. As they approached the city of Najaf, south of the capital, they were stalled by small bands of assailants, the *Fedayeen*, who employed sniper tactics and seemed to have an endless supply of rocket-propelled grenades. In what would become one of many intelligence failures, the U.S. had assumed Saddam would order these forces to suppress rebels inside the Iraqi population, not fight the Americans. The military did not want to hear about the *Fedayeen*, so they ignored the small-unit forces.

In what would become a harbinger of word games played back in the Pentagon, an order came down banning the use of the term itself, which means "men who sacrifice themselves for a cause," because it conferred too much dignity to them. They would be called "paramilitaries" or "terrorist death squads." Whatever they were called, the army easily beat back the attacks from the AK-47-brandishing foes making suicidal runs in Toyota pickups. But Petraeus couldn't ignore the rapidly dwindling fuel supply and other logistical issues such as getting enough food and water to the troops. "This thing is turning to shit," he told Atkinson.[1] The 3rd Infantry Division was in danger of running out of food and water. The entire operation appeared to be in jeopardy because of bad logistical planning. Ammunition levels were running dangerously low.

Working with the *Post*'s senior Pentagon reporter, Tom Ricks, Atkinson dictated the details of the growing debacle over his satellite phone. The next day, Ricks and Atkinson had a joint byline on the front page, with the headline, "War Could Last Months." The article began: "Despite the rapid advance of Army and Marine forces across Iraq over the past week, some senior U.S. military officers are now convinced the war is likely to last months and will require considerably more combat power than is now on hand there and in Kuwait, senior defense officials said yesterday."[2]

The story scored a direct hit along the Potomac. President Bush was asked about the report and how long he thought the war would last. "However long it takes," he snapped. Privately, Petraeus began to voice his doubts about the war's outcome. The general could see the growing resistance to the Americans, including some Iraqis waving white flags to feign surrender. In what would become a prophetic rhetorical question, Petraeus asked his embedded reporter, "Tell me how this ends. Eight years and eight divisions." This was an allusion to advice given to the Eisenhower White House in the early 1950s about what it would take to prop up French forces in South Vietnam.[3]

While he exposed some of the shortcomings of the U.S. logistical effort in Iraq, Atkinson did not expose Petraeus to more withering fire back home by reporting the general's growing doubts. Asked why he waited a year to publish Petraeus's battlefield musings, until the 2004 release of his combat memoir, Atkinson replied, "It would have come down on his head. I think when you're embedded, you have to use discretion." Petraeus was asking "the right question," Atkinson told me in 2007. "Four years later, it's still the right question. Anyone who'd read Mesopotamian history knew it didn't end well."

Dusty and tired, the *Post* reporter made his own tactical decisions about how to report what he was seeing behind the scenes with Petraeus without getting the general in trouble or even removed from command. It was a delicate balancing act. A subsequent March 30, 2003, report in the *Post* quoted Petraeus's superior, Lt. Gen. William Scott Wallace, the V Corps commander, about the need to pause the invasion and build logistical strength. Subduing Najaf could tie up the 101st Airborne for weeks, he warned, and subduing Baghdad could take longer.[4]

Later, Atkinson would hear in a satellite phone call from Washington that Wallace's comments generated controversy about the conduct of the war, raising serious questions about the administration's quick-strike, light-force strategy. Press spokesmen at the Pentagon and Central Command in Qatar reacted defensively to anyone who dared asked tough questions about the invasion. Gen. Richard B. Myers, chairman of the Joint Chiefs of Staff at the time, defended the U.S. operation as "a brilliant plan." President Bush was described as "irritated" by Wallace's frank assessment.

Atkinson told me, "Certainly the stuff with Wallace was candid. His remarks caused a shit storm back in Washington. He was only stating the obvious. It shows the extent to which the White House was being mendacious, conniving, and creating a tissue of lies." But the reporter could see how the drama was being played back home, so he asked Ricks to pull his byline from their combined front-page story. "I didn't want it to fall on Petraeus's head," Atkinson explained.

Reporting unfettered views of army commanders under duress was causing heartburn in high places, especially since it went against the carefully orchestrated good-news story line crafted by the Bush administration and its military minions. The TV news operations in particular were in no mood to hear any doubts or shades of difference about the glorious war. Why would they? Iraq was a ratings bonanza and a career booster for news anchors and correspondents alike. It had all the elements of a round-the-clock version of *The Sands of Iwo Jima* (including lots of sand) and *The Longest Day*, with gritty, determined American doughboys—and now doughgirls—bravely marching into the unknown in order to bring down a nefarious despot. In this black-and-white moral universe, America was right and true and brave, and everyone else was wrong and false and cowardly . . . and probably liberal.

Given their first chance since 9/11 to cover a war against an Arab nation, the networks were fully engaged not in news coverage, but in image making. They unabashedly waved the flag—or at least wore the flag on their anchors' lapels. "We report, you decide," became Fox's mantra. Its breathless, unapologetically pro-Bush coverage reaped immediate ratings results. By early April 2003, Fox became the first news network to win the cable-ratings race since the 1991 Persian Gulf War, averaging 2.16 million viewers daily—an 83 percent gain from the year before.

Fox also led with viewers between ages twenty-five and fifty-four, one of the most coveted demographics in television advertising. Part of it was appearance, with Fox's producers creating a red, white, and blue studio motif, including the stars and stripes in a corner of the screen. Part of Fox's appeal also came from lowering its journalistic standards, effectively knocking down the walls between commentators and the story they were covering. Objectivity was checked at the studio door; subjectivity and emotionalism were encouraged.

As TV critic Dusty Saunders noted, "While other network anchors use terms like 'U.S. forces' or 'coalition troops,' [Fox anchors Shepard Smith and John Gibson, and others] talk regularly about 'we' while using other personal references when describing troop movement or battle situations."[5] Fox's cheerleading fit the tenor of the times as polls showed about 70 percent of Americans favored the war. "Still," Saunders wrote, "I wince when Fox anchors breathlessly say, 'We have unconfirmed reports . . .' when a U.S. victory is expected on the battlefield. Just the facts, please." Other media critics noted Fox's mass appeal, including one who noted the "cheeky approach" of vilifying Iraqi officials, such as Information Minister Mohammed al-Sahaf, who was dubbed "Baghdad Bob." Larry Eichel of the *Philadelphia Inquirer* chronicled Fox's Iraq script:

- Playing a few seconds of upbeat martial music before and after each commercial break.
- Labeling the coverage "Operation Iraqi Freedom" rather than "War in Iraq."
- Letting news anchors, who wore American flag buttons in lapels, inject their opinions.
- Encouraging viewers to send in patriotic photographs to be showcased as "Friends of America."

Eichel noted with some understatement that "those elements— some of which have been adopted by other television news operations—tend to be at odds with the traditional canons of objective journalism." While some critics wondered how Fox was managing to beat CNN in the ratings, Eichel quoted a media professor who told

him, "In times of crisis . . . a lot of Americans aren't looking for journalistic detachment or an international perspective."

No detachment or international perspective was allowed on the
red, white, and blue network, where a *Fox & Friends* co-host referred
to a meeting of some of the war's opponents—France, Germany, and
Russia—as "the so-called weasel summit." Anchor John Gibson speculated about postwar Iraq, observing that the notion that "we would
ever turn it over to the United Nations to bumble it is incomprehensi-
ble."[6] Obviously, Eichel wrote, such talk "appeals to people who agree
with those viewpoints."

Other media analysts cited what Eichel described as a "David-versus-
Goliath" attitude as part of the network's appeal. Bill O'Reilly, host of
Fox's primetime *The O'Reilly Factor*, targeted a *New York Times* story
about Fox and other media companies owned by media baron Rupert Murdoch. "Here's a flash for the *Times*," O'Reilly said. "It's not just conservative Americans who watch. That's the reason the *Times* and other
newspapers are furious. They know they are losing power to this network."

TV critic Saunders suggested the kind of separation of news and
opinion that newspapers traditionally have maintained by having separate editorial pages. In Fox's case, he suggested leaving the cheerleading
to its sometimes shrill stars O'Reilly and Sean Hannity.[7] Most of Fox's
embedded reporters and other correspondents "seem mostly free of the
'patriotic' atmosphere that permeates the anchor desk," Saunders noted.

Still, like a dark star with its own gravitational pull, Fox forced competitors to either mute their criticism of the government or wave the flag
and jump on board the war wagon. Walter Isaacson, president of CNN at
the time, later conceded a massive failure of good journalism. "We didn't
question our sources enough," he told Bill Moyers. Why? Isaacson said
there was "almost a patriotism police" after 9/11. When CNN showed
dead Iraqis in the rubble in Baghdad, it received outraged calls from
advertisers and the Bush administration and, Isaacson said, from "big
people in corporations" who said, "You're being anti-American here."[8]

One of the most egregious acts of network censorship occurred at
MSNBC, where talk show host Phil Donahue had jumpstarted his career

on the cable channel owned by NBC only to be fired in February 2003. According to *Editor and Publisher*, Donahue "was told he could not feature war dissenters alone on his MSNBC talk show and always had to have 'two conservatives for every liberal.'"[9] A leaked NBC memo about Donahue's firing declared he "presents a difficult public face for NBC in a time of war. At the same time our competitors are waving the flag at every opportunity."[10]

Even Dan Rather, a favorite target of conservative pundits as the epitome of the New York liberal, told Moyers, "I don't think there is any excuse for, you know, my performance and the performance of the press in general in the roll up to the war. . . . We didn't dig enough. And we shouldn't have been fooled in this way."

But as Moyers's stinging documentary on PBS shows, it was hard to counter the planetlike gravitational pull into war exerted by the Bush media machine. William Safire, a columnist for the *New York Times*, predicted a "quick war" with Iraqis cheering eloquently. Safire alone wrote twenty-seven opinion pieces advocating an invasion, according to *Editor and Publisher*. The *Washington Post*, though a favorite target of conservative critics, nonetheless carried some 140 front-page stories making the Bush administration's case for war. Finally, of 414 Iraq stories broadcast on nightly news broadcasts on NBC, ABC, and CBS in the six months before the invasion, "almost all could be traced back to sources solely in the White House, Pentagon or State Department," Moyers said.[11]

Meanwhile, over at the Pentagon, the pugnacious Donald Rumsfeld began firing the first shots in what would become an ongoing offensive against the media. Along with Joint Chiefs chairman Myers, he blasted so-called "armchair generals" for second-guessing the Pentagon's Iraq invasion plan.

This kill-the-messenger mood was easy to exploit, since polls showed overwhelming public support for President Bush and this second Gulf War. A *USA Today*/CNN/Gallup poll showed that 70 percent of Americans supported the war. Only one third of respondents said the administration intentionally understated how hard the war would be.[12]

Still, *USA Today* noted some of the public's concerns as it read or heard about the unexpected assaults of the *Fedayeen* and the logistical issues such as those raised by Atkinson. "Although the battle began just 13 days ago and has put U.S. troops within 50 miles of Baghdad, the optimistic talk that launched it has contributed to a sense that the war hasn't gone as quickly or as well as expected," wrote *USA Today*'s Susan Page. General Myers "four weeks ago . . . spoke with reporters about a 'short, short conflict' against an Iraqi force that was 'much weaker' than it was in the 1991 Gulf War."[13]

In a town hall–style meeting with Pentagon employees, Rumsfeld and Myers criticized the media coverage as "inaccurate" and "conflicting." According to the *Post*'s Ricks, Rumsfeld complained that not long ago, "people were saying that the plan was terrible, and . . . there weren't enough people, and . . . there was to be, you know, tens of thousands of casualties, and it was going to take forever." Rumsfeld blasted retired military officers who seemed to exaggerate problems, or as he put it, "That constantly, you know, blare big headlines of 'Henny Penny: The Sky is Falling,' 'It's Just Terrible,' 'Isn't It Awful?'"

MSNBC, which already had muzzled Phil Donahue, called the Pentagon leaders' remarks more than just a "brushback pitch" against the media. "They were throwing at our heads," said MSNBC chief Erik Sorenson. Chastened by Rumsfeld's rhetoric, Sorenson said, "This is not a primary in New Hampshire. This is life and death and people in harm's way, and we have to be careful. Helping us understand what's going on is different from criticizing strategy in a half-informed way. That can potentially undermine confidence and compromise lives on the battlefield."[14]

Other network executives defended their use of retired generals to provide informed perspective on Bush's Operation Enduring Freedom in Afghanistan. "If nobody ever had an opinion that differed from the party line, then we'd only have one line and that would be the Pentagon's, and that's not what this country is all about," said CBS hard news chief Marcy McGinnis. "Generals in studios are not going to turn the tide of war or make our soldiers get into depths of depression." She bluntly told *USA Today*: "If Rumsfeld and his generals have the courage of their convictions, they should just say, 'We made a plan, it was the right plan, and frankly, we don't care what any of you say.'"[15]

The flag-waving to draw a larger audience share, the political pull of a media magnate, a failure to report the news dispassionately and objectively as possible—the media's first major test of the twenty-first century was eerily reminiscent of another war in another century.

William Randolph Hearst, the rich son of a California silver miner and industrialist, had come east to New York in the 1890s and—just as the Australian-born Murdoch would a century later—gladly battle the eastern media establishment. Like Murdoch, Hearst brought the same outsider's disdain for the way things were usually done, including objectivity and fairness in news coverage. At the age of thirty-two, Hearst had a rare gift—some might say curse—for feeding the public's insatiable appetite for lurid news and easily digestible views of the world.

In the bustling world of 1890s New York, Hearst successfully exploited and titillated the public's fascination with pseudoscience and crime, with such headlines as "Are Sea Serpents Real?" and "How It Feels to be a Murderer." He had a wildly popular cartoon, "The Yellow Kid," chronicling the adventures of a personable street urchin. The cartoon character sparked competition with Joseph Pulitzer's rival *New York World*. Thus the term "yellow journalism" was born.[16]

The tabloid's ability to tap into the basest instincts of readers—many of them newly arrived immigrants—led Hearst to follow a marketing strategy that seems to have come full circle to today. In a first "birthday" editorial on November 8, 1896, Hearst bragged that his *New York Journal* "realized what is frequently forgotten in journalism, that if news is wanted it often has to be sent for . . . for the public is even more fond of entertainment than it is of information."[17]

As he pursued what became known as his "crime and underwear" marketing strategy, Hearst made his indelible mark on American history with a shameless prodding of public opinion that led to the nation's 1898 invasion of Cuba in the Spanish-American War. Here again, the similarities to the American invasion of Iraq are eerie.

As a rebellion against Spanish authority grew in Cuba, Democratic President Grover Cleveland maintained a policy of neutrality. After Republican William McKinley entered the White House in 1897, Hearst, himself a Democrat, urged the president to go to war to help the freedom fighters—the Spanish called them "insurgents"—off America's southern shore. More than a century before Fox's Murdoch dispatched such media stars as Ollie North and Geraldo Rivera to Iraq, Hearst created the mold by sending the leading media figures of his day, such as painter and illustrator Frederick Remington, to cover the Cuban uprising for what was then the princely sum of $3,000 a month.

Flag-waving headlines were drawn up, including one five-column headline asking, "DOES OUR FLAG PROTECT WOMEN?" It breathlessly related the lurid tale of three pretty Cuban girls boarding the American vessel *Olivette* in Havana, bound for New York. As the ship was about to sail, Spanish policemen rushed aboard, declaring that the girls were suspected of carrying insurgent dispatches and therefore had to be searched. The salacious and sensational reporting strategy worked, sparking a storm of protest around the country as Congress hopped on the war wagon with a resolution demanding that the secretary of state provide "any information he may have concerning the incident of the stripping of three lady passengers . . . as related by the correspondent of the New York Journal."

The media frenzy, which also was fueled by Hearst's main competitor, Pulitzer, reached its climax with the explosion and sinking of the twenty-four-gun battleship, the USS *Maine*, in Havana harbor on January 25, 1898. Though Spanish sailors joined in the effort to rescue surviving U.S. sailors, the loss of 260 Americans—even to a mysterious explosion—was enough to push America over the brink into war: "THE WARSHIP MAINE WAS SPLIT IN TWO BY AN ENEMY'S SECRET INFERNAL MACHINE," Hearst's *Journal* declared. The cause of the blast was never determined, but like the mysterious WMDs that Bush guaranteed would be found in Iraq, logic was not the issue. It was all about fear and payback.

Hearst, for all of his deceit and follies, was at least honest when he wrote that a newspaper "is the greatest force in civilization," and among its duties in a republican government, "They declare wars." Or as he put in a more candid moment to Remington, who had sent a telegram requesting to return to New York from Cuba: "Please remain," Hearst replied. "You furnish the pictures and I'll furnish the war."[18]

Chapter Five

"A MOMENT OF REAL WAR"

As Charlie Company of the 1st Battalion, 1st Marines, rumbled along near the Tigris River, Rex Bowman had a front-row seat to history. His amtrac was following the path of earlier foreign invaders, including the Greek warrior and author Xenophon, a disciple of Socrates and author of the classic *Anabasis*. The account chronicles what Bing West and Maj. Gen. Ray L. Smith called "the march up Mesopotamia—now Iraq—in 400 B.C. by ten thousand indomitable Greek fighters, called hoplites, who hacked their way through every army that charged them."[1] The Greeks, like the marines, prided themselves on their warrior ethic and toughness in the face of fear and adversity—two emotions that Bowman experienced firsthand even as the American invaders easily overwhelmed their overmatched foe.

"The flotsam of Saddam Hussein's regime flowed south along the road from Baghdad," he wrote in the April 6, 2003, *Richmond Times-Dispatch*. "Hundreds of beat-up cars puttered away from the capital, filled with young Iraqi men fleeing war." Bowman inventoried the detritus of the sacking of Iraq. Cars were piled with family possessions and had pillows and mattresses lashed to the roofs, along with stacks of luggage. Women, old men, and young men alike gave the universal hand gesture for approval—a thumbs-up—to the Americans. Some cars bore white flags on their antennas. "The Marines, holding their rifles, waved back good-naturedly," Bowman wrote. "Up ahead, a massive plume of black smoke rose above Baghdad. The battle for the capital was underway."

It looked like the Americans were being hailed as liberators from the yoke of Saddam's murderous regime—just the kind of liberation-of-Paris welcome the Bush administration predicted. "I think things have gotten so bad inside Iraq . . . we will, in fact, be greeted as liberators," Vice President Dick Cheney said on NBC's *Meet the Press*. Cheney also said the war would "go relatively quickly . . . [in] weeks rather than months." Not to be outdone, Deputy Defense Secretary Paul Wolfowitz mined the mother lode of American patriotism: the liberation of Europe by Allied forces in World War II. "The Iraqi people understand what this crisis is all about," Wolfowitz told the Veterans of Foreign Wars in 2003. "Like the people of France in the 1940s, they view us as their hoped-for liberator."

Bowman, stuck in the rear of an amtrac, was too busy observing and reporting to reflect much on the historical significance of his ride-along with the marines. "I didn't know if I was right or wrong, wise or foolish," he reflected later. "I have the same attitude about abortion and the death penalty. I can write [with] indifference, and I don't know who's right or wrong." He wryly noted that most reporters like him get on-the-job training in how to stay neutral when they cover long, boring municipal meetings.

"It's very easy to be disinterested when you cover planning commissions," he said. This training in objectivity extends to any topic, whether it's in war or peace, he said. He compared his role to that of a professional mediator who is able to see multiple sides of an issue with equanimity. "Why can't we accept that journalists can be even-handed?" he asked. "That's the way I went into the war. I did not know who was right or wrong, did not care if they were right or wrong. All I knew was that it was a story to be covered."

He noted, however, that "disinterested isn't the same as *uninterested*." His interest peaked along Route 7 as the marines entered the city of Al Kut, a key crossroads along the banks of the Tigris. His April 4, 2003, dispatch began with this teasing opening line: "Yesterday must have been my lucky day." He gave a quick scene-setter to explain:

> It must have been a lucky day as well for the 16 Marines I've been traveling with in an amphibious assault vehicle because every Marine knows a rocket-propelled grenade can tear a hole through an AAV and ruin the day for anybody inside.
>
> That's why, later in the day, as soon as they lowered the back ramp on the AAV, the Marines poured out and ran to the right side of the vehicle, to see where the rocket-powered explosive had hit.
>
> But that's getting ahead of the story.

In the best tradition of Ernie Pyle, Bowman slowed his narrative to explain how they'd gotten into a jam after what looked like a good day for the marines. Ordered to test Al Kut's outer defenses, the marines found abandoned bunkers and artillery pieces, antiaircraft guns, and boxes of ammunition—signs that any Iraqi resistance had evaporated. There were even abandoned uniforms, with Republican Guard garb left on the ground. Presumably, the fleeing Iraqi soldiers were blending in with the population.

But as they rolled north, along the city streets, their luck turned. "Snipers began firing down on us from buildings. Some of them ran out, fired off a rocket-propelled grenade and ran back into the shadows." The surrounded marines blasted back at the shadowy foe. The gunner in Bowman's amtrac opened up with his .50-caliber machine gun as riflemen in the rear readied their M-16s to fire through the hatch. Tanks, followed by Cobra attack helicopters, arrived on the scene to help Charlie Company escape the tight spot.

Amid the firefight, Bowman stayed put and took note of this first taste of true war, including his first near-death experience. A rocket-propelled grenade (RPG) was fired at his amtrac. Then another. Bowman had to see this for himself. "I climbed out the top hatch to get a look at the battle raging around us," he wrote. "Just then—wham!—a loud bang and the sound of exploding metal. The vehicle shook. I fell back down the hatch."

The amtrac was hit by one of the RPGs, as Bowman soon learned from the shouts of the pumped-up Marines. "We all were supposed to be dead or wounded right about now," Bowman wrote. One Marine reported feeling the RPG strike "right behind my head." In the confusion, Sgt. Shant Postoyan of California declared, "You can't say there is no God after that! We just took an RPG shot!"

When the firing died down, the Marines inspected the damage to their armored vehicle, which was remarkably intact. "In my corner of the AAV," Bowman wrote, "I pulled out a pack of Charms hard candies. They come in the ration packets, but nobody in Charlie Company eats them because they think the candies bring bad luck. But then and there, Sgt. Gray and I decided to split a pack. If our luck was good enough to help us survive a direct hit by a rocket-propelled grenade, nothing a Charms candy could throw at us could be that bad. As we prepared to pull out of the city, I opened my mouth and popped in a red piece of candy. It tasted sweet, so very sweet."

In retrospect, Bowman saw the fighting at Al Kut as the climax of his Iraq reporting. "At that point I was undeniably in combat, undeniably among courageous men, undeniably having that adventure that I'd sought," he told me. "This was everything I wanted—having been shot at and survived, I could now say I'd been in combat. I know what Churchill meant when he said there's 'nothing so exhilarating as being shot at without result.' I knew exactly what he meant."

After the RPG attack, Bowman sat on a mound of dirt about three feet high, opened his laptop, checked his notes, and wrote the story in only twenty minutes. "I didn't even reread it," he said. The story reported "exactly the way I feel, exactly what happened."

Though this was his first combat experience, the battle of Al Kut wasn't his only bump on the road to Baghdad. After the early drive-by shooting from the Toyota pickup destroyed by the marines, Bowman followed Charlie Company when the Marines were ordered out of their vehicles and told to run over to a line of palm trees. Running with his head down, Bowman thought to himself, "I could be killed right here. How foolish would that be?"

That turned out to be a non-event, and the 1/1 kept pushing onward. Bowman's scariest moment—even worse than the RPG strike—came on a moonless night. Because of cloud cover, it was a pitch black. "The Marines had night vision goggles," he said later. "I had nothing." It happened before the RPG attack, so Charlie Company was not yet battle-tested. They were ordered to set up observation points along the highway, braced for a night assault by the *Fedayeen*. "This was the night the Marines offered me their weapons," Bowman explained. To maintain his detachment and remain a noncombatant, he turned them down. Staying unarmed, he said, simply "was part of what you signed up for." Still, several Marines tried to give him quick lessons in firing a 9mm pistol in case they were overrun and Bowman had to take a weapon out of their dead hands.

Captain Collins, the company commander, "was steeling his men," Bowman recalled, telling them, "I'm not telling you it's a *possible* attack. I'm telling you it's a *probable* attack." The vibe was ominous. "I hesitate to call the Marines scared," Bowman said, but at this point "no one was battle-tested. I picked up on the terror everyone felt, out in the middle of nowhere."

Charlie Company formed a thin defensive line, with the nearest marine thirty feet away. "It was like being in a coal mine. You couldn't see a foot in front of your face." Bowman suddenly had a strange thought: Maybe he was going blind from fear and stress. "I thought maybe there was something like a terror blindness. . . . It was the scariest night of my life." He became convinced that "there could be a thousand guys crawling up in the grass field."

Hours passed before anything happened. Then, just before sunrise, the sound of several cars or small trucks could be heard racing toward them. When the vehicles didn't stop at a nearby checkpoint, the marines unleashed a torrent of gunfire, starting with the green tracer rounds that allowed the riflemen to see where they were firing. Bowman watched in amazement as the rapid fire machine gun and semiautomatic rounds slammed into the hapless caravan.

Charlie Company held its fire, though, in case the *Fedayeen* were attacking the highway checkpoint as a diversionary tactic. Soon after that, Bowman's long, solitary night finally came to a merciful end. It was still pitch dark. "One of the Marines had to find me," he said. "I was grateful. I was just sitting on the ground. It was raining. My fleece sleeping bag was totally soaked, totally useless. This marine put his hand on my shoulder and said, 'Let's go.' I put my hand on his shoulder and followed him."

After "the darkest night of my life," Bowman was elated to climb back into the close confines of the amtrac. When a silver ray of sunlight sliced across the horizon, he reflected on the deep trauma of the night. "That was a moment of real war for me," he said.

Later that morning, as he peeked out at the burned-out hulks of the vehicles destroyed at the checkpoint, Bowman listened to the young marines chattering excitedly about what they'd seen. This was their first sight of dead bodies, though not his. He'd seen murder and accident victims before in his reporting back home. "They still had to wear the mask of bravado," he recalled of the marines. "I didn't. I could stay quiet. It was the nervous day after excitement. It was their first taste of combat."

What did Bowman learn about himself during his long night in the dark, not knowing if his throat was going to be slit by a silent enemy? "I guess it has do with confidence," he said. He discussed the values of the Greek warriors in *The Odyssey* and *Anabasis*: courage, loyalty, perseverance. Part of his motivation for embedding, he said, was "to see these values in the context of combat."

What he found, though, transcended merely reading about such values in the classics. Rather, he was struck by a more modern phenomenon, what he called "the evolution of competence in combat" that he saw develop among the men of Charlie Company. When they had started their mission into Iraq, they were still green, stuck in "29 Palms training," he said, alluding to the California training base where they trained for desert combat. It had taken weeks of hard work and experience, first in Kuwait and now Iraq, before the marines were transformed from green combatants into true warriors.

"To see on-the-job training," he said, "was truly amazing. That was the take-away revelation."

Such experiences echoed those of earlier correspondents, including Joe Galloway, the legendary UPI reporter whose Vietnam reporting led to the modern combat classic, written with Lt. Gen. Harold Moore, *We Were Soldiers Once . . . And Young.*

"On the surface covering wars is deceptively enticing," Galloway told journalist Michael Tharp in 2006. "War stories are fairly simple and direct and center around raw human emotions: love, hate, fear. You see soldiers and civilians alike stripped of all pretense, stripped down to the bare essence. Because it is an important subject, there is always room in the newspaper or on the air for the correspondent's story every day, day after day. It is enough to keep a certain small hard corps of correspondents going back to war after war until they burn out or they are consumed by war itself, dead or wounded."[2]

That was the fate of Bowman's hero, Ernie Pyle, who became a national hero for his combat dispatches in 1944. At that point, Pyle was writing in 300 daily newspapers and 10,000 weeklies, arguably riding the crest of the power of the press in twentieth-century America. Because of Pyle's crusading reporting, for example, Congress approved a measure called "the Ernie Pyle bill" that granted combat infantrymen an extra $10 a month in pay. Even the military loved Pyle. As Gen.

Omar Bradley said, "Our soldiers always seemed to fight a little better when Ernie was around."

But such celebrity status, even when it was done for a noble cause, was fleeting, Phillip Knightley noted. "The sad thing was that Pyle genuinely did not understand the magnetism he had for soldiers, and the emotional responsibility it involved became a burden for him."[3] By the summer of 1944, Pyle was burned out, declaring, "If I heard one more shot or saw one more dead man, I'd go off my nut."[4] After writing his epic dispatches from Europe, this "slight, gnome-like man" resisted the military's pressure for him to report from the Pacific theater.[5] "The old romanticism about getting itchy feet to get back to the front is a myth as far as I am concerned."

But he finally relented, flying to the Pacific to report on war with Japan. But this time the military, so eager to use Pyle to bolster morale, overprotected him and cut into the access to frontline troops that gave his reporting such grit and humanity. Pyle grew resentful and wound up angering his core audience when he said the real action was in Europe and those in the Pacific theater had "no conception whatever of what our war was like."[6] Pyle died from a sniper's bullet on the island of Ie Shima, "renowned and rich, but lonely and frustrated covering a war theater he did not want to know."[7]

Pyle's experiences were a precursor to Joe Galloway's Vietnam coverage. "You pay a price even if you survive unscratched. You find yourself by no means untouched by what you have witnessed," he told Tharp. "The memories of young men dying before their time, some of them in your arms; the memories of what it feels like to be hit by pieces of human flesh flying through the air; the never-to-be-forgotten smells of human flesh fried by napalm, or rent or torn by hot shrapnel; the hideous odor of the battlefield after three or four days of fighting and dying in the tropical heat. You don't just turn off those memories and get on with life untouched."[8]

Galloway nonetheless professed his admiration and even love for the men of the infantry, where "no one will lie to you; no one will try to spin the truth. Those for whom death waits around the next bend or across the next rice paddy have no time and little taste for games that are played with such relish in the rear. No one ever lied to me within the sound of guns. . . . There you earn the sort of friendship that cannot be acquired in any other field of human endeavor—there you forge bonds that will endure for a lifetime."

Rick Atkinson also managed to capture much of the suffering, sacrifice, and bonding he experienced with the men of the 101st Airborne as they slugged their way toward Baghdad. Yet he also managed to provide a portrait of the broader action with the analytical detachment of a David Halberstam or Neil Sheehan in Vietnam.

Atkinson's Iraq coverage was interrupted by the award of a Pulitzer Prize for his research into the war of his father's generation. As he wrote later in *In the Company of Soldiers*, "At 11:30 P.M. I had finished my day's story in the public-affairs tent when an e-mail message arrived asking me to call the foreign desk in Washington. Swearing vividly at the intrusion into my sleeping time, I rigged the satellite phone and dialed the number." *Post* Executive Editor Leonard Downie Jr. answered and informed him that *An Army at Dawn*, the first of three volumes on the liberation of Europe in World War II, had been awarded the 2003 Pulitzer Prize for history. "It was thrilling and discombobulating," Atkinson wrote, "like a bolt from the heavens, and only the stars kept me company in the sleeping camp."[9]

He had little time to think about his latest prize (his second Pulitzer, with a third one still to come for his work at the *Post*). The 101st Airborne was caught up in the kind of fighting that Petraeus dreaded—house-to-house urban warfare, with the inevitable loss of life of children, women, and the elderly, not to mention the dangers to the GIs on the front line.

Over time, Atkinson won Petraeus's trust and became a sounding board for a commander trying to make sense of a dangerous, shifting situation. Looking for signs of success in this war-ravaged land, the hard-charging general faced enormous pressures from above and below in deciding how hard to press the battle. He repeatedly asked Atkinson, "Tell me how this ends."[10]

For a while, the illusion of total victory continued to play out on the streets of Mesopotamia and on the TV screens of America, as though Hollywood had scripted a classic war movie produced by George Bush, Dick Cheney, and Donald Rumsfeld, with Gen. Tommy Franks directing the action.

"Across the river," Atkinson wrote, "boys capered on a stony soccer field with goals fashioned from plastic tubing. They turned to wave, as did a little girl in braids and a print dress. 'This is a hell of an experience,' Petraeus said. 'We have won over the children of Iraq.'"

Atkinson stuck to reporting the progress of the 101st. A year later, in his memoir, he shared the doubts he harbored along the way. Noting Iraq's more than 5,000-year history of invasion and describing how "invaders here had been greeted with the open, toothy smile that surely was a Mesopotamian cultural trait," he wrote, "And usually, in short order, life had soured. Liberator had become occupier, occupier had become oppressor, and oppressor had become someone whose throat needed cutting."[11]

Atkinson had his own close calls. He was talking with a Humvee driver about the relative pleasures of sex or beer, when a fusillade whizzed overheard and an orange flash exploded nearby. "As we spilled from the Humvee," he wrote, "I saw bullets chew the dirt berm ahead and heard the sharp ping of ricochets. Several dozen riflemen had taken cover on both sides of the road." Petraeus had been ambushed by a small group of Iraqis. A sergeant major, I. T. Savusa, squelched the attack by rushing forward and hurling a hand grenade, killing two Iraqis and dispersing the rest.[12] The fighting continued and Atkinson dove for cover. "I found myself facedown, embracing the dirt ten feet from the two dead Iraqi soldiers dispatched by Savusa's grenade."[13]

Afterward, the reporter turned to Petraeus. "It would have been really bad if they got a cheap kill on a major general."

"They probably wouldn't even know it," Petraeus replied.

Atkinson demurred. "Everybody in the United States would know it."

Arriving in Baghdad with the 101st, Atkinson witnessed the looting of the nation's art and cultural treasures. Only hours after Saddam's statue fell, he wrote, "The liberation of Iraq had become the plundering of Baghdad." He saw the Iraqis pillaging their own country and carrying away pipes, electrical wiring, sinks—the entire country's infrastructure. But the army never expected to stay longer than six months, he noted, and senior officers "even avoided uttering what they referred to as the O-word"—that is, occupation.[14]

At the time, though, even expert observers like Atkinson couldn't have known how formidable—perhaps impossible—a task America faced or how foolish the lack of postwar planning would prove to be. However, after spending so much time at the elbow of the ultimate Type A general, Atkinson did predict Petraeus's destiny to become the top American general in Iraq:

> He had taken care of his troops and executed his mission, the two essentials of command, while asking no more of subordinates than he asked of himself. If others found him hard to love—his intensity, competitiveness, and serrated intellect made adoration difficult—he was nevertheless broadly respected and instantly obeyed.
>
> I was certain he would excel in the netherworld between war and peace that no doubt would characterize the occupation of Iraq. His pragmatism and broad peacekeeping experiences in Haiti and Bosnia had prepared him for the thankless work of a proconsul in the American imperium.[15]

But it was the soldiers that he would remember most. Like Rex Bowman, Atkinson said he believed it possible to write about solders with objectivity "and to bear witness with cool detachment." But he admitted, "I also knew that every subsequent report of a 101st Airborne

Division soldier killed in action or grievously wounded would break my heart."[16]

Back home, Donald Rumsfeld did everything he could to pull a curtain over the media's coverage of the war dead. On the eve of the invasion, in March 2003, the Pentagon issued a directive that tried to stage-manage the inevitable loss of life. "There will be no arrival ceremonies for, or media coverage of, deceased military personnel returning to or departing from Ramstein [Germany] airbase or Dover [Delaware] base, to include interim stops," the defense department directive said, referring to the major posts for returning remains of deceased service members.

A Pentagon spokesman told Dana Milbank of the *Washington Post* that the military-wide policy actually began in November 2000, in the waning days of the Clinton administration. "But it apparently went unheeded and unenforced, as images of caskets returning from the Afghanistan war appeared on television broadcasts and in newspapers" until early 2003, Milbank reported.[17]

Bush's critics seized on the issue but, outside of media circles, received little support from a nation still reveling in the demise of Saddam Hussein and the quick seizure of Baghdad. "This administration manipulates and takes great care to manage events, and sometimes that goes too far," said Joe Lockhart, Clinton's former press secretary.

The Pentagon earlier had noted the effect on public opinion of what Milbank called "the grim tableau of caskets being carried from transport planes to hangars or hearses." Army general Henry H. Shelton, then chairman of the Joint Chiefs of Staff, said a decision to use military force is based in part on whether it will pass "the Dover test," as the public reacts to fatalities, according to Milbank.

This time around, Rumsfeld made sure that there would be no Dover test and that the American public would see no images of flag-draped coffins coming off planes at Dover Air Force Base. The returning war dead were put off limits to the press. And the president, while saying he met privately with families of fallen soldiers, kept his distance from memorials and funerals for soldiers killed in action, ending a long, bipartisan tradition of presidents attending such gut-wrenching ceremonies for the fallen—a tradition that included his father, George H. W. Bush, who attended ceremonies at Dover and Andrews Air Force Base for Americans killed in Panama and Lebanon and aboard the USS *Iowa*.

Such questions of access and remembrance were, in military parlance, "outside the lane" for embedded reporters such as Rex Bowman. He tried to stay alert, file stories, and survive a once-in-a-lifetime adventure that lasted more than six weeks and drove him to write twenty-nine articles for the *Richmond Times-Dispatch*.

Often, it was the little things that captured his attention, such as the moment the marines of Charlie Company were allowed finally to remove their chemical warfare protection suits. They had donned the bulky protective wear the day they began the operation, March 20, and didn't get to strip them off until April 9, nearly three weeks later. "We were fetid," Bowman recalled. The protective gear absorbed each man's body odor, holding it in until the day of release. "My God, it was amazing," he said of the mass body odor.

He also remembered the awe and wonder he experienced when they finally crossed the river into Baghdad, where his unit encountered no armed resistance. "Just a bunch of Iraqis looting a building, waving at us." Driving along the streets of a city he'd only seen before on CNN— usually as American cruise missiles and bombs fell—he reflected on how far he'd come from Roanoke, Virginia. He knew it was a cliché, but for him, this was history in the making.

"I was raised Southern Baptist, and I couldn't believe I was standing in the streams of ancient Baghdad." The NBC station in Roanoke happened to reach him by satellite phone and he proclaimed, "Hey, I'm in Baghdad!"

When the Marines saw him calling home, they asked if they could use his satellite phone. After gaining approval from his managing editor in Richmond, which he needed because of the high cost of the satellite minutes, he gladly shared his technology. "Hey honey!" one marine after another called out to their wife or girlfriend. "I'm in Baghdad!"

Such exhilaration was understandable considering the mood swings they had experienced in the day before entering the capital. The marines had been ordered to cross the Diyala River on the approach to Baghdad, and because they couldn't use any bridges, they were told they'd have to ford the river in their bulky amtracs. A somber mood enveloped Charlie Company. Asked if the mission was doable, the commander of the vehicles, Maj. Jim Swafford of Dallas, replied, "Yes, if they're willing to lose 10 to 15 percent."

The value of giving reporters a front seat or rear view of the military was evident in Bowman's April 8, 2003 account. The fog of war, with all its doubts, confusions, grumblings, and resignation to bad decisions from commanders up the chain of command—all this comes through loud and clear. That, and the sense of pathos among young men wondering whether or not they will cross to a distant shore, even as victory seems so close at hand.

Swafford was "plainly opposed to the plan," Bowman wrote. "The amphibious vehicles were in horrible condition. Several were being towed, and all of them were in need of serious repairs."

Lt. Brendan Egan, who'd asked for the major's frank assessment, asked Swafford to join him at battalion headquarters in a last-ditch attempt to talk the higher-ups out of the plan.

After the officers left, the marines whom Bowman had gotten to know so well—the ones who hadn't left him on that dark night of "terror blindness," the ones who shared their Charms candies after surviving the RPG direct hit—all gathered to ponder their collective fate. "The men began looking at maps," he wrote. "The Diyala River looked wide, very wide. They knew the vehicles were beat up, and they didn't relish having to swim for their lives if the vehicles stalled in the middle of the stream. The mission seemed to have a semi-suicidal bent to it."

When Egan and Swafford returned, they regretfully announced the amphibious assault was on. "No one knew how many of the vehicles would make it across," Bowman wrote, "and no one knew how many enemy troops waited for them on the other side.

"The mood at camp was like a funeral parlor. Marines began showing each other pictures of their families and girlfriends. The men packed up their gear while joking bleakly about drowning. Swafford figured his own vehicle had an 80 percent chance of making it." Others put their chances at 60 percent.

Bowman kept his thoughts to himself, but later recounted, "I felt like things can't turn bad now." He'd already written home about his charmed life, an attitude, he could see now, that reflected "confidence born of ignorance."

The marines quietly rode toward the river crossing. "The usual happy, dirty banter was missing. Instead, Marines rode silently in the dark confines of the vehicles as they clutched their M-16s."

But as they neared the Diyala River, a wonderful sight greeted the marines with the best views in the amtracs' top hatches. "The river lay before them. It was no more than 50 or 60 yards wide. It looked shallow enough that the vehicles could drive across. It wasn't the threat they had imagined."

War rarely operates with the linear sameness of everyday life. Rather, it has slow times, endless lulls, then quick bursts of action. It has climaxes, followed by anticlimaxes, and back again—sometimes in the same day. Bowman experienced this roller-coaster reality as he prepared to leave Iraq and say good-bye to the marines. After Charlie Company was assigned to a relatively placid neighborhood in east Baghdad, he felt his work was done. The invasion was over. The marines seemed to be preparing for mop-up duty. "So I didn't see any interesting stories coming out of it."

He'd been told to give five days' notice when he wanted to fly out of Iraq and head for home—what the military, in its endless use of jargon, calls "disembedding." So Bowman gave what he thought was advance notice, thinking he'd have several days to say good-bye to this group of young men with whom he'd become so attached. Much to his chagrin, though, later that night a lieutenant interrupted his trip to the latrine and said they had a helicopter ready to start him on his way back to Kuwait and the flight home. Bowman rushed to grab his gear and realized he was bailing out on his friends. When they saw their reporter leaving, several marines rushed up and jotted down their home addresses, urging Bowman to say in touch.

Then he drove off with the lieutenant. Later that night, sniper fire prevented the helicopter from taking off. But by then, Bowman had been taken away across Baghdad and couldn't get back to Charlie Company unless he wanted to jeopardize his ticket out of the country. He cooled his heels for several days, regretting his inelegant exit from the marines. "It was a shame to leave these guys," he recalled.

He finally reached Kuwait City to wait awhile for a flight home. In the meantime, he took four showers. It had been a month since he had last bathed. "I felt dirty to my bones."

After the fourteen-hour flight back to Virginia, Bowman was stunned to see his return covered by the local NBC station, which had been following his exploits. The station, WSLS-10, is part of the same media conglomerate that owns the *Richmond Times-Dispatch*.

Bowman remembers being "dead tired." He was also surprised to read hundreds of emails sent from around the country from the wives, fathers, mothers, and other friends of Charlie Company, 1/1. They told him how much they appreciated his coverage and all the human stories he'd told about their exploits. "They appreciated the way I wrote the story about the men, not the war," he said.

Bowman was invited to speak at various functions around the country and even to be a guest of honor at homecoming parades. Thanks, but no thanks, he said.

"They all wanted to make a celebrity out of me," Bowman said. But he was satisfied being a reporter.

Chapter Six

GERALDO TO JESSICA:
THE SHOW CONTINUES

ixing the media and the military is a bit like making nitroglycerine: it can always blow up in your face. Case in point: Fox News correspondent Geraldo Rivera. During a live broadcast in the early hours of the invasion, Rivera told his cameraman to tilt the camera to the ground. He proceeded to outline a map of Iraq in the sand, marking Baghdad and taking his best guess at the current location of Petraeus's 101st Airborne, which he had joined on temporary assignment. The Fox star's homespun cartography was a major breach of security, but Rivera only compounded his mistake by mapping out where the 101st was going next.

Giving away his unit's location was a clear violation of the ground rules for news media, which Rivera—like the more than 700 embeds operating with Multi-National Force Iraq—signed as a condition of embedding with the American military. The second page of the four-page document lists fifteen categories of information banned from release by the media "since the publication or broadcast of such information could jeopardize operations and endanger lives." Rivera violated rule 14c, which prohibits "information, photography or imagery that would reveal the specific location of military forces or show the level of security at military installations or encampments."

Initially, senior Pentagon officials said they had decided to expel Rivera from the war zone. "He was giving away the big-picture stuff," one senior military official told CNN. "He went down in the sand and drew where the forces are going."

Pentagon spokesman Bryan Whitman further explained, "He was with a military unit in the field and the commander felt that he had compromised operational information by reporting the position and movement of the troops. The commander thought it best to get the reporter out of his battle space."

Rivera was not officially embedded with the division, but only on temporary duty. He was to be escorted to the Kuwaiti border and sent packing. But after the flap unfolded, he appeared in another live report from Iraq hours after the Pentagon announced his expulsion. "In fact, I'm further in Iraq than I've ever been. It sounds like some rats from my former network, NBC, are trying to stab me in the back," he said, alluding to his late 2001 departure from NBC subsidiary CNBC in order to report from Afghanistan for Fox News. Rivera said he had heard nothing about his expulsion until he called network headquarters for a scheduled live broadcast.

After he was forced out of the battle zone—only to return later—the controversial correspondent unleashed a broadside at his former network, which he blamed for stirring the pot. "MSNBC is so pathetic a cable news network that they have to do anything to attract attention," Rivera said. "You can rest assured that whatever they're saying is a pack of lies."

Whatever the merits of his argument, Rivera was right in one respect: MSNBC did grab plenty of attention over his misdeed. Not only did it play up the story on its newscast, the cable network broadcast a promotional spot promising to never "compromise military security or jeopardize a single American life." Fox, not to be outhyped, responded with its own broadside. It maintained that the network had decided to extract Rivera from the battle zone and that he wasn't forced out by the Pentagon.

Like warships taking aim at each other across New York harbor, the two networks kept trading advertising ammo. William Randolph Hearst, who always enjoyed a good fight with competing newspapers, probably would have appreciated the flap. In one corner was Fox, with Rupert Murdoch and his parent company, Nucor, the global holding company with assets topping $60 billion and a diverse portfolio in eight industry segments, including TV, cable, film, newspapers, and book publishing. In the other corner was MSNBC, the cable network owned by megabillionaire Bill Gates's Microsoft Corporation and General Electric.

In its counterpunching promotions, Fox arguably hit below the belt, seizing on the fact that NBC fired Peter Arnett in the early days of the Iraq invasion. NBC reportedly was angered because Arnett gave an unauthorized interview in which he voiced opposition to the U.S.-led operation. Arnett was seen on Iraqi television saying the U.S. was reconsidering its invasion plan because "the first war plan has failed."

The network said it got thousands of e-mails and phone calls protesting Arnett's remarks, including 1,000 e-mails to MSNBC President Erik Sorenson alone. Arnett, best known for his 1991 reporting for CNN on the first Gulf War and a Pulitzer Prize winner for reporting in Vietnam in 1966, issued a muted apology for his "misjudgment," adding, "I said over the weekend what we all know about the war."

But the American public still supported the crusade against Saddam Hussein, cheering the toppling of his Soviet-style statue and marveling at the rescue of Army PFC Jessica Lynch after what appeared to be a heroic rescue by special forces. It was only a matter of time before the WMDs—which provided the main argument for invading a sovereign nation—would be discovered and destroyed. Administration officials continued to insist, as Donald Rumsfeld did on the March 30, 2003, broadcast of ABC's *This Week*, that they knew where to find the hidden weapons. "They're in the area around Tikrit and Baghdad and east, west, south, and north somewhat."

Against this bullish backdrop, it was easy enough for Fox to exploit NBC's embarrassment over Arnett's apparent disloyalty to his adopted country (born in New Zealand, Arnett was a naturalized American citizen). After the correspondent's resignation, Fox aired a promotional spot that showed Arnett's Iraqi TV interview as an announcer intoned, "He spoke out against America's armed forces; he said America's war against terrorism had failed; he even vilified America's leadership. And he worked for MSNBC." Fox dismissed MSNBC's claim to be "America's News Channel" with this question: "Now, ask yourself, is this America's news channel?" Murdoch's network flashed the answer in the form of its own slogan: "Real Journalism, Fair and Balanced."

My efforts to reach Geraldo Rivera through a Fox spokeswoman proved unsuccessful. After a request to interview other newsmen at the cable channel, only one made himself available for a telephone interview: Oliver North, the former marine lieutenant colonel who had made a remarkable career revival at the cable network, positioning himself as a kind of hybrid: a combat correspondent and a documentary filmmaker.

"I've been to Iraq eight times for Fox," North said in September 2007, "and twice to Afghanistan. My only beat is U.S. military personnel." His goal, he said, is "to document the first draft of history. We have hundreds and hundreds of hours [of tape] that we've shot, and over a thousand interviews with U.S. military personnel."

Asked about the embedding reporting program, North said, "My sense is that the embedding process was unexpectedly successful in terms of news gathering, and showing the American people what was transpiring and allowing me to show how remarkable America's sons and daughters are." Even foreign reporters who covered the war, he said, could see what a great job the American soldiers and marines did in 2003. "You could not point a camera and not get a very positive impression of who these guys were."

North defended Fox's performance, despite criticism of its on-air objectivity. "Sean Hannity is a dear close personal friend," he said, "and Bill O'Reilly is our number-one show. What they do on their shows is different than what I do on our show, because they do not document the war." North continued, "I don't think my documentaries are biased. Anyone who wants to be at war never wants to see another one. I've been to a lot of them, and war brings out the best and worst in people. I consider my job to fairly document what's done there." He said he hoped that in 100 years, his archives could be used to provide honest, firsthand interviews with the troops in Iraq.

North's long view was understandable, considering the short-term memory loss his fellow countrymen seemed to be experiencing. "Close to 98 percent of Americans don't know the name of anyone serving" in Iraq, he said, "whereas in World War II, everyone knew someone serving."

Rivera's blunder was the most highly publicized clash between military authorities and the media, but there were plenty of other problems occurring behind the scenes. Marine captain Kelly Frushour, the public-affairs officer for the First Marine Expeditionary Force (I MEF), scrambled to accommodate all sorts of requests. She recalled that the NBC crew from Miami wasn't supposed to get to use its own "NBC Humvee" and should have been on temporary assignment with one battalion and not allowed to stay with it for the push into Iraq. "I went to the battalion commander and asked him what was going on, and he pretty much said, 'I'm keeping them.'"

Frushour often found herself caught in the middle. "It was hard enough to get any of the battalion commanders to embrace the media, so it became my job to make it legitimate for NBC to stay," she recalled. Working her way up the chain of command, Frushour recalled one higher-ranking officer in public affairs agreed with her strategy to work things out for Kerry Sanders of NBC, who had befriended the battalion commander. "What's DOD going to do?" the higher ranking officer told Frushour, "Shave my head and send me to Iraq?"

Some of the issues could be mundane, but they're nonetheless vital to any war effort—transportation and logistics, for example. "One of the issues we had was with media vehicles," Frushour said. "The battalions were concerned about giving up valuable vehicle space. Some of the media had their own vehicles." Others didn't. "There was a question of fairness, since the big organizations had all kinds of money to support their reports, but the smaller ones couldn't afford fancy Humvees. So the decision was made to have the embedded media ride in military vehicles."

That didn't stop some entrepreneurial correspondents from trying to hide their vehicles, sometimes with the full knowledge of the marine commanders who were only too happy to let the journalists find their own rides. Inevitably, the reporters and photographers who "gave up their vehicles were real ticked at the ones who ignored the rule and seemed to get away with it," Frushour said. "In the end, no media crossed the border in their own vehicles. Several media vehicles were abandoned at the border."

She advised marine commanders to give reporters access to classified briefings so that they could better understand the military. "If you felt like you could trust them, then you were encouraged to let them attend the planning meetings," Frushour explained. "Then, when they went on the mission they would have a better understanding of what the mission was, how it was planned, what the purpose was, and how effective it was." Mission planning is secret, but only *before* the combat occurs. Afterward, she said, "The planning that went into that is no longer classified." Letting reporters see the planning also saved time, Frushour said. "We didn't have to explain the planning after the fact—the reporter already knew."

By and large, opening up to the media worked well for the military, with one major exception: When the French equivalent of the Associated Press—Agence France Presse, or AFP—photographed a map in a slide show that inadvertently showed the marines' invasion route. The briefing officer had approved a low-resolution reproduction of AFP's picture, not realizing that when it was altered for publication in a high-resolution format, it would clearly show the classified map. "It was on the front page of the *New York Times* one or two days before we went in," Frushour said. The inadvertent leak caused a major blowup among the marine commanders, but apparently, Saddam Hussein wasn't reading the *New York Times*. "Obviously, it didn't hurt us." As the 45,000-strong force entered Iraq, said Frushour, "It was very much making it up as we went along. . . . No plan lasts the first few hours of a battle."

This was especially true the night of "the Polish media incident." Frushour was awakened in her tent when a senior officer informed her that two members of the Polish media showed up unannounced. She went to the security guards holding the exhausted reporters, who explained they had left their assigned unit for embedding and decided to drive across Iraq in two cars "because it looked more exciting," Frushour said. "They had put 'TV' in duct tape on the side of the vehicles," then took off across the desert.

Unfortunately for the Poles, some Iraqi soldiers stopped them—an event that was captured on tape as the Poles in the front car were filmed by their friends trailing behind. When the Iraqis pointed weapons at their friends, making them get down on their knees, "You can hear them say, 'oh crap,' then reverse the car and do a California 180 and take off." The Americans might have dismissed the claim except for the tape which the Poles turned over as proof.

Since they weren't embedded with the I MEF, though, Frushour regretfully told the wayward scribes they would have to try to make it to Baghdad and contact the Polish embassy. "'We have a mission here,'" she told them. "'Our mission is not to find your guys.' It was a hard thing to say." Later, Frushour heard that the captive Poles had escaped, and everyone made it out alive.

Summarizing her experience with embedded reporters, she said, "It all came down to personalities. Some of the marines loved them, and some couldn't stand them. One reporter, he just rubbed the marines the wrong way. The marines felt like the stories he was filing didn't accurately reflect what had happened." After reading the reporter's work, Frushour agreed. "They weren't biased—just bad reporting."

Frushour found the unpopular reporter at a regimental command post. "They disembedded me," the reporter told her. The regimental commander arrived and heard the same thing: the marines at his assigned battalion had kicked him out. "The regimental commander sighed and told him to get in his truck. He took him back down to the battalion and re-embedded him with the explanation that you can't just randomly kick the reporter out."

Al Eskalis, a soft-spoken marine captain, had his own front seat of history in Iraq—and his own unique viewpoints of the ensuing culture clash.

A native of Egypt, he was born into a family of Coptic Christians living among the Muslims in Alexandria. "My father was a captain in the Egyptian Army and fought in the 1967 and 1973 wars" against Israel, Eskalis said. Trained as a chemical engineer, the elder Eskalis flew to New York in 1979 in search of a better job. Like so many emigrants, he had to settle for odd jobs in warehouses and grocery stores. But in 1980, he had earned enough money to send three plane tickets back to Egypt—one for his wife, one for his son, Al, and one for his daughter.

They settled in a one-room shack outside New York City in New Jersey. "I failed English my first two or three years of school," Eskalis recalled. "My parents really made sure I spoke this language. We spent a lot of nights reading from the English Bible, reciting verses." Later, they moved to Hackensack, New Jersey, where he grew up in a neighborhood with Italians, Greeks, and Syrians.

His father pushed him to go to college, but Al had other plans. His next door neighbor had just left the U.S. Marine Corps and spun tales about going on cruises to exotic ports of call. Eskalis thought, "Yeah, I'm going to party for four years and find myself."

But after he joined, the glamour quickly wore off, especially after he was chosen to become a cook. "I never pictured myself baking pies for the rest of my life." One day he heard about tests for something he'd never heard of—public affairs. He was selected because he was the fastest typist in his group, the result of taking a high-school typing course. "To this day, I say it's the reason I'm a marine public-affairs officer, that one course I took in Hackensack."

Eskalis quickly took to the work, mastering the writing, photography, and editing skills it took to work in the public-affairs department. And his ability to read and speak Arabic at a minimal level—what he calls "Jersey Arabic"—gave him a competitive edge over his peers within the corps when it was time to pick who would get the first crack at Iraq.

His Arabic roots were tapped one night near Nasiriyah when he heard about the rescue of a young army private who'd been held hostage at a local hospital. Eskalis, a lieutenant at the time, was working as a media officer for the I MEF, where he was helping embedded media following the MEF's commander, Gen. James Conway.

Word came down about the rescue of Jessica Lynch, but Eskalis knew very little at the time because "CNN wasn't piped in in the middle of the desert." Eskalis learned more from some of the reporters who'd heard the Pentagon was hailing Lynch's rescue from her captors after some members of the army's 507th Ordnance Maintenance Company made a wrong turn at Nasiriyah on the banks of the Euphrates River on March 23. The attack, one of the first setbacks for the U.S. in the war, drew attention because it was conducted by Saddam's *Fedayeen*, the militia formed by Saddam Hussein's son Uday.

Nine of Lynch's fellow soldiers died, five were captured, and seven were listed as missing in action. The key to the early story, though, was the Defense Department's first account that said Lynch fought bravely to avoid capture, returning fire at the *Fedayeen*.

Eskalis knew nothing about this official legend being created back home. He first learned about the Jessica Lynch rescue after a command brief when an officer explained that an Iraqi family was nearby who had helped the American soldier escape. "You might translate for them," the officer said.

So Eskalis found the family headed by a man the military called simply "Mohammed" to protect their safety. The thirty-two-year-old lawyer was married to a nurse who worked in the hospital. They had brought out their nine-year-old daughter as well. "They looked ragged and hungry," Eskalis said. "I got to talking to him. He kept talking about this blond-haired girl at the hospital, asking, 'How is she? How is she?'"

Four reporters—among them Peter Baker from the *Washington Post*, Mark Manzetti of the *Los Angeles Times*, and reporters for *USA Today* and the *Orlando Sentinel*—listened as Eskalis talked with Mohammed and translated.

"We sat around a chem-light camp fire in the middle of the desert," Eskalis explained. "They asked questions through me, and I translated the best I could." The Iraqi couple "told them this great story about how he knew the invasion was coming, that he knew the Americans were coming. These *Fedayeen* forces were wreaking havoc on him and his family and town." Mohammed had risked arrest or even execution by sneaking a satellite TV into his home, hiding a VCR under his bed.

"He went to the hospital to visit his wife and saw this girl there, and saw the *Fedayeen* staking out the floor of the hospital. Word was getting around that they were going to amputate her legs." Mohammed suspected the *Fedayeen* were simply trying to torture the young American. "He wanted to do something," Eskalis said. "He felt a bond with her," even though Lynch was unconscious at the time. She was an American, and he viewed them as liberators.

Mohammed "went back to the American line," Eskalis said. "I imagine he was met with some skepticism. They didn't know who this guy was. He literally risked his life to talk to these forces. He walked up to the control point with his hand up in the air." Mohammed met the marines of Task Force Tarawa, and under question with intelligence specialists, he sketched a map of the hospital.

When he returned to his house, he found it had been ransacked. "The secret police and the *Fedayeen* knew he was conspiring with the Americans," Eskalis said. "His family was in danger, so he sought refuge. That's when we linked up."

Eskalis was gripped by the story of the family who wore sweatshirts to protect them against the cold of April in the desert. It was a day after Lynch's rescue. The nighttime interview provided "a great perspective,"

Eskalis said. "This guy was just happy. He kept saying it was a turning point—his country was going to get better. He had a real patriotism."

The brave Nasiriyan's full name was Mohammed al-Rehaief. He later wrote an autobiography describing his hard life living as a member of the oppressed Shiite majority. He was arrested and beaten for owning a satellite dish; his daughter lost a lung to misdiagnosis and unneeded surgery; a cousin was hanged for joining an Islamic political group. Despite all of these hardships, he felt sympathy for the injured girl in the hospital. "I cannot say how I pictured this American POW, but I never imagined her as quite so small or quite so young. She was a child, really. Her bed had been raised to a forty-five degree angle and faced me head-on, so I could see her clearly. She was mostly covered by a white blanket. Her forehead was bandaged. Her mouth was knit in pain."[1]

Mohammed snuck into the hospital with help from his wife and sister-in-law, who were nurses, and began plotting his rescue of Lynch. "This girl's future still held possibilities. . . . I felt strangely tied to her. She was my responsibility now."[2]

The story of sacrifice and rescue played to rave reviews back in the U.S. "Mohammed, a gregarious 32-year-old Iraqi lawyer, went by the hospital in Nasiriyah one day last week to visit his wife, who worked there as a nurse, when he noticed the ominous presence of security agents," Baker wrote in a front page story in the *Washington Post*. "Curious, he asked around, and a doctor friend told him an American soldier was being held there. Something made him want to go see. The doctor took him to a first-floor emergency wing where he pointed out the soldier through a glass interior window—a young woman lying in a bed, bandaged and covered in a white blanket."[3]

Baker described Mohammed's account of his hospital visit, as the security agent "slapped the American woman with his open palm, then again with the back of his hand," and how "in that instant . . . he resolved to do something."

That decision, Baker wrote from the battlefield, "set in motion one of the most dramatic moments in the first two weeks of the war in Iraq. Five days after Mohammed located U.S. Marines and told them what he knew, Black Hawk helicopters swooped in under cover of darkness, touching down next to the six-story hospital, and a team of heavily-armed commandos stormed the building. With hand-scrawled maps from Mohammed and his wife, the commandos quickly found the injured PFC Jessica Lynch and spirited her away to safety."

The made-for-TV script would have been fine on its own merits. Unfortunately, the Pentagon—eager for a good news story to offset early reports of U.S. forces getting bogged down on en route to Baghdad—could not let the story speak for itself. The military spinmeisters inflated Lynch's role, saying she valiantly fired away at the *Fedayeen* before being captured. As the *Los Angeles Times* reported later, "A 19-year-old soldier from rural West Virginia . . . became the face of American heroism and grit in the war against the regime of Saddam Hussein."

But as in so much of combat, the truth was not made for TV. "Although news accounts at first suggested that Lynch was wounded as she bravely tried to shoot her way out of the ambush, the Army now believes that she was 'severely injured' only after the Humvee in which she was riding was hit by gunfire and then slammed into a stalled tractor-trailer."[4]

"Both inside and outside the government," the *Los Angeles Times* wrote, "the Iraq war has been described as a textbook example of superior planning and precise execution. But the incident on the morning of March 23 involving the 507th Maintenance Company continues to haunt the U.S. military, particularly as families of the 11 soldiers killed and nine wounded demand answers and accountability for what the [army] report called the 'tragic results' of error."

The Jessica Lynch episode—filled with misdirection and misinformation—would come back to hurt the military's credibility. Testifying before Congress in 2007, a still-limping Lynch reportedly walked slowly to the witness table and took a seat next to another family whose loss had become headline news, that of Cpl. Pat Tillman, the U.S. Army Ranger who left a pro football career to enlist. Tillman was killed accidentally by fire from his own unit. But according to his brother, Kevin, who also enlisted in the army to fight terrorism, officials chose to put "a patriotic glow" on Pat Tillman's friendly-fire death. Tillman said the decision to award his brother a Silver Star and to say that he died heroically fighting the Taliban was "utter fiction" intended to "exploit Pat's death."

Lynch leveled the same kind of charges before the House Committee on Oversight and Government Reform. "The Rambo from West Virginia" told lawmakers she never understood why the army chose to cast her in a role right out of a Jerry Bruckheimer action film. "I'm confused why they lied," she said. Lynch said other members of her unit had acted with real heroism and deserved the recognition accorded to her. "The bottom line is, the American people are capable of their own ideas of heroes, and they don't need to be told elaborate lies."

For military historians, though, it was a familiar tale, reminiscent of Sen. Hiram Johnson's sober assessment in 1917: "The first casualty when war comes is truth."

Chapter Seven

PATRIOT GAMES

I n late 2002, when U.S. Marine lieutenant Josh Rushing received orders to report to U.S. Central Command in Doha, Qatar, he was ecstatic. The young Texan was stuck in a post that, at first blush, sounds idyllic—the U.S. Marine Corps' Los Angeles Motion Picture and Television Liaison Office. In this capacity, he served as a coordinator with the movie and television industry in Hollywood.

He regularly reviewed requests from producers to use Marine Corps bases and equipment, reviewing scripts to check for verisimilitude and to make sure the marines wouldn't be portrayed in a harsh light. Rushing worked with producers of a number of films, including *Windtalkers* and *War of the Worlds*, continuing the corps' long tradition of partnering—and trying to exploit—the motion picture industry. This included providing equipment, locations, technical advisers, and extras for MGM's film *Tell It to the Marines* and Fox's *What Price Glory?* in 1926. Hollywood moguls fought legal battles and debated whether they might obtain the copyright to "Marine Corps." The lines blurred between reality and fiction as Camp Pendleton was made over to represent Central America, China, New Zealand, and Vietnam. The marines played along with Hollywood because whether it was Jack Webb's *The DI* or Stanley Kubrick's *Full Metal Jacket*, the silver screen usually produced spikes in the number of young men—and later young women—signing up as recruits.

If there was an Academy Award for pure propaganda, it surely would go to the U.S. Marine Corps for *Sands of Iwo Jima*, a 1949 film that used actual combat footage taken by marine combat correspondents at the epic—and bloody—battles of Tarawa and Iwo Jima during World War II. The film, which reviewer John Nesbit calls "good old fashioned U.S. military propaganda," is best known for John Wayne's performance as Sgt. John N. Stryker, a troubled sergeant taking his men from training into combat, all the while practicing the kind of tough love on his charges that in real life would have ended with a court martial.

Sands also featured cameo appearances by three heroes of the battle—Rene Gagnon, Ira Hayes, and John Bradley—just before the legendary flag-raising on Mount Suribachi as "The Marine Hymn" swells in the background. The outpouring of public support for the marines led one of their biggest detractors, President Harry S. Truman, to comment that the corps had "a propaganda machine bigger than Josef Stalin's." Truman was forced to apologize later—after the 1st Marine Division fought gallantly in Korea.

For Rushing, such Hollywood-produced hagiographies were practically ancient history. He handled much more mundane tasks, such as arranging for a tank or a fighter jet to be used in a production. The luster of Tinseltown soon faded. The bane of his existence became CBS's primetime hit *JAG*, an adventure drama about elite lawyers of the military's Judge Advocate General group. He came to dread dealing with the show, which he thought traded in ridiculous, Norman Rockwell–like stereotypes of the military.

By late 2002, he jumped at the chance to leave Los Angeles for a job he hoped would be more authentic: serving as a public-relations officer with U.S. Central Command (CentCom) in the Middle East as America prepared to topple Saddam. But it didn't take long to realize that America's fantasy factory had been exported to Qatar, where Cent-

Com set up shop. (Qatar, a tiny, oil-rich nation on the northeastern coast of the Arabian Sea, remains a key American ally in the region, a crucial partner in the Middle East after Saudi Arabia asked U.S. forces to leave to placate increasingly restive anti-West mullahs.)

Arriving at CentCom's sprawling desert headquarters in Qatar's capital city, Doha, Rushing was surprised to learn that no one on the military's public-affairs staff was fluent in Arabic. How would he communicate effectively with the audience of their host nation, not to mention the hundreds of millions of Arab-speaking TV viewers?

Rushing was bothered by something else—the division of labor in this oil rich nation, where the base's civilian workers weren't from the host country but rather were euphemistically known as "third-country nationals," i.e., hired hands from Nepal, India, and Bangladesh seeking better jobs and higher wages than they could find in their native lands. It smacked of neocolonialism, only with a down-home, Texas flavor.

Still, he did his best. Before the 2003 invasion, he waited to be assigned to the arriving journalists. He recalled it was like the NBA lottery, with the highest-ranking officers taking Fox, NBC, and the larger networks. Such alliances were sealed by the goodies doled out by the networks—hats, coffee mugs, and T-shirts. Rushing was assigned to ABC, the European Broadcasting Union, and China's Xinhua News. Then, in what would become a fateful request, he was asked if he'd mind working with Qatar's homegrown satellite TV network, Al Jazeera. At first, he felt complimented by the scope of the request, since he would be on the air in front of tens of millions of viewers around the Middle East. Only later did he realize he was chosen as CentCom's face to the Arab world for all the wrong reasons. He was the junior guy, even though he would be appearing on camera before millions of Arabs.

As the American invasion began, Rumsfeld and others vilified Al Jazeera as a willing accomplice of the terrorists' propaganda machine. But Rushing had a different take on the network, which was funded by the emir of Qatar, Hamad bin Khalifa Al Thani. He came to believe the station was an authentic news-gathering organization, and not, as Rumsfeld argued, a front for anti-American propaganda. The Al Jazeera reporters were not a monolithic force, as some of his colleagues believed. Rather, he came to learn it had a mix of traditionalists—Islamists and Ba'athists—and a variety of people who were progressives and what he called "just good, old-fashioned cynics as well." The Al Jazeerans were united in one thing: they were Arabs covering a war against other Arabs.

Soon enough, Rushing witnessed the high-level antagonism toward his new friends, including the reply Franks gave when Rushing asked the general to call on one of the leading Al Jazeera reporters at a press conference as a sign of respect to the Arab world. "Sure, right after I rip off his head and shit down his throat!"[1]

Franks's diatribe was one of many eye-popping moments that put Rushing on a rather improbable professional path that led him from the Marine Corps into the newsroom of Al Jazeera—an odyssey whose origins are captured in *Control Room*, a documentary about Al Jazeera's war coverage.

From his front-row seat in Qatar, Rushing watched—and felt—the long hand of control exercised from the Bush White House. In particular, he witnessed the influence of a minion of Karl Rove, the Texas political consigliore who came to be known as "Bush's Brain." The president called him "the architect" of Bush's 2004 defeat of John Kerry. In those halcyon days for the GOP, Rove was seen as the mastermind of a political strategy that would extend the Republicans' hegemony well into the new century—something akin to the stretch of Republican dominance that followed the 1896 election of President William McKinley (the same president, incidentally, who had been bullied into war by William Randolph Hearst).[2] Rove's surrogate and enforcer in Doha was a young political operative named Jim Wilkinson, whose power surpassed the military's own media director, U.S. Air Force colonel Ray Shepherd. Wilkinson, though not in the service, donned a uniform and became CentCom's communications czar.

Rushing grew alarmed over the blurring of the lines between political and military interests. Yet it barely raised an eyebrow among the reporters, especially aspiring anchormen and anchorwomen from the major networks who seemed more interested in getting primetime exposure than in grilling the American command.

Rushing was amazed at the spineless behavior he saw around him, as reporters played footsie with the military in return for sound bites during press conferences. "I would actually go around to reporters and ask, 'What are you going to ask at the press conference today?'" Rushing told me later. "And they would tell me! Because they want their moment in the sun—they want to be included in the newscast, and if they ask a general a question and he doesn't have the information, he'll say, 'I'm sorry, I don't know. We'll get back to you later,' and move on to the next reporter. No reporter wants that. They want to engage and get out an answer out of a guy."

TV reporters started lobbing softball questions to avoid alienating Franks, Wilkinson, or anyone in the command structure, Rushing recalled. "They knew the access game. Wilkinson played hardball and you didn't screw with him. And if you asked a question that was out of line, no more questions for you. And that's the way it is at the White House—they play that kind of game. They give access to those who play that kind of game."

Yet Rushing asked the fundamental—and troubling—question raised by such sucking up: "What's the point of journalism if you're not asking the hard questions? You might as well just set up a TV station in the White House and let them say whatever they want." Is it pure propaganda? "Absolutely," Rushing replied. "It's not a new idea. Absolute power corrupts absolutely—that goes back to the Romans. You need someone asking the hard questions."

Even in this intimidating environment, a few reporters did step up to the pitcher's mound and toss hard pitches right down the middle. CNN correspondent Tom Mintier "asked tougher questions and didn't suck up for access," Rushing recalled. Another standout was AP correspondent Nicole Winfield, who grilled CentCom spokesman Brig. Gen. Vincent Brooks about the official version of the looting of national treasures, which put the blame squarely—and totally—on the shoulders of the Iraqi populace run wild. Rushing later called Brooks's response "ridiculous." Mintier and Winfield had a common trait that may have toughened their reporting, Rushing noted. They were Americans living abroad and had not been exposed to what he called "the not-so-subtle war marketing" back in the U.S.

The other journalist who swam against the tide of conformity in Doha was Michael Wolff, a media columnist for *New York* magazine. He became highly critical of the information void at CentCom. "It is not just that the general and his staff and the military communications people seem secretive or averse to supplying information, it's that they don't seem to know what information is. The press office wouldn't even provide the *Newsweek* correspondent with the first name of one of the generals."[3]

Wolff finally asked Brooks one morning, live on international TV, "I mean no disrespect, but what is the value proposition? Why are we here? Why should we stay? What's the value of what we're learning at this million-dollar press center?"[4] It was the 800-pound question mark lurking in the back of the briefing room, according to Wolff's hilarious account in *New York*, "My Big Fat Question." It was met "with a sudden, disruptive, even slightly anarchic round of applause" from the frustrated press corps—"not dissimilar to the whoops when a kid drops a tray in the school cafeteria—and I knew I was in a little trouble." Rush Limbaugh later broadcast Wolff's e-mail address, and 3,000 emails poured in, he wrote later, "full of righteous fury . . . which all, in some way, helps explain why we're in Iraq."

The accounts by Rushing and Wolff serve to illustrate the Orwellian world faced by journalists operating in the hothouse environment of the early days of Bush's war—a show that was getting high ratings back home. In this star-making machinery, far from hampering the war effort, most of the American media actually helped push the images and story lines of CentCom's information assembly line in Doha. "You can't have a taping without a studio audience," Rushing wrote. "We were the pretext for the show—and for delivering the message."[5]

No doubt, the military's public-affairs leaders could rationalize their behavior. They could say they were limiting their comments because they feared putting American soldiers at risk. But despite the openness that Rumsfeld's minions had apparently shown by enforcing the embedding process, the command and control in Doha—and the systematic manipulation of the media—set a dangerous precedent for future wars and future tests of a fair and open media. Military public affairs had been used to achieve political gains. It would not be the last time in the war such suspicions were aired, and until the last American leaves Iraq, it is an issue and a danger that will hover over the media-military landscape as the dust and pollution hangs over the Baghdad skyline.

"We have in our mind in the military that we are not part of the political process," Rushing told me later. "That we aren't a tool of the government. But this administration more than any has really brought the military in and used them in the political process."

The friction and fantasy may have started in Doha, but it was played out daily thousands of miles away, in another briefing room, with an authority figure who outranked any four-star general, a government mogul who seemed to revel in the daily battle of wits with some of the nation's top reporters: Donald Rumsfeld.

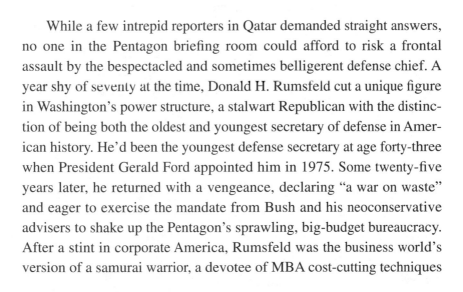

While a few intrepid reporters in Qatar demanded straight answers, no one in the Pentagon briefing room could afford to risk a frontal assault by the bespectacled and sometimes belligerent defense chief. A year shy of seventy at the time, Donald H. Rumsfeld cut a unique figure in Washington's power structure, a stalwart Republican with the distinction of being both the oldest and youngest secretary of defense in American history. He'd been the youngest defense secretary at age forty-three when President Gerald Ford appointed him in 1975. Some twenty-five years later, he returned with a vengeance, declaring "a war on waste" and eager to exercise the mandate from Bush and his neoconservative advisers to shake up the Pentagon's sprawling, big-budget bureaucracy. After a stint in corporate America, Rumsfeld was the business world's version of a samurai warrior, a devotee of MBA cost-cutting techniques that led to widespread worker layoffs, but he was admired on Wall Street and in Republican circles since it helped fuel the economic boom of the 1980s and 1990s.

As chief executive of the pharmaceutical giant G. D. Searle and Company from 1976 to 1985, Rumsfeld sold several subsidiaries, cut the payroll by more than half, and made *Fortune*'s list of the ten toughest bosses in America. He also managed to gain government approval of NutraSweet, a product that did not seem to sweeten his public behavior or his relations with the press.

He also had maintained his ties within the Republican Party, serving as an advisor during the Reagan years, and visited Saddam Hussein in Iraq in 1983–84. He knew how to play both sides of the political fence, making campaign contributions to two Democratic presidential hopefuls, Bill Bradley and John Glenn, and led President Clinton's commission on a national missile-defense system.

Before 9/11, however, in his efforts to trim the Pentagon budget with a corporate bean counter's relish, Rumsfeld had stepped on enough polished toes in the military and Congress that many considered him an early favorite to be ousted from the Bush cabinet.[6] But the former champion wrestler at Princeton also was known as a master of political in-fighting, once writing in a document known as "Rumsfeld's Rules," "Amidst all the clutter, beyond all the obstacles, aside from the static, are the goals set. Put your head down, do the best job possible, let the flak pass, and work towards those goals."[7] He survived as secretary.

Soon after the invasion, Rumsfeld turned on former generals who dared to question the invasion plan he'd spent more than a year refining with Tommy Franks and dozens of other military and defense officials. Air force general Richard Myers, chairman of the Joint Chiefs of Staff, also had told retired generals who'd become TV pundits to put a lid on it. Rumsfeld and Myers were especially irked by the critical views aired by retired generals Wesley Clark and Don Sheppard on CNN and Dan Petrosky on MSNBC.

Perhaps the most authoritative face on the tube was retired U.S. Army general Barry McAffrey, who led a mechanized infantry division during the 1991 Persian Gulf War and had other extensive combat and security experience in Bosnia, Serbia, Croatia, Latin America, and Southeast Asia. After Rumsfeld and Myers chided the retired generals at a Capitol Hill press conference, McAffrey returned fire on TV, saying he "resented the implication that my voice not have a place at the table and that it shouldn't be listened to with some deference based on my experience. The problem," McAffrey continued, "isn't that . . . retired senior officers are commenting on television. The problem is that they chose to attack 250 miles into Iraq with one armored division and no rear-area security and no second front."

(Rumsfeld's ire may have been fueled by a dirty little secret about the Pentagon's massaging and management of the retired generals. The *New York Times* would later report on a secret "information apparatus that has used those analysts in a campaign to generate favorable news coverage" of the war effort—a campaign that continued well into 2008. The *Times* chronicled the cozy relationship between many of the top generals and showed how the retired officers parlayed their high-level access inside the Pentagon into lucrative business deals for defense contracting clients. One internal strategy memorandum called the generals "surrogates and message-force multipliers" and noted how in 2005 retired military officers aided the Bush administration's attempts to deflect rising international outrage at the human rights abuses at the American prison at Guantanamo Bay.)[8]

Later, military commentator and analyst Ralph Peters, a McAffrey protege, lashed out at what he viewed as shabby treatment of retired officers. It is interesting to note Peters's unique take. A retired army officer with a deep knowledge of geopolitical realities, Peters did not object to toppling Saddam Hussein. Rather, he opposed what he viewed as the arrogance and hubris of Rumsfeld's "fawning train of courtiers." Rumsfeld's minions had tried to muzzle McAffrey and others, though these civilians "had never tied on a combat boot."[9] Peters believed Rumsfeld to be "a man of deeply flawed greatness (but of greatness, nonetheless)" and saw similarities between him and Robert S. McNamara, secretary of defense during much of the Vietnam War.

Rumsfeld was hard not only on retired generals, but also on the journalists who jousted with him daily in the Pentagon briefing room. The verbal combat actually began long before the Iraq war, including the signature moment on February 12, 2002—a full year before the invasion—when Jim Miklaszewski, chief Pentagon correspondent for NBC News, pressed Rumsfeld on the question of terrorists and weapons of mass destruction.

"In regard to Iraq weapons of mass destruction, is there any evidence to indicate that Iraq has attempted to or is willing to supply terrorists with weapons of mass destruction?" Miklaszweski asked. "Because there are reports that there is no evidence of a direct link between Baghdad and some of these terrorist organizations."

Rumsfeld replied: "Reports that say that something hasn't happened are always interesting to me, because as we know, there are known knowns; there are things we know we know. We also know there are known unknowns; that is to say, we know there are some things we do not know. But there are also unknown unknowns—the ones we don't know we don't know. And if one looks throughout the history of our country and other free countries, it is the latter category that tends to be the difficult one."

As the members of the press corps tried to follow Rumsfeld's train of thought, which was a bit like trying to hold on to a roller coaster that suddenly flips on its side and follows a mobius strip of track into a dark tunnel, Rumsfeld concluded, "And so people who have the omniscience that they can say with high certainty that something has not happened or is not being tried, have capabilities that are—what was the word you used, Pam, earlier?"

UPI reporter Pam Hess replied, "Free associate?" Laughter filled the room.

"Yeah. They can," Rumsfeld said with a chuckle, "they can do things I can't do."

Another reporter asked, "Excuse me. But is this an unknown unknown?"

Rumsfeld hesitated, "I'm not—"

"Because you said several unknowns," someone else asked, "and I'm just wondering if this is an unknown unknown."

This surreal line of question stopped for a while, until Rumsfeld was asked to answer Miklaszweski's question. "He didn't ask you something that was unknowable," said the reporter, who's not identified in the official transcript. "He asked you if you knew of evidence that Iraq was supplying—or willing to supply weapons of mass destruction to terrorists—"

Rumsfeld replied, "He cited reports where people said that was not the case."

"But we just want to know, are you aware of any evidence?" Rumsfeld was asked again. "Because that would increase our level of belief from faith to something that would be based on evidence."

Rumsfeld finally ended this line of questioning, saying, "Yeah, I am aware of a lot of evidence involving Iraq on a lot of subjects. And it is not for me to make public judgments about my assessment or others' assessment of that evidence."

Miklaszewski ruefully recalled his verbal duals with the wily secretary. "Who doesn't remember Donald Rumsfeld's news briefings when it was not enough to deny the premise, but to demean the individual reporters?" During a 2007 panel discussion sponsored by Harvard's Kennedy School of Government, the veteran Pentagon reporter described the Rumsfeld treatment: "Excoriate them, as he attempted to answer questions, and in most cases, didn't answer them adequately." Whether by design or not, this not only had a chilling effect on military-media relations, but also managed to resurrect what Miklaszewski called "the ghosts of Vietnam . . . this idea that the media is losing the war. I hear those undertones."

The military's blame game eventually extended to internal finger-pointing. Miklaszewski recalled a conversation with a senior public-affairs officer who was berated by a senior member of the Joint Chiefs of Staff for "losing" the war in Iraq. "And he didn't say, 'The media is losing the war,'" Miklaszewski said. "He looked at the public-affairs officer and said, 'You're losing the war. Because you're not getting enough of the good news, the positive news that's coming out of Iraq.'"

The veteran NBC Pentagon correspondent added, "Now, when you got out in the field, and work with the individual commanders and soldiers on the ground, I have never, ever felt any of those kinds of pressures. And, I think it does emanate, or trickle-down from the top. The leadership, at that time, [was] Donald Rumsfeld, and some of the military commanders, quite frankly."

Like Tom Glavine, who once threw a variety of curve balls, Rumsfeld could pitch his evasions in different ways, from citing history to using semantics to making personal asides and even jokes—sometimes within one answer. Usually, though, he threw hardballs right down the middle of the media's plate. Such was the case on March 21, 2003, the day after President Bush announced the Iraq invasion, when a reporter had the audacity to ask about possible collateral damage from America's high-tech bombing campaign.

"You mentioned the allusion to bombing campaigns in World War II and that they were an inappropriate historical analogy," a questioner asked.

Rumsfeld interjected, "Those were dumb bombs and they were spread across large areas."

The reporter (not identified in the official transcript) replied, "Can I finish my point?"

"Those weren't very precise weapons," Rumsfeld insisted.

The questioner conceded the point. "But one thing that characterized those campaigns and the bombing . . . of Hanoi was that the public, their spirit did not diminish; they hunkered down, they pretty much resisted the bombing. What makes you so certain that in this case, even though it's precise, that 'shock and awe' won't just force the Iraqis to hunker down and wait it out like the Brits, the Germans, the Vietnamese, and the Japanese in World War II, and in Vietnam?"

Rumsfeld replied, "Well, for one thing, the people here are a repressed people. And everyone there, I think, while it has to be a terribly unpleasant circumstance, will have an opportunity to see the precision with which we're going about this task, and that the targets are military targets, and that we—this is not an attack on the Iraqi people, it's not an attack on the country of Iraq. It's an attack on that regime that has refused to disarm peacefully."

Later in the press conference, when reporters clamored to ask more questions, Rumsfeld hushed them like a schoolteacher, with a chiding "Shh, shh."

The Defense Department's official transcripts note times when Rumsfeld mocked reporters, such as this exchange on April 15, 2003:

> Question: Mr. Secretary, how confident are you that Iraq still has Scud missiles? And during your evaluation of the battle damage assessments of your bombing in the western part of Iraq, have you found any sort of evidence there?
>
> Rumsfeld: Not to my knowledge.
>
> Question: None at all? Not even like shells or anything like that?
>
> Rumsfeld: (Mocking) "Please? A little?" (Laughter.) A half one of one, is that what you want?

Later Rumsfeld explained, "Look—look, there are still people shooting and getting killed in that country. The western area where the Scud baskets were is enormous! It's enormous!" Once the fighting died down, he promised, there would be a chance to find the elusive Scud missiles.

A month after the invasion, on April 21, 2003, Rumsfeld dismissed the ongoing resistance as coming from "some number of dead-enders that remain in the country." He also downplayed any potential problems stemming from demonstrations by Sunni and Shia factions. "Many of those demonstrators are calling for an Islamic republic to take over in Iraq," one reporter noted.

"Well, I don't know what the definition of 'many' is," Rumsfeld shot back. "Portions of this country have been free for 15 minutes, others for a day or two, or three or a week. Characterizing anything as 'many' or implying that there are large numbers that happen to have that view, it seems to me, reflects a much more insightful knowledge of the situation than I think is permitted at the present time."

Rumsfeld also denied that the U.S. had any intention of occupying Iraq:

> Question: Mr. Secretary, I want to close the loop on the Iraq base question. Was your answer intended to say that you are not currently considering—you haven't considered yet having permanent bases there, or is that you've ruled it out? Because it seems to me that in places where there are U.S. military bases, there tends to be more stability.
>
> Rumsfeld: I have never, that I can recall, heard the subject of a permanent base discussed in any meeting.

The body count mounted, and by mid-July 2003, the fighting had claimed 148 American lives, surpassing the number of deaths in the 1991 Persian Gulf War, as well as thousands of Iraqis. Yet Rumsfeld and Myers continued to deny the obvious: that American troops were fighting small units of highly armed, often well-trained opponents.

Jamie McIntyre, CNN's senior Pentagon correspondent, had been pondering a way to get Rumsfeld to admit the obvious. "Rumsfeld was a very sharp guy and could make very compelling arguments," McIntyre told me. "He could skewer your arguments pretty effectively if you didn't have all the facts." Before the July 1, 2003, press conference, McIntyre recalled, "I'd been trying to figure out if all the upbeat pronouncements were matching what happened in the field."

McIntyre has covered military affairs since 1992, so trying to match the ground truth with official pronouncements was old hat. "We're constantly trying to figure out if what the Pentagon is telling us matches reality on the ground. We get these briefings at the Pentagon with power-point charts, and invariably, when you get out into the field and talk to local commanders and the troops on the front line, you find it's completely different." Generals often say the same thing, he noted.

As American troops kept getting hit by small, organized bands of Iraqis, McIntyre grew increasingly leery of the official story being spun from the Pentagon's podium. "Rumsfeld kept saying they're just mopping up the remnants, and everything is going great." To the veteran reporter, though, "It began to look more and more like a counterinsurgency, and it looked to me like it was being waged by guerrillas."

McIntyre pondered how to break through the secretary's rhetorical defenses. "Rumsfeld has a lot of rhetorical techniques to disarm his foes. The classic one is to change the premise of your question, debate that, and never answer your question." After several years of verbal combat with the prickly, but wily, official, the CNN reporter said, "I learned two things: Either have a rock-solid premise for your question or ask a question with no premise at all."

As he prepared for the next press conference, McIntyre realized his best debating tactic came from employing Rumsfeld's own resources against him, much as a wrestler does when he scores a reversal on his opponent. "It turns out the military has its own dictionary of military terms. I came armed with the military's own definition of guerrilla warfare."

The transcript of their exchange provides a blow-by-blow account of a crafty, experienced reporter managing—however briefly—to surprise a usually unflappable foe:

> McIntyre: Mr. Secretary, I'd like to ask you about a couple of words and phrases that keep popping up in the commentary about what's going on. One of them is "guerrilla war," and the other one is "quagmire." Now, I know you've admonished us not to—
>
> Rumsfeld: I never have admonished you.
>
> McIntrye: —not to rush to any judgment about a quagmire just because things are getting tough. But can you remind us again why this isn't a "quagmire"? And can you tell us why you're so reluctant to say that what's going on in Iraq now is a guerrilla war?

Rumsfeld: I'll do my best. I guess the reason I don't use the phrase "guerrilla war" is because there isn't one, and it would be a misunderstanding and a miscommunication to you and to the people of the country and to the world. If you think what I just answered on the first question—looters, criminals, remnants of the Ba'athist regime, foreign terrorists who came in to assist and try to harm the coalition forces, and those influenced by Iran—I would say that those are five . . . different things.

They're all slightly different in why they're there and what they're doing. That . . . doesn't make it anything like a guerrilla war or an organized resistance. It makes it like five different things going on that are functioning much more like terrorists.

I mean, if you think of what the Ba'athists and the remnants are doing, well, think what they did during the war, the *Fedayeen Saddam*. They put civilian clothes on, went around and took women and children and shoved them in front of them in Basra, as I recall, during the early part of the war, and attempted to use human shields and that kind of approach. Now that . . . doesn't fit the word.

McIntyre listened closely, getting ready to pounce. "So," Rumsfeld continued, I think that if one analyzes what is going on in that country, they would find a different way to characterize it. I know it's nice to . . . have a bumper sticker, but it's the wrong bumper sticker."

McIntyre made his move: "Well, I know. But appreciating, as I do, your appreciation of precision in language . . ."

"You've got the dictionary definition?" Rumsfeld asked. "I was afraid you would have—I should have looked it up. I knew I should have looked it up . . ."

The room laughed. McIntyre kept reading, knowing the secretary was playing his charm card: "According to the Pentagon's own definition . . ."

"I could die that I didn't look it up!" Rumsfeld interjected.

McIntyre continued: " . . . military and paramilitary operations conducted in enemy-held or hostile territory by regular . . . indigenous forces. This seems to fit a lot of what's going on in Iraq."

Rumsfeld, while initially taken aback, gathered himself. "It really doesn't." The press corps laughed. "Now the other part of your question. Quagmire. Quagmire. We had several quagmires that weren't thus far, and I don't know—I didn't look that word up, either. I should have, knowing you. But why don't I think it is one? Well, I opened my remarks today about the United States of America. Were we in a quagmire for eight years?" (Rumsfeld had started his remarks before Independence Day by comparing America's celebration of liberty—with its various stages of "chaos and confusion" in its formative years—to "the difficulties that the Afghans and Iraqis face today. This transition to democracy is never easy.") "I would think not," he continued in his pedantic fashion. "What happened in Eastern Europe? Were they in a quagmire when the Berlin Wall fell down and they started struggling and working their way towards democracy?"

And on Rumsfeld went, telling his CNN questioner, "If you want to call that a quagmire, do it. I don't."

Reflecting back on the media's performance in covering the war and its aftermath, McIntyre said it's easy to criticize the press for not being more skeptical long before the invasion. "The press is constantly criticized for not asking the tough questions" about such things as the administration's linchpin for entering Iraq, the threat of Saddam's WMDs, which never materialized.

While such scrutiny is fair enough, McIntyre said responsible journalism is a deductive process in which one fact leads to another. While some critics of Bush made their own leaps of logic early on, he said, "part of the question is that responsible news media are limited by what facts can be ascertained, and what the facts show. The available facts don't often answer the question. . . . It's the age-old question in intelligence: Tell me what you think. Tell me what you know. And make it damn clear which is which. Responsible reporters are limited by the facts and can't make the leap to what they think." With the spread of bloggers and other Internet writers, he said, "The problem with some journalism is that some reporters want to leap to a conclusion. If they leap to the right conclusion, they want to be congratulated. But if they leap to the wrong conclusion, they don't want to hear about it."

During the early weeks of the war, "Overall coverage was fairly positive," McIntyre said. "Reporters were under pressure not to be too critical. Every time I'd ask questions such as 'are there enough troops on the ground?' I'd get nasty e-mails from people asking, 'Why are you second-guessing the president? What makes you so smart?' There was a lot of patriotic fervor."

McIntyre didn't stop asking tough questions, but he acknowledged, "As you began to ask questions, you had to frame questions in a neutral way. . . . I think it did have a chilling effect. Reporters who are critical of the war, or how it was fought, or challenging the military leadership, were seen as unpatriotic or undermining the U.S. soldiers."

Yet he disagreed with the notion that news divisions of the major networks ordered Pentagon correspondents such as McIntyre to lighten up on Rumsfeld or other Pentagon officials. "Actually, the kiss of death, and the way to lose your job, is to appear you've gone *soft* and lost your critical faculties," McIntyre told me. "Few reporters get fired for being overly critical. Reporters are shipped out all of the time when they appear to be going soft. People think we have an incentive to protect our sources" by lightening up on the military, "but the reality is opposite of that case. It doesn't matter what the Pentagon thinks of us. It only matters what our news organizations thinks of us."

Covering the Pentagon, with its Byzantine power structure, politics, and hard-charging players, can be a difficult balancing act. "To stay on this beat, you have to earn the respect of those you cover, and the respect of the people you work for," McIntyre said. "It's a delicate balance and takes a degree of sophistication."

As Rumsfeld and others began to complain about the tenor of the coverage, his reply was simple, McIntyre said. He told them, "If you want better coverage, the simple answer is that the war has to be going better."

On one flight with Rumsfeld, McIntyre said he watched the award-winning documentary about Robert McNamara, *The Fog of War: Eleven Lessons From the Life of Robert McNamara*, and was struck by the uncanny resemblance between the defense secretaries. This was true of their looks, their speech patterns, and even "the way they formulate thoughts," McIntyre said. In this, he agreed with Ralph Peters, who cited Rumsfeld's "deeply flawed greatness" and described the historical parallel. After the in-flight film, McIntyre asked Rumsfeld later if he'd watched it. "Nah," he told McIntyre, "I was busy working."

McNamara spent years explaining and apologizing for his mistakes in Vietnam, but McIntyre said, "I don't think Rumsfeld will have an epiphany and decide he made all the wrong decisions."

Chapter Eight

THE POLITICAL THEATER OF WAR

O n May 1, 2003, President Bush, formerly of the Texas Air National Guard, donned a flight suit and climbed into the copilot's seat of a U.S. Navy Lockheed S-3B Viking jet. The twin-engine aircraft—given the call sign "Navy One" and marked on the outside with "George W. Bush, Commander in Chief"—made two passes over the USS *Abraham Lincoln*, an aircraft that had just returned from combat operations in the Persian Gulf. With service in the Afghanistan and Iraqi theaters of war, the *Lincoln* deployed for 290 days and sailed an estimated 100,000 miles, longer than any other nuclear-powered aircraft carrier in history. At the time, however, the carrier was only about thirty miles off the coast of San Diego, California, close enough that the Marine One helicopter could have flown him to the *Lincoln*—an inconvenient fact that would later crop up after Bush landed on its deck.

After he landed, Bush traded his flight suit for a dark suit and red tie. As thousands of sailors looked on, he strode purposefully to a lectern on the carrier deck. "Yeah!" a sailor hollered, and the rest of the crew burst into what sounded like spontaneous applause. In his best low-key, Texas Ranger tone of voice, the president thanked the commanders and sailors of the *Lincoln*. Then he announced, "Major combat operations in Iraq have ended. In the battle of Iraq, the United States and our allies have prevailed."

About six weeks after the invasion, Bush walked a fine rhetorical line. He wanted to declare victory without saying the fighting and dying were over. "We have difficult work to do in Iraq. We're bringing order to parts of that country that remain dangerous. We're pursuing and finding leaders of the old regime, who will be held to account for their crimes. We've begun to search for hidden chemical and biological weapons and already know of hundreds of sites that will be investigated. We're helping to rebuild Iraq, where the dictator builds palaces for himself, instead of hospitals and schools."

At times, Bush delivered melodramatic lines like "the tyrant has fallen, and Iraq is free." His speechwriters linked the Iraq invasion to Normandy, Iwo Jima, and other signature moments from history, including the events of 9/11. He vowed that the war on terror would not last forever: "We have seen the turning of the tide."

But the headline for the day didn't come from Bush's hushed speech. It came from a wide banner hung on the carrier's bridge, displayed prominently above the president: "Mission Accomplished."

Combined with Bush's dramatic landing off the California coast, the high-definition day was later seized upon as evidence that the president was playing politics with the war. Bush later told reporters the sign was put up by the navy, not the White House. But as attacks on American forces continued, and the body count climbed, the May 1 declaration began to receive new scrutiny from an increasingly skeptical Washington press corps. That summer, some reports said that the banner was the navy's idea to signify that the *Lincoln* had completed its cruise, but the White House actually made it, according to Dana Bash, CNN's Washington correspondent. "What was once viewed as a premier presidential photo op continues to dog President Bush six months after he landed on an aircraft carrier to declare 'one victory' in the war on terrorism and an end to major combat operations in Iraq," Bash said.

Donald Rumsfeld later told Bob Woodward that he had seen an advance copy of the president's speech during a trip to Baghdad. The rhetoric was meant to echo the formal surrender of Japan in Tokyo Bay on the deck of the battleship *Missouri* at the end of War II, Woodward wrote in *State of Denial*. "The draft borrowed General MacArthur's memorable remarks—'the guns are silent'—and according to Rumsfeld included the line, 'Mission Accomplished.'"[1] Rumsfeld said he deleted the line. "I was in Baghdad and I was given a draft of that thing and I just died. And I said, it's too inclusive. And I fixed it and sent it back. They fixed the speech but not the sign."[2]

Within six months of Bush's carrier landing—and with the 2004 presidential election heating up—the banner issue was seized upon by Democrats "as evidence of bravado and an unclear sense of how dangerous the postwar conflict in Iraq would be," Bash reported.

By the fall of 2003, American casualties reached into the hundreds, easily surpassing 125 killed in action during the initial invasion. When navy officials defended the president's assertion that he was only honoring the carrier's wishes by standing in front of the "Mission Accomplished" sign, Bush's political foes seized on the image making issue. When it was revealed that the White House ordered the banner, some said the carrier landing appeared to be the handiwork of Karl Rove in an attempt to store TV footage for his boss's 2004 reelection bid.

Furthermore, White House spokesman Ari Fleischer admitted Bush "could have helicoptered" out to the carrier, but the plan was already in place. Plus, he said, the president "wanted to see a landing the way aviators see it." Democrats seized on the easy target of a president-turned-flyboy as American troops were fighting and dying halfway across the world. "Landing on an aircraft carrier and saying 'mission accomplished' didn't end a war, and standing in the Rose Garden and stating that 'Iraq is a dangerous place' does nothing to make American troops safer," said Sen. John Kerry of Massachusetts, whose 2004 presidency run taught him his own hard-won lesson about the power of war imagery.

Another presidential hopeful at that time, former Vermont governor Howard Dean, jumped on the Bush-bashing bandwagon. "We heard him try to walk away from the USS *Abraham Lincoln* 'end of major combat operations' announcement, absurdly claiming that the White House was not responsible for the 'Mission Accomplished' banner that decorated the flight deck."

The old adage that a picture is worth a thousand words still applied. And in the age of the Internet and cell phones, it was a lesson that the military would learn the hard way as it tried to channel, if not stop, the free flow of words, pictures, and videos from Iraq.

As the president declared an end to major combat operations, media critics began to question their performance in the dramatic invasion. "They reported from the trenches, hitched rides in tanks, slogged through sandstorms, dodged enemy fire and used whiz-bang technology to bring the war, live and unfiltered into living rooms around the world," wrote *Washington Post* media critic Howard Kurtz on April 28, 2003. "And yet despite the investment of tens of millions of dollars and deployment of hundreds of journalists, the collective picture they produced was often blurry."

Robert Lichter of the Center for Media and Public Affairs told Kurtz: "The fog of war makes for foggy news. War is too messy to package into sound bites and two-minute stories."

With the worst combat seemingly ended—a natural assumption that Kurtz and other media critics made—he wondered about "what the media accomplished during the most intensively and instantaneously covered war in history? Did the presence of all those journalists capture the harsh realities of war or simply breed a new generation of Scud studs?" Was there too much information, he asked, and what did the coverage portend for future wars?

Many of the early politically tinged disputes continued. Kathryn Kross, CNN's Washington bureau chief, told Kurtz that "journalists serve their audience by being appropriately skeptical. If viewers are after cheerleading, they're looking the wrong place. It doesn't mean we're not patriotic."

Fox News Vice President John Moody said that despite the network's flag-waving start to the war, "There were moments when I wanted to make sure we did not cheerlead," such as barring correspondents from referring to "good guys and bad guys."[3]

The broadcast networks quietly began retreating from their much-ballyhooed commitment to cover the American fighting men and women in the nation's first war of the new century. They began pulling correspondents and left live coverage to the cable networks, including Fox, according to Kurtz.

In this post-invasion period, some academic critics said the American networks had sanitized their coverage, showing a "war devoid of blood," wrote Sean Aday and Steven Livingston of George Washington University. This was a minority viewpoint, however. The viewing public still liked what it saw. A Pew Research survey in early April found that 74 percent gave excellent or good marks to the war coverage. Even President Bush praised the journalists, and Vice President Cheney said "the troops have come to know reporters who are willing to accept the hardships and dangers of war in order to get the story right."[4]

Mark Strassman, a CBS News correspondent who rode with the 101st Airborne Division, said the test of the embedding process for him came when he had to report on one of the most startling stories in the war when a U.S. Army soldier who had recently converted to Islam used hand grenades to kill two fellow American commanders.

"It was a very bad story from the military's standpoint, not only because it was a sneak attack in the dead of night," but also because it targeted the brigade's senior officers, Strassman told *NewsHour* on PBS. "But the story behind the story was that as the first real test of the embedding process, it did work." Strassman praised the access from the military, even before the army arrested the soldier who rolled the hand grenades into the tent. There was sensitivity about releasing the soldier's picture and about the fact he had recently converted to Islam. "But in the end," Strassman said, "both those details got out simply because there was nothing about the embed's rules of engagement that prevented that."

George C. Wilson, veteran military writer for the *National Journal*, was less satisfied with his embed experience, complaining that "the view is too narrow" for his taste. Wilson told *NewsHour* about his experiences with the 1st Marine Division. "You were somewhat like the second dog on the dogsled team, and if you saw an interesting story to the left or the right, you couldn't break out of the dogsled team without losing your place because we were moving all the time. Also, the smaller the unit, the more action you saw, but also the less chance of getting your story transmitted."

Because of the fast pace, Wilson said, "I had to go the old-fashioned way of dictating a lot of stories through the satellite phone, and then the military, in its wisdom, confiscated my satellite phone for reasons that I never really understood." He found himself "at the mercy of finding a larger unit which had the transmission capability of my story."

PBS commentator Terrence Smith wondered if the military had cracked down on his satellite phone use for security reasons. Some said such phones have global positioning systems (GPS) that could be picked up by enemy intelligence and thus posed a risk to the military's operational security. "They gave me three different reasons," Wilson replied, "none of which made sense to me."

Were there other restrictions that hindered good reporting? "Not direct restrictions," Wilson replied, "but the higher up you went, like if you went to the 1st Marine Division headquarters, you couldn't sit in on the command briefings. But if you went to the smaller outfits, like the regimental level, they were much more cooperative and you could sit in on the briefings and they kind of trusted you not to give away the store. . . . It depended where you were." Wilson said he heard from other reporters "who were told that they couldn't sit in the command briefing unless they agreed to show their stories" before they were transmitted. "So that was indirect censorship."

CBS's Strassman expressed an entirely different viewpoint. He said he had so much access that "there were times when I felt like . . . a character in some Tom Clancy novel in progress. I mean, I wasn't Jack Ryan, but I was definitely somebody sitting in there listening to what was the battle plan and how it was all going to take shape. And there was never any attempt by anybody there to sort of restrict us."

Wilson stuck to his criticism of the embedding process—not, as some academic critics alleged, because it compromised a reporter's objectivity in covering the military, but instead, because embedding simply didn't give him enough freedom to observe and report on those things that caught his eye. "You had no wheels of your own, you had to wait in line basically for vehicles to become available." This restricted his mobility. He also faulted unnamed marine generals who, he said, "spoke a good game, but they didn't play it" to help embeds such as himself.

Wilson, who has reported from Vietnam, Latin America, and the Middle East, called himself "a willing propagandist" for the U.S. military, explaining, "I think it was set up that way . . . you were put in a position where you would certainly not be antagonistic to the kids that you were involved with and admired and you went in . . . without having the ability like I had in other wars to check things out for myself, which was great for the Pentagon, but not so great for the readers."

Yet the readers—and viewers—repeatedly gave a thumbs-up to the early coverage. Americans in April 2003 gave generally high marks to the coverage, the Pew survey showed. The nonpartisan center found most Americans (55 percent) felt the media gave the war the right amount of coverage, but a significant minority (40 percent) said it was giving too much coverage to antiwar protesters. More than one in three Americans felt there was too much attention to commentary by retired military officers—that is, the leaders Rumsfeld disparaged as "armchair generals."

Whatever their views, the Pew results and other indicators showed how the public's views on news coverage are closely linked to opinions about the war and to partisan politics. With 69 percent of those surveyed approving of Bush's job performance, the percentage who said military action in Iraq was the right decision was even higher (72 percent), according to Pew. The pollster also found that the viewing audience was starting to feel its own kind of combat fatigue: 39 percent said they felt as if they "can't stop watching news about the war."

Yet the story emerging on the ground in Iraq wasn't developing in the neatly scripted fashion that marked the president's photo-op landing on the *Abraham Lincoln*. On August 20, 2003, a bomb ripped through the United Nations headquarters in Baghdad, killing Sergio Vieira de Mello, the UN's special representative in Iraq, and at least 16 more workers, while wounding 100 others. The attack led the UN to close its offices in Iraq, arguably the one place in the world that most needed that body's peacekeeping efforts.

The bombing followed by a month Bush's provocative statement about the Iraqis who continued to attack and kill American and allied forces. "We'll stay the course in Iraq," Bush said on July 2, 2003. "We're not leaving until we accomplish the task, and the task is going to be a free country run by the Iraqi people." Neither Bush nor his aides offered a timetable for withdrawal of American forces. The president continued to assert that the attacks would not weaken his resolve to bring democracy and order. "There are some who feel like that the conditions are such that they can attack us there," he said. "My answer is bring them on. We've got the force necessary to deal with the security situation."

Bush's cowboy chatter drew an immediate response not from insurgent leaders in Iraq—who let their bombs do the talking—but rather from the president's political foes in Washington. Sen. Frank Lautenberg, a New Jersey Democrat, called the president's language "irresponsible and inciteful," *USA Today* reported. "I am shaking my head in disbelief," Lautenberg said. "When I served in the army in Europe during World War II, I never heard any military commander—let alone the commander in chief—invite enemies to attack U.S. troops." Rep. Dick Gephardt of Missouri thundered, "Enough of the phony, macho rhetoric. . . . We need a serious attempt to develop a postwar plan for Iraq, and not more shoot-from-the-hip one liners." White House spokesman Ari

Fleischer sought to deflect the criticism of Bush's combative tone, saying the president was trying to express "his confidence in the men and women of the military to handle the military mission they still remain in the middle of."

In what would become a precursor to the next few years, Bush attempted to forcefully defend his decision to upend Iraq but rejected questions about the growing sense of an intelligence failure about WMDs. "Saddam Hussein had a weapons program," Bush said, employing the past tense. "Remember, he used them—he used chemical weapons on his own people." The president didn't mention the failure of U.S. teams to find evidence of WMDs, instead focusing on the broader mission that had been accomplished. "We're bringing some order to the country and we're beginning to learn the truth." He vowed that "it's a just a matter of time" before the secret weapons caches would be found. As the search continued, the Iraqi insurgents (a word that took months to gain traction, at least in the establishment media) had no shortage of conventional weapons to attack U.S. and British forces. On the day Bush talked about restoring order, assailants traveling in a vehicle in central Baghdad fired a rocket-propelled grenade at U.S. troops, wounding three soldiers. Another grenade slammed into an American truck south of Baghdad, injuring three U.S. soldiers, one of whom later died.

As Bush began his mantra to "stay the course," one American military commander who decided to check out of the action was Tommy Franks, the architect of Bush's invasion plan. Franks announced his retirement in August 2003 and reportedly stood to earn $1 million from public appearances and millions more from a book contract.

Through the late summer and early fall of 2003, the story line of Bush's invasion of Mesopotamia unraveled as quickly as Saddam's regime. Former Ambassador Joseph Wilson wrote an op-ed piece in the *New York Times*, casting serious doubts on the president's 2003 inaugural speech claims about Iraq trying to buy materiel in Niger to build a nuclear bomb. Condoleezza Rice declared that if there were doubts about WMDs "these doubts were not communicated to the president."

Post-invasion reports by the joint chiefs of staff and the state department confirmed the suspicions of the war's critics that the planning process was rushed and sloppy, with little planning for the post-invasion occupation and handover of power to the Iraqi people. Even the December 13, 2003, capture of Saddam Hussein—unshaven and apparently disoriented in a hole near a farmhouse outside Tikrit—provided only a brief boost to the administration's war news.

As the number of American dead began to mount—it would surpass 500 by early January 2004—the media started to report the bad news ahead. One of the most influential stories came from Thomas Ricks, the *Washington Post*'s chief Pentagon correspondent, on October 19, 2003: "Reduction in U.S. Troops Eyed for '04—Gradual Exit Strategy Tied to Iraq's Stability." Drawing from interviews with "several senior Army officers," Ricks described planning to cut back troop levels in Iraq in 2004.

"There are now 130,000 U.S. troops in Iraq," he wrote. "The plan to cut that number is well advanced and has been described in a broad outline to Defense Secretary Donald H. Rumsfeld but has not yet been approved by him. It would begin to draw down forces next spring, cutting the number of troops to fewer than 100,000 by next summer and then to 50,000 by mid-2005, officers involved in the planning said."[5]

Ricks reported that troop reductions could lower the political heat on the Bush Administration ahead of the 2004 presidential race. But even as the plan envisioned limited troop withdrawals from some "well-policed" neighborhoods in Baghdad, Ricks quoted an unnamed Army general who posed a question that proved prophetic, and could serve as the epitaph on several thousand American graves:

"What will it take to sustain the conditions under which you can have political and economic progress?"

Chapter Nine

WASHINGTON ON THE EUPHRATES

When Lt. Col. Dan Williams landed in Baghdad in late 2003, he could see there was plenty of peacekeeping work to do—not with the Iraqis, but rather with the American media. As a military spokesman at the Combined Press Information Center (CPIC), Williams was greeted by a restive press clamoring for answers to the mounting rebellion in Iraq. They were getting stonewalled by senior U.S. commanders reluctant to deliver honest appraisals of the deteriorating situation on the ground.

By early 2004, the CIA was warning the White House about the danger of the outbreak of civil war in Iraq, a caution that surprised nobody who had actually seen the suffering and loss of lives. Shortly after arriving in the Green Zone, Williams tried to sort through a flood of e-mails from reporters searching for answers.

"The e-mail was bitter about things," Williams recalled. The complaints ranged from little things, such as the military command's proclivity for long-winded e-mails nobody had time to read, to larger issues of access to top commanders. "I knew we had animosity here," he told me.

CPIC is the intake center for any journalist wishing to gain press credentials to cover the war in Iraq. It's located inside the four-square-mile area known as the Green Zone, a military designation for the area of Baghdad considered safe for Americans (the rest of the city is designated the Red Zone because it's not safe). The press center was built as part of a rabbit warren of offices located in the Republican Palace, formerly the home and playground of Saddam Hussein.

U.S. engineers transformed the palace into an American playground, with a huge mess hall where red and white linens covered the tables and a dessert table was piled high with cakes and cookies. Halliburton, the Texas-based engineering company once headed by Vice President Dick Cheney, served as a kind of outsourced municipal government, providing food, water, electrical generation, and other services.

If one had any doubt about the role that 9/11 played in Bush's decision to go to war in Iraq, it would be quickly dispelled by the red, white, and blue imagery in the dining room of the conquered palace. A World Trade Center mural was at one of the entrances. According to the *Washington Post*'s Baghdad bureau chief, Rajiv Chandrasekaran, "The Twin Towers were framed within the outstretched wings of a bald eagle. Each branch of the U.S. military . . . had its seals on a different corner of the mural. In the middle were the logos of the New York City Police and Fire departments, and atop the towers were the words THANK GOD FOR THE COALITION FORCES AND FREEDOM FIGHTERS AT HOME AND ABROAD."[1]

Chandrasekaran chronicled other signs of the Americanization of the occupied city, which reflected what he called the "imperial life" of the invaders. These ranged from the Bible studies posted around the dining room to the distrust of the Iraqis in food preparation. "Halliburton had hired dozens of Pakistanis and Indians to cook and serve and clean, but no Iraqis. Nobody ever explained why, but everyone knew. They could poison the food."[2]

A new economy, based on outsourcing to politically plugged-in contractors, was established. Saddam's *Republican* Palace took on a new, unintentionally partisan meaning. The soldiers, private contractors, and security guards from growing firms such as Blackwater USA all spoke from the same page—the same one used in Doha, Washington, and now Baghdad.

The walling-off of Baghdad wasn't limited to the Iraqi populace. American reporters also struggled to break down walls to gain access to facts, plans, stories, or anything of value from the military command. Lieutenant Colonel Williams said he tried to link reporters with senior leaders, but it was difficult. Lt. Gen. Ricardo Sanchez, the top military commander in Iraq, was press shy, and Williams found it hard to change his mind, despite his argument that the media deserved better access to the decision-makers. "They're our customers," Williams said. "You don't want the customer to walk away. Then we have no one to deal with. We need them to carry the message back home. We can't afford to lose them."

One media "customer" was Anthony Shadid, foreign correspondent for the *Washington Post*. Baghdad in 2003 "was a story . . . for foreign correspondents unlike anything we'd ever seen before," Shadid reflected. A typical assignment in another country involved "trying to understand the country, trying to make sense of the place, trying to understand where events were going, and how they were unfolding. But in Iraq we had a different situation, because all of a sudden we had, almost, the infrastructure of Washington imposed on that story at the same time."[3]

The key figure in this Bush-based command-and-control structure was L. Paul "Jerry" Bremer, a Yale alumnus like the president. Unlike his boss, though, Bremer was a workaholic. After earning a master's degree in business administration from Harvard, he entered the Foreign Service and traveled with Henry Kissinger during his "shuttle diplomacy" after the 1973 Arab-Israeli War. Bremer also was a devout Catholic who reportedly attended Mass every Sunday in the palace chapel, which Chandrasekaran described as a "vast room adorned with a mural of a Scud missile."[4] Bremer's closely held leadership methods—some called them dictatorial tendencies—only made matters worse between the media and military.

Col. Steve Boylan, who would later become General Petreaus's chief spokesman, fought his own battles to provide factual information to the press under the strictures of the U.S. military command then in place. "It seemed to me there was a risk-avoidance environment" in dealing with the press, Boylan told me. From August 2004 to December 2005, Boylan headed CPIC, but he was "too far down the totem pole" to understand the mindset of Gen. George Casey, the senior commander at the time. "But with all the requests for interviews that came through my desk, they were rarely if ever granted."

One explanation for the reticence was that Casey and other senior commanders wished to let the Iraqi military and government speak for itself. But, Boylan added, "It was too soon to just hand over the media engagement to the Iraqis as they were not talking, and to be fair, the American public does not want to hear from the Iraqi government on what our soldiers are doing, why they are getting wounded and so on. The media knew this and so the coverage reflected it."

Boylan struggled to work with the restive reporters inside CPIC's cramped offices. "I am quite surprised I wasn't fired for being the daily spokesperson," he told me. "I rarely asked permission, as director of the combined press center. I answered questions to the best of my ability and continued to engage with the media."

Boylan was adamant about the importance for the military to keep communicating through the media, even when it's hard. "We have an obligation to tell our audience, the American public, what is happening with their sons, daughters, friends, family members. We have America's treasure here and we have to tell them what is happening." It must be done "within the bounds of the operational security concerns, and issues of privacy, where warranted."

During this 2004–05 period, there was continuing "frustration from the media about not being able to talk to the senior level," Boylan said. Did this hurt the media's relations with the military and, ultimately, how the story of Iraq was told to the American people? "Most definitely," Boylan replied. "Part of the mantra or philosophy on public affairs, or the larger information environment, is that an informed public makes an informed decision. That is a bedrock issue for us." By keeping the American public informed, he said, "by being transparent, giving the media the access they need and what we should desire, within the operational security environment, goes a long way to make this happen."

But Boylan, Williams, and numerous reporters said this wasn't happening for several years after the invasion during the Bremer-Sanchez-Casey period. "I found that one of the most bewildering experiences of my life," Shadid said. "I've never, I don't think, questioned my sense of the story so much as I did back in 2003 . . . trying to make sense of that. At times I felt intimidated, there's no question about that. And, at other times, I felt by going to news conferences in the Green Zone, I understood the story less, and I got confused even more. Trying to keep your sense as a journalist, your sense as a reporter, in that kind of environment, I found one of the . . . most difficult challenges I've come across as a reporter."[5]

Chandrasekaran agreed: "We didn't do a nearly good enough job at writing about the 'what comes next' after Saddam is overthrown when it comes to governance and reconstruction in Iraq." There was scant coverage of the failure of Iraq's exiled leaders before the 2003 invasion to come to any agreement about how their country might be governed, and what the U.S. was trying to do "to foster some sort of political consensus among Iraqis in exile. What were the plans for a post-Saddam political transition?"[6]

Reporters and editors fixated on the search for WMDs and the backbiting within the Bush administration, such as Secretary of State Colin Powell's admission in February 2004 that he'd not been fully informed about the weakness of the CIA's intelligence about Saddam's secret weapons program. It was an important story, but one that would take years to nail down because of the many levels of national security involved. Not getting the WMD story out right away is understandable, given the difficulty of getting credible sources to speak on the record. But, Chandrasekaran said, "When it came to governance and reconstruction-related issues, a lot of those things were fairly get-able. And the press corps should have done a much better, much more aggressive job of asking questions, and truth-squadding claims made by the administration."

The Bush administration's claims about how it intended to handle Iraq should have been put under the microscope, from its belief that the country's oil resources were sufficient to fund the reconstruction and its assertion that Iraq had a modern infrastructure that wouldn't be hard to fix to the notion that "Iraqis would quickly unite to form a postwar administration—all [claims] which we have now learned the hard way were woefully inaccurate," Chandrasekaran said.

Reporters missed a big opportunity to tell more of the story soon after the American forces rolled into Baghdad. Before the war, reporting in Saddam Hussein's police state was a tough, restrictive assignment. "You couldn't go anywhere without permission from the Ministry of Information, you couldn't speak with Iraqis openly and honestly," Chandrasekran said. All that changed after the Americans arrived. "All of a sudden that lid had been lifted off. And you had that rare window in time where you could, literally, travel anywhere, talk to anybody," with none of the security concerns that would crop up by 2004. But reporters didn't key in on the main story, he said. Instead of focusing on the underlying problems of the reconstruction—everything from restoring the country's power grid to paying its civil servants to forming a stable government—"a lot of us in the press corps were off in a dozen different directions," especially when it came to covering attacks on U.S. forces, Chandrasekaran said. "We were sort of playing cops and robber reporter by going out and covering a shooting at a checkpoint, and going and writing about this and that, and there was no systematic focus on the broader American effort in Baghdad to try to forge political consensus, to administer this country. We would go into the Green Zone to try to write about the world of Coalition Provisional Authority, but it was a scatter-shot deal." Even though there were still dozens of reporters embedded with military units in late 2003 and early 2004, he said, "I don't think there were any reporters who were actually embedded with the Coalition Provisional Authority."

As a result, the overarching question of why the Iraqis couldn't forge a political compromise remained unanswered. "That's the issue that this nation is wringing its hands over today," Chandrasekaran said in 2007. "The roots of all that could be seen back in 2003 and 2004."

During a Harvard-sponsored conference in 2007, the former foreign and military correspondents pondered the lessons of Iraq. What could they have done differently then, and what are the warning signs in future foreign engagements? The answers can be found by examining the standards of reporting, specifically how these can inadvertently lead to conventional articles that don't dig far enough below the surface even today in Iraq.

"Did the conventions of the profession prevent us from covering the story as forthrightly as we should have?" Shadid asked. "I ask myself that a lot. Were we too slow in understanding the scope of . . . the tragedy of the disaster . . . how bad things were going in America? I think we probably were."

Media critic Michael Massing noted the stir created in 2004 when a *Wall Street Journal* reporter, Farnaz Fassihi, wrote an e-mail to her friends about the difficulty of reporting from Iraq and her fear of being kidnapped. The e-mail appeared to give Fassihi a freedom and openness that normal reporting lacks. "It created such a stir," Massing said, "because it got through to people" more than a conventional article ever could.

Fassihi wrote in September 2004: "Being a foreign correspondent in Baghdad these days is like being under virtual house arrest." She described the paranoid atmosphere gripping the capital. "I avoid going to people's homes and never walk in the streets. I can't go grocery shopping any more, can't eat in restaurants . . . can't look for stories . . . can't take a road trip, can't say I'm an American, can't linger at checkpoints, can't be curious about what people are saying, doing, feeling. And can't and can't. There has been one too many close calls, including a car bomb near our house that blew out all the windows. So now my most pressing concern every day is not to write a kick-ass story but to stay alive and make sure our Iraqi employees stay alive. In Baghdad I am a security personnel first, a reporter second."[7]

In her email, which spread like wildfire on the Internet, the young journalist told friends it was hard to pinpoint when things took a turn for the worse. Was it April 2004, when Americans lost control of the city of Fallujah, which became a magnet for foreign fighters? Or was it when various Islamic clerics declared war on the U.S.? "Despite President Bush's rosy assessment," she wrote with a brutal frankness impossible in a regular "objective" newspaper article, "Iraq remains a disaster. If under Saddam it was a 'potential' threat, under the Americans it has been transformed to 'imminent and active threat,' a foreign policy failure bound to haunt the United States for decades to come."

After her confessional e-mail, Fassihi "was attacked . . . vehemently in the blogosophere [and] on some of these talk shows," Massing said. "She made a comment that the Bush policy is failing [and] they jumped on her for being non-objective."

Chandrasekaran concurred that too often the conventions of reporting—which require comment from both sides or no comment at all— "left me in a position where . . . in seeking balance, I wasn't . . . telling the story."

The battle of Fallujah is one of the prime examples of the cataclysmic failure of America's political and military leaders in understanding the importance of 24/7 news on the battlefield. It's a place where Al Qaeda in Iraq scored major propaganda victories, and it should serve as a cautionary tale of how not to take the bait when an enemy uses the media to goad you into a fight.

The city's downward spiral into murder and violence began in March 2004 when four American security contractors from the North Carolina-based Blackwater Security Consulting Company made the mistake of taking a shortcut as they escorted a supply run through the city known to be the most dangerous in Iraq. The contractors, driving two Mitsubishi Pajero sport utility vehicles on the main thoroughfare, Highway 10, got stuck in a traffic jam as they passed the main police station and the walled compound of the city, formerly the headquarters for the Baath Party.[8]

A gruesome scene unfolded after the ambush: a boy doused the SUVs with gasoline, creating a conflagration. Boys in the town dragged the smoking corpses onto the street and beat the charred flesh with their flip-flops "to show that Americans were scum under the soles of their shoes," wrote Bing West in *No True Glory*, his account of the battle for Fallujah. "A body was ripped apart, and a leg attached to a rope was tossed over a power line above the highway."

The bloody scene unfolded throughout the day, with townspeople spurring each other on, shouting, "Viva mujahedeen! Long live the resistance!" And after this blood lust, as two of the bodies were dragged behind a car down the main street of the city, came the awful, defining image of the lynching—one captured in photos and TV images broadcast around the world. The mob hung two of the charred bodies from an overhead girder on the bridge over the Euphrates River. The Fallujah massacre was recorded by an unmanned aerial vehicle (UAV), providing real-time footage to horrified military planners and government officials from Iraq to Washington.

The horribly graphic footage sparked a precipitous decision by the Bush administration to order an immediate retaking of the city by the marines. The commanding general of the Marine Expeditionary Force, Lt. Gen. James T. Conway, argued against rushing back into the heavily armed town and engaging in urban combat reminiscent of an earlier war. As West noted, "The last time American troops fought street by street had been twenty-six years before in Hue City [in Vietnam]. That battle had raged for a month, and blocks of houses were leveled. Hundreds of Americans and thousands of Vietnamese had died. The Marines knew that in Fallujah rough stuff lay ahead. They wished others understood that."

But Conway was overruled by the president, a fateful decision that led to a nearly two-year-long conflict with 15,000 combatants and left 153 Americans and thousands more Iraqis dead. "Fallujah provides a cautionary tale about mixing the combustible ingredients of battle and politics, and illustrates the role of the media on the battlefield of the twenty-first century," wrote Bing West. "Al Jazeera's repeated assertion of horrendous civilian casualties, buttressed by selected pictures, evoked sympathy and anger in Iraq and worldwide." Even British generals complained to Prime Minister Tony Blair about America's alleged "heavy-handed tactics," and President Bush expressed concern about the rising casualty count.

"Every battle now has a global audience," West wrote, echoing Marshall McCluhan's prediction of a "global village" from the 1960s. "The April 2004 siege of Fallujah was lost on the playing fields of digital technology. As Conway put it, 'Al Jazeera kicked our butts.'"[9]

The digital age—with its endless steam of videos, webcasts, and cell phone photos—quickly created an information-based war like no other before it. And 2004 witnessed numerous low points for American forces, including the gruesome kidnappings and beheadings organized by arch-terrorist Abu Musab al Zarqawi and the growing casualty count, with an American death toll that topped 1,000 by early September.

But nothing did more damage to America's image both at home and abroad than the release of photographs and videos taken by army soldiers at Abu Ghraib, twenty miles west of Baghdad. Under Saddam, wrote Seymour M. Hersch in the May 10, 2004, *New Yorker*, Abu Ghraib "was one of the world's most notorious prisons, with torture, weekly executions, and vile living conditions. As many as fifty thousand men and women . . . were jammed into Abu Ghraib at one time, in twelve-by-twelve-foot cells that were little more than holding pits."

In the days of looting that followed the 2003 invasion, looters stripped this symbol of Saddam's sadistic power of everything, including doors, windows, and bricks. "The coalition authorities had the floors tiled, cells cleaned and repaired, and toilets, showers, and a new medical center added," Hersch wrote. "Things were so clean," commented the army general in charge of Abu Ghraib, that "at one point we were concerned that they wouldn't want to leave," she told the *St. Petersburg Times*.

The warm fuzzy feeling didn't last long. An internal report written by Maj. Gen. Antonio M. Taguba in early 2004 "found that between October and December of 2003 there were numerous instances of 'sadistic, blatant, and wanton criminal abuses' at Abu Ghraib." Among the more blatant cases Hersch cited from the Taguba report were pouring cold water on naked detainees, beating them with a broom handle and chair, and threatening male detainees with rape.[10]

Photographs and videos taken by the soldiers as the abuses occurred were left out of the report, Taguba said, because of their "extremely sensitive nature." But the photographs were leaked to CBS's *60 Minutes 2* and showed leering GIs taunting naked Iraqi prisoners who were forced into humiliating poses. Charges were brought against six suspects, and one, Pvt. Lynndie England, was reassigned to Fort Bragg, North Carolina, after becoming pregnant.

"The photographs tell it all," Hersch wrote. "Private England, a cigarette dangling from her mouth, is giving a jaunty thumbs-up sign and pointing at the genitals of a young Iraqi, who is naked except a sandbag over his head, as he masturbates." Other equally odious photos emerged, including one that became the signature image for the scandal: Spc. Charles A. Graner grinning behind a female soldier and a cluster of naked soldiers piled like animals in a pyramid.

Secretary of State Colin Powell later admitted the prisoner abuse scandal had "a terrible impact" on America's international image. But Powell, who had put his stellar reputation on the line for his commander in chief, told foreign leaders: "Watch America. Watch how we deal with this. Watch how America will do the right thing."

The investigations and subsequent trials of soldiers were a double-edged sword for the Bush administration, however, especially amid allegations of similarly sadistic and degrading techniques used at the U.S. detention facility at Guantanamo Bay, Cuba. According to subsequent testimony before the Senate Armed Services Committee, Rumsfeld approved techniques such as forcing a stubborn detainee to wear women's underwear on his head and confronting prisoners with snarling dogs. Military investigators who briefed the Senate committee called the tactics "creative" and "aggressive" but said they never crossed the line into torture. That testimony drew a link between the interrogation practices at Guantanamo and Abu Ghraib and some of the military figures who oversaw both facilities. Some of the Abu Ghraib soldiers said they were following directions of military intelligence officers to "soften up" detainees for interrogation.

In May 2004, Rumsfeld made a surprise visit to Baghdad and visited Abu Ghraib. "We wanted to have a chance to look you folks in the eye to tell you how proud we are and what a wonderful job you are doing," Rumsfeld told troops after visiting the prison site. He told them the president "said to give you his respect—he knows what you're doing. It's noble work, he knows it's important, he values it and appreciates it and wanted to send his personal regards."

As he tried to offset the growing outrage over America's behavior in the prison, Rumsfeld tried to put a good face on things by focusing on the civil reconstruction work the troops performed. "In recent days," he said, "there's been a focus on a few that have betrayed our values and sullied the reputation of our country." But the actions of a few, he said, do not represent "the values of America."

In a later meeting with troops, Rumsfeld admitted the Abu Ghraib scandal "was a body blow" to the military. But, he added, "Don't let anyone tell you that America's what's wrong with this world 'cause it's not true. . . . It's a great country, the American people are wonderful people, and we'll get through this tough period, let there be no question."

Then Rumsfeld took the media to the woodshed. With so much negative reporting out of Iraq, he charged, "You don't read a lot about the schools are open, the hospitals are open. They've got a new dinar and the dinar's been steady and strong." With its currency on the upswing and its infrastructure starting to arise, Rumsfeld proclaimed, "This country has a future . . . it has every opportunity in the world to be an engine and an energy source here in this region for good. Goodness knows it has not been an engine for good for many decades." Then he trumpeted plans to reduce the prisoner population at Abu Ghraib and build a new prison called "Camp Redemption."

But redemption at Abu Ghraib would take more than a name change. Though President Bush later apologized on Arab television and expressed sorrow over prisoner abuse, the damage was done—not only to the nation's credibility around the world, but also to any chance of smoothing relations between the military and media. "I'm sure everybody in the public affairs operation at the Pentagon knows that the basic rule when you get bad news is fast and full disclosure," said Bradley Graham, the *Washington Post*'s Pentagon correspondent. Speaking at a 2005 conference of the McCormick Tribune Foundation, Graham said, "That certainly was not the case when Abu Ghraib began to surface. The determining consideration was about how disclosure of the scandal might affect military operations in Iraq, how it might affect the morale of the troops, how it might affect the training of Iraq security forces, how it would play in Iraq and in the Middle East." As a result, the Pentagon's official statement on the matter early in 2004 was "this case was being investigated," Graham said. "The full impact of what had happened was not revealed until the *New Yorker* article and broadcast stories appeared."[11]

Lt. Col. Williams told me "there was always a nagging question" among the senior public affairs officers in Baghdad about the lid that was kept on the prison investigation. "A lot of us knew from the get-go what was going on." They urged Lieutenant General Sanchez "to get in front of it" and tell the media about Taguba's investigation in January 2004. But it was March before Sanchez talked about it with reporters. "I'm not sure if he was the decision-maker, or if he got bad advice," Williams said.

An army inspector general later cleared senior army officials, including Sanchez, of wrongdoing. At least seven low-ranking soldiers faced charges in the sexual humiliation and physical abuse cases. "But the legacy of Abu Ghraib and its photographs of prisoner mistreatment that prompted world outrage dogged General Sanchez and ensured that any promotion would ignite a political storm on Capitol Hill over holding senior military officers and top Pentagon officials accountable for the misconduct," wrote the *New York Times*'s Eric Schmitt in a January 2006 report from Iraq. Pentagon leaders feared any effort to appoint Sanchez to a new job, which requires Senate approval for generals at the three-star level and above, would "stir up too much political news in an election year."[12]

By this time, Sanchez had left the war zone to command the U.S. Army's V Corps in Germany. The independent panel that investigated the Abu Ghraib scandal, headed by former Defense Secretary James R. Schlesinger, found that Sanchez was derelict in overseeing detention in Iraq. Despite finding that Sanchez approved the use of severe interrogation techniques similar to those used at Guantanamo, Sanchez and his deputies "consistently maintained that the only practices they authorized for use in Iraq were consistent with the Geneva Conventions, which cover the care and treatment of detainees," Schmitt reported.

After he left the army, Sanchez blasted the media for describing the thirty-three-year army veteran with phrases like "dictatorial and somewhat dense," "liar," and "torturer." Media relations soured to the point where he refused to talk to the military newspaper, *Stars and Stripes*, for two years.

"But Sanchez reserved most of his venom . . . for U.S. officials, saying the U.S. government still has not brought all resources needed to win in Iraq," *Stars and Stripes* reported. "From a catastrophically flawed, unrealistically optimistic war plan, to the administration's latest surge strategy, this administration has failed to employ and synchronize the political, economic and military power." General Sanchez predicted that ongoing changes in American strategy would not achieve victory, but rather only "stave off defeat."

It was a long way from the heady days of the president's carrier land and the banner declaring "Mission Accomplished."

Chapter Ten

"WAR IS ABOUT KILLING PEOPLE"

The first anniversary of the American invasion passed uncelebrated—and actually began to be the object of weak humor by the president himself. Iraq was rocked by a seemingly endless string of IED explosions, shootings, kidnappings, and battles, with the number of killed and wounded rising on all sides. Yet Bush joked at the Radio and Television Correspondents' Association Dinner in late March 2004: "Those weapons of mass destruction have got to be somewhere."

As the Iraq invasion morphed into an occupation, the debate turned to that question Rumsfeld himself had deflected early on: the Vietnam quagmire. The historical comparison began to be made more often as the 2004 presidential race heated up. The Democratic candidate, Sen. John Kerry of Massachusetts, demanded that Bush set a date for a pullout of American troops, and Bush's own Vietnam-era service came under scrutiny. The White House was forced to release Bush's military records after it was reported that he joined the Texas Air National Guard twelve days before his student deferment was to expire in 1968. That was the height of the Vietnam War, when more than 300 American troops were being killed every week.

Bush's stint as an air guard pilot occurred during an earlier debate about that deadlier and more controversial war. In February 1968, the most trusted broadcaster in modern television history, Walter Cronkite, departed from his normal duties as a newsman and delivered his own analysis of what he had just seen and heard in Vietnam.

Until the night of February 27, 1968, Cronkite's views of the war "had mostly been balanced, nearly bland," Stanley Karnow wrote. Then he decided to deliver "a fresh verdict" on Vietnam based on his recent visit during the Tet offensive, when North Vietnamese and Viet Cong insurgents shattered the official façade that the U.S. was close to winning the war.[1] Cronkite, like the reporters who covered Iraq in the confusing days of 2003–04, appeared to have decided that sticking with journalistic conventions would prevent him from leveling with his audience about the whole story of Vietnam, which had become a national debacle. His remarks are instructive in showing the difficulty of drawing lessons from one battle or war and the problems of the United States placing trust in foreign governments. Cronkite said:

> Tonight back in more familiar surroundings in New York, we'd like to sum up our findings in Vietnam, an analysis that must be speculative, personal, subjective. Who won and who lost in the great Tet offensive against the cities? I'm not sure. The Vietcong did not win by a knockout, but neither did we. The referees of history may make it a draw. . . . On the political front, past performance gives no confidence that the Vietnamese government can cope with its problems, now compounded by the attacks on the cities. It may not fall, it may hold on, but it probably won't show the dynamic qualities demanded of this young nation. Another standoff.
>
> We have been too often disappointed by the optimism of the American leaders, both in Vietnam and Washington, to have faith any longer in the silver lin-

ings they find in the darkest clouds. They may be right, that Hanoi's winter-spring offensive has been forced by the Communist realization that they could not win the longer war of attrition. . . . For it seems now more certain than ever that the bloody experience of Vietnam is to end in a stalemate. This summer's almost certain standoff will either end in real give-and-take negotiations or terrible escalation; and for every means we have to escalate, the enemy can match us, and that applies to invasion of the North, the use of nuclear weapons, or the mere commitment of one hundred, or two hundred, or three hundred thousand more American troops to the battle. And with each escalation, the world comes closer to the brink of cosmic disaster.

To say that we are closer to victory today is to believe, in the face of the evidence, the optimists who have been wrong in the past. To suggest we are on the edge of defeat is to yield to unreasonable pessimism. To stay that we are mired in stalemate seems the only realistic, yet unsatisfactory, conclusion. On the off chance that military and political analysts are right in the next few months we must test the enemy's intentions, in case this is indeed his last big gasp before negotiations. But it is increasingly clear to this reporter that the only rational way out then will be to negotiate, not as victors, but as an honorable people who have lived up to their pledge to defend democracy, and did the best they could.[2]

For better or worse, the Iraq war had no Cronkite figure, no one who spoke with enough authority to give the whole affair a thumbs-up or thumbs-down. Cronkite was a towering figure who, according to Karnow, "by a mere inflection of his deep baritone voice or by a lifting

Rex Bowman, who dreamed of following in Ernie Pyle's footsteps, got his wish with Charlie Company of the 1st Battalion, 1st Marines.
REX BOWMAN

Rick Atkinson put aside his research for his books on World War II to follow Gen. David Petraeus and the U.S. Army's 101st Airborne Division in Iraq. RICK ATKINSON

Jim Lehrer on the set of PBS's *NewsHour*, where his straight news approach stands in contrast to the puffy content on other channels.
PBS

Oliver North of Fox News sees himself as a modern-day Plutarch, chronicling the lives of noble Americans in combat. U.S. MARINE CORPS / PHOTO BY CPL. MIKE ESCOBAR

New York Times reporter Damien Cave (second from right) on a day-long operation with an Army Stryker platoon that took a tragic turn. ROBERT NICKELSBERG / GETTY IMAGES

Donald Rumsfeld holding forth at a press briefing at the Pentagon. The pugnacious defense leader spent months denying that an insurgency or guerrilla war had broken out. DEPARTMENT OF DEFENSE

Former Marine Corps Commandant and NATO Commander
Gen. James L. Jones advocates active engagement with the media.

U.S. Army PFC Jessica Lynch became an early, if unwitting, poster girl for the American war effort.

What would Honest Abe say? President Bush's dramatic arrival on the USS *Abraham Lincoln*, with a banner saying "Mission Accomplished," later backfired. U.S. NAVY / PHOTO BY MAHLON K. MILLER

U.S. Marine Corps major general W. E. Gaskin wondered why his countrymen cared more about Paris Hilton than his troops risking their lives. CHARLES JONES

Lauren Frayer, Associated Press correspondent, at work in Baghdad. Frayer worried that too few of her friends back home cared about the news out of Iraq. CHARLES JONES

Master Gunnery Sgt. Phil Mehringer's bulletin board at Camp Fallujah. The flag offers this wry commentary about the Marines: "Arriving over water uninvited for 231 years." CHARLES JONES

Cpl. Christopher Stankiewicz, son of a school superintendent, always had an erudite point to add to the discussion in the Marine Corps' public-affairs office in Fallujah. CHARLES JONES

The author on a U.S. Air Force C-130 transport plane in Kuwait, awaiting takeoff for Baghdad. A helmet and body armor were required, along with a bottle of water to stave off dehydration.
MATTHEW MACLEAN

Maj. Al Eskalis, an Egyptian-born Marine, put his "Jersey Arabic" to good use helping journalists during the invasion. AL ESKALIS

U.S. Marine brigadier general John Allen (center) greets Iraqi Army and police officers in Haditha, with his cultural officer, Capt. Sherif Aziz (foreground). CHARLES JONES

NO BAGS
OF ANY TYPE
ALLOWED
IN DFAC

HANDWASH STATION
ALL PATRONS MUST WASH HANDS BEFORE
ENTERING THE DINING FACILITY.
GOOD HYGIENE = GOOD HEALTH!!!

Outside the dining hall at Ali Al Salem, the American air base in Kuwait. The sign warns, "No bags of any type allowed"—a precaution against suicide bombers. CHARLES JONES

Americans and Iraqis heading to a meeting in Haditha. The marines flew in Iraqi officials by helicopter for speed and safety. CHARLES JONES

Provincial officials in Anbar Province walking with local counterparts for a day-long conference to strengthen ties with Iraq's central government. CHARLES JONES

Anbar's Governor Ma'Moun (right) expresses his hopes from improving water, electricity, and other basic services in Haditha. CHARLES JONES

Holding court. Governor Ma'Moun talks with American officials and one reporter. CHARLES JONES

The golden arches in Kuwait at Ali Al Salem. Note Arabic translation below the "M." CHARLES JONES

Abandoned outpost in Haditha provides wry commentary on fierce fighting: "HiDeatha." CHARLES JONES

PFC Aaron Barnum sprints from kitchen in a Baghdad apartment after retrieving the helmet of his wounded sergeant. The blood of Sgt. Hector Leija lines the floor. ROBERT NICKELSBERG / GETTY IMAGES

Hollywood Marine. After serving as a liaison to the entertainment industry, the allure of Tinseltown soon wore off for Josh Rushing. JOSH RUSHING

Rushing was transferred to Central Command in Qatar, where he became the designated American spokesman to *Al Jazeera*. The marine stirred controversy when he later became a military analyst for the Arabic TV network. JOSH RUSHING

of his well-known bushy eyebrows . . . might well change the vote of thousands of people."[3]

The Vietnam-Iraq debate spun like a carousel with an unreachable brass ring of historical certainty. Spinning from the right, Oliver North used his own service in the U.S. Marine Corps to deride comparisons of Iraq to Vietnam. "Purveyors of the 'news' in our so-called mainstream media picked up the beat—though many of them are too young to know anything more about Vietnam than what they learned from a movie," North wrote on Fox's website on October 27, 2006.[4]

North went on to describe how Iraq differed from Vietnam. First, the adversaries the U.S. faced were "radically dissimilar." In Vietnam, the U.S. confronted hundreds of thousands of soldiers and insurgents who received aid from the Soviet Union and other communist countries and fell under the "centralized command and control [of] the authorities in Hanoi. None of that is true in Iraq," where the more diffuse and less organized enemy—called "jihadis" by North—"has no ability to mount any kind of protracted offensive against U.S. or even lightly armed Iraqi government forces."

While noting how difficult it is to make comparisons in death and casualty rates, North said he did a "reality check" that showed that in 1968–69, when he and his brother served in Vietnam, thirty-nine Americans died every day. In Iraq, that number is 2.06 per day. And during the Tet offensive that so alarmed Cronkite, North said, "There were more than 2,100 U.S. casualties per week." In Iraq, by contrast, the monthly casualty rate "has never exceeded 490 troops." North continued, "Unfortunately, our media intends to use every one of those killed to make their point. It's a lesson they learned in Vietnam."

He then excoriated Cronkite for proclaiming "that the Tet Offensive had proven to him that the Vietnam War was no longer winnable. . . . It didn't matter that Tet had been a decisive victory for the U.S. and South Vietnamese." In a line worthy of Spiro Agnew's worst alliterations ("nattering nabobs of negativism"), the Fox commentator concluded, "Today's potentates of the press are trying to deliver the same message: that Iraq, like Vietnam, is un-winnable. . . . The war in Vietnam wasn't lost during 'Tet '68' no matter what Walter Cronkite said. Rather, it was lost in the pages of America's newspapers, on our televisions, our college campuses—and eventually in the corridors of power in Washington. We need to pray that this war isn't lost the same way."

Even some commentators who opposed the Vietnam War, such as Christopher Hitchens, cried foul at playing the Vietnam card. "The principles of the antiwar epoch still mean a great deal to me," Hitchens wrote. "That's why I retch every time I hear these principles recycled, by narrow minds or in a shallow manner, in order to pass off third-rate excuses for Baathism or jihadism. But one must also be capable of being offended objectively. The Vietnam/Iraq babble is, from any point of view, a busted flush. . . . It's passed on. It has ceased to be. It's joined the choir invisible. It's turned up its toes. It's gone. It's an ex-analogy."[5]

The historical brass ring proved alluring for those on the left as well. Liberal critics began by decrying the conservatives' media bashing. Shortly before the November 2004 presidential election, *New York Times* columnist Paul Krugman wrote about the charges and countercharges over the failure to capture or kill Osama bin Laden in late 2001 at Tora Bora in Afghanistan. If Bush happened to lose the election, he wrote, "Just in case, the right is already explaining away President Bush's defeat: it's all the fault of the 'liberal media,' particularly the *New York Times*, which, so the conspiracy theory goes, deliberately timed its report on the looted Al Qaqaa explosives—a report all the more dastardly because it was true—for the week before the election. [U.S. soldiers had passed through a munitions dump at Al Qaqaa in Iraq, allowing the weapons cache to fall into insurgent hands.] It's remarkable that the right-wingers who dominate cable news and talk radio are still complaining about a liberal stranglehold over the media," Krugman wrote. "But, that absurdity aside, they're missing a crucial point: Al Qaqaa is hardly the only tale of incompetence and mendacity to break to the surface in the last few days."

Krugman detailed the failed military planning that allowed bin Laden to slip away at Tora Bora, allegedly "because the administration 'outsourced' the job of closing off escape routes to local Afghan war-lords." Quoting terrorism expert Peter Bergen, Krugman noted that Kerry's charge—refuted by Tommy Franks and Dick Cheney alike—"is an accurate reflection of the historical record."

Once again the ground truth was lost in the fog of politics. "No matter how you try to blame it on the president," said former New York mayor Rudy Giuliani, who was setting his eyes on the White House, "the actual responsibility for it really would be for the troops that were there. Did they search carefully enough?"

Krugman ruefully observed of Giuliani: "Support the troops!"

Though pundits and politicians couldn't resist reaching for historical comparison, one veteran newsman, Sam Donaldson, cautioned against drawing too many parallels between the wars. For one thing, in Vietnam the military made it easier to hop aboard its aircraft, making things easier for reporters. "We all moved around at our own pace," he told me. "There was no permission from the commanders."

"Now in Iraq most reporters don't get out of the Green Zone," ABC's former White House correspondent said. "You can understand why. In Vietnam, the other side did not target journalists." In Iraq, "There's no effort to spare journalists."

Donaldson's comments reflected the disturbing statistics that showed Iraq had become the deadliest country for journalists in the last twenty-five years, according to the Committee to Protect Journalists.

In 2005, twenty-two journalists were killed in Iraq, raising the total at that time to sixty-one since the 2003 invasion. That number surpassed the fifty-eight journalists killed in the Algerian conflict from 1993 to 1996. The committee has been tracking journalists' deaths since 1981 and counts only those who die as a direct result of combat or hostile action. The *New York Times* reported a separate tally showing that twenty-three media-support people, including drivers and translators, were killed in Iraq in 2005. The latter number continued to rise as talking to Iraqis became crucial to getting firsthand accounts for the newspapers, such as the *New York Times* and *Washington Post*, that kept reporting from Baghdad.

For all of the bad feelings engendered in Iraq, Donaldson said it appeared to him that the dislike of the media by the military appeared greater in Vietnam, "where they *really* hated the media."

I asked Donaldson if he agreed with Bill Moyers and others that the American media generally failed in covering the Iraq war. "Obviously, there was a failure, but the extent to which the media, taken as a whole, can be faulted is open to question," he replied. "I am really not one of those who think we should put ashes and sackcloths on our heads. No one outside the CIA . . . had access to information" about the WMDs, he noted.

It's easy to blame Fox for beating the war drum, Donaldson said, "but Fox to me preaches to the choir. And Rush Limbaugh doesn't convert a bunch of liberals. But they do reinforce [Bush's policies] and harden the attitudes out there."

Another veteran of Vietnam War coverage pointed out a major difference in reporting from a war zone that was far away and hard to reach, compared to today's instant access to Iraq. "What was remarkable was how distant Washington was from us," said Elizabeth Becker, who covered Cambodia for the *Washington Post* and later was Pentagon reporter for the *New York Times*. "We could set a context, which is impossible nowadays. Not only were your editors far away—there were no computers, and most of the time, there were no telephones. So you could file; you set your context."[6]

Moreover, she said, "And you also did not have the bully pulpit of the administration the way you felt it during this war, of constant e-mails . . . they are able to set a context, not just in Washington, but in the war you're covering. . . . It's hard to break out of that Washington box, even though you're in a different war." Unlike Iraq, in Vietnam, when the White House or Pentagon could comment, complain, and criticize an article or story within minutes of filing or broadcast, "my editors would not listen to the Administration for two seconds."

They may not have been as bad as in Vietnam, but relations between the Pentagon and its press corps continued to head south during 2005. Jonathan Karl, ABC News' senior national security correspondent, described the foul mood in the Pentagon he found when he switched from covering the state department to defense in 2005. "I was struck by how much the embedded reporters at the Pentagon were seen as almost like a hostile force," he said at a Harvard-sponsored seminar in 2007. Karl recalled that Rumsfeld's point at the briefings was never to answer the question, but "to tell you why the questioner was an idiot for asking the question."

The military wasn't to blame, Karl said, but rather, the civilian side of the department of defense's public-affairs operation was "set up to counter the media—not to facilitate, not to get information out, but to counter the media." Some of the countermeasures were "little annoying things that just kind of rubbed it in our faces, like the *Early Bird*," the Pentagon's daily digest of news stories. Widely read by military and civilian analysts around the world, the *Early Bird* typically begins with the biggest news stories of the day. During Rumsfeld's regime, though, "the standard practice became to put the corrections first—even if it was correcting the spelling of a guy's name in the *New York Times*."

The finger-pointing was relentless, Karl said, including an entire "machinery" within the Pentagon to bash the media. This included "letters to the editor that were written by the assistant secretary for public affairs or somebody else in the military," whose intent was to lash the media for its alleged "gross inaccuracies and horrible stories."[7] If Rumsfeld's goal was to drive a wedge between the Pentagon press corps and military sources, he seems to have succeeded, at least for a time. "I think that in some cases you would get a real standoffish, deep suspicion of the media," Karl said.

Bradley Graham of the *Washington Post* expressed the frustration. "We often have layers and layers of public-affairs people to go through," he said in 2005 at a McCormick Tribune Conference. "I had one interview last week where there were about ten people involved in the briefing, and four of them were public-affairs officers."

Graham also noticed "increased efforts at regional outreach" to smaller news organizations which "we've seen have come at the expense of attention to larger media organizations." His complaint was echoed by colleagues at the *Post* and other large organizations who also would question the time and access given to independent bloggers—those independent, usually self-appointed experts who were starting web logs, or "blogs," to give their perspectives on the war.

Jane Arraf, senior Baghdad correspondent for CNN, said at the same conference in 2005, "It is extremely hard to overemphasize how much reporting has changed there over the last year. A year and a half ago, we had unimaginable freedom. We could be in Baghdad, we could drive to Karbala, to Mosul or to Fallujah. We did not have to be embedded. We could stay in Iraqi hotels and speak with Iraqis and the military as well. That's impossible these days. The only way I've been able to show our viewers parts of the country that normally don't get covered—and, ironically, the only way I've been able to talk to large numbers of Iraqis—is to be embedded with the Army and with the Marines." As Americans wondered about the morale of troops and conditions on the ground, she said, "We can't be behind the front lines. We need to be there showing people what's it's like in Iraq."

Even as Pentagon officials and the White House complained about the lack of "positive" stories, Arraf observed that she has done numerous "good news stories" "because I've been in Iraq for a long time and I can see the changes." But she still received complaints from the military. "It's not black and white—we all know that," she said. "And there has to be a balanced picture. But the best thing you can do for the military's credibility is to show us everything and let us make up our own minds."[8]

Arraf noted that some editors and viewers only want to see "the sensational stuff: the explosions, the gunfire, people dying," and not the stories about rebuilding Fallujah. "They either get knocked off the air by a missing girl in Aruba or by our people at the network and viewers who want the daily violence," Arraf said. "That's more exciting than people rebuilding. And that is a serious problem that we really have to try to face."

As the number of embedded reporters dropped—there were only 26 in 2005, down from about 200 in 2004 and the more than 700 in

2003—Arraf suggested that the military needed to open itself up to wider coverage. "You need to embrace the Iraqi media," she advised. "I know there is a concern about security, but I'm surprised to hear that reporters are under suspicion of being insurgents. Almost every news organization I know has had a stringer of some sort—cameramen, not necessarily reporters—in jail at some time. I'm not sure that it's in your best interest as the military not to reach out to Iraqi media . . . I've been on bases where they've refused to deal with a specific news agency because they don't like one of their stringers. I've been on bases where they've said that they would rather deal with another network that's seen as more patriotic. You have to talk to everyone. You cannot complain that we're not telling your story if you're not letting us tell the story."

If base commanders were turning away CNN reporters or Iraqi stringers, perhaps they were just mirroring the messages they were receiving from the Pentagon. Secretary Rumsfeld, in his internal musings to his staff known as "snowflakes," tried to counter the news stories on the deteriorating conditions in Iraq, according to Robin Wright of the *Washington Post*. In a 2004 memo, "Rumsfeld concluded that the challenges in Iraq are 'not unusual' and he mused that 'our public risks falling prey to the argument that all is lost.'"

Two years later, after a number of retired generals denounced Rumsfeld and called for his resignation, Rumsfeld wrote about a conference call with military analysts, "Talk about Somalia, the Philippines, etc. Make the American people realize they are surrounded by violent extremists." People will "rally" to sacrifice, he wrote. "They are looking for leadership. Sacrifice=Victory," Rumsfeld wrote, according to Wright's account of the memos.[9]

She reported these other revelations about Rumsfeld's "snowflakes," written at the rate of twenty to sixty per day:

- He argued that Muslims avoid "physical labor" and wrote of the need to keep "elevating the threat," "link Iraq to Iran," and develop "bumper sticker statements" to rally public support for the increasingly unpopular war.

- Rumsfeld said he needed a team to help him "go out and push people back, rather than simply defending" Iraq policy and strategy. "I am always on the defense," he complained, perhaps with unintended irony. "They say I do it well, but you can't win on the defense. We can't just keep taking hits."
- "Rumsfeld suggested that the public should know that there will be no 'terminal event' in the fight against terrorism like the signing ceremony on the USS Missouri when Japan surrendered to end World War II." The secretary wrote, "It is going to be a long war. Iraq is only one battleground. . . . Iran is the concern of the American people, and if we fail in Iraq, it will advantage Iran."
- In May 2004, Rumsfeld "considered whether to redefine the terrorism fight as a 'worldwide insurgency.'" He wrote that the enemy's goal is to "end the state system, using terrorism, to drive the non-radicals from the world." Drawing on his corporate marketing experience, Rumsfeld instructed aides "to test what the results could be" if the war on terrorism were renamed.
- He also complained that oil wealth had spoiled many Muslims, detaching them "from the reality of work, effort and investment . . . too often Muslims are against physical labor, so they bring in Koreans and Pakistanis while their young people remain unemployed. . . . An unemployed population is easy to recruit to radicalism."

Rumsfeld also wasn't above targeting specific columnists, such as former U.S. Army lieutenant colonel Ralph Peters, who had written a harsh assessment of the defense secretary and his "fawning train of courtiers" in 2003 but who nevertheless supported the war. The retired officer had clearly gotten under Rumsfeld's skin. "I think you ought to get out a letter about Ralph Peters' op-ed in the *New York Post*," he wrote on February 6, 2006. "It is terrible." Peters had criticized the "chronic troop shortages in Iraq" while the Pentagon buys "high-tech toys that have no missions."

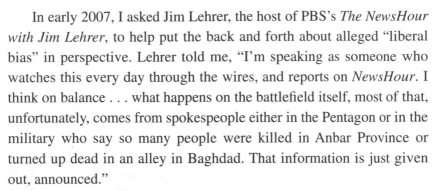

In early 2007, I asked Jim Lehrer, the host of PBS's *The NewsHour with Jim Lehrer*, to help put the back and forth about alleged "liberal bias" in perspective. Lehrer told me, "I'm speaking as someone who watches this every day through the wires, and reports on *NewsHour*. I think on balance . . . what happens on the battlefield itself, most of that, unfortunately, comes from spokespeople either in the Pentagon or in the military who say so many people were killed in Anbar Province or turned up dead in an alley in Baghdad. That information is just given out, announced."

Lehrer continued, "Then there's the big-picture stuff that comes from the generals at the Pentagon . . . [and] the third element comes from reporters on the ground, the embed reporters. . . . In general, all three of these elements are required . . . you can't cover a war with just one of those three—just embeds, or just big shots from the Pentagon, or do it with individual battle reports. It takes the whole mix. Plus, what I consider a fourth element is to use analysts of various kinds, former military officers who understand warfare and the region."

Lehrer, a former marine, dismissed the complaints by some that the media had ignored "positive" news on the war. "I can't imagine someone saying there's not enough good news from war. That's absurd. War is about killing people, and war reporting is about why they do it and how they do it. It's details of the killing. To say, 'Oh, no one died, or fewer died, and thirty went to school . . .' We've done those stories, too, but we're covering a war. We are there to cover the [soldiers] in harm's way. I'm very comfortable about that. If that offends anyone, that's too bad. They don't [understand] what our function is."

Lehrer noted that his program tries to pay tribute to the sacrifices of America's fighting men and women by running "every picture of everyone, every American, who dies in Iraq and Afghanistan . . . our honor roll. . . . We media are there to cover them and what's happening to them."

Lehrer's overall assessment of the media's performance in Iraq? "I'm sure there have been things done better than others, but nothing leaps to mind as a particular episode" of bad journalism, adding, "Keeping in mind that in daily journalism, if you screw it up one day, you can fix it the next."

While the veteran news anchor could accept the ups and downs of daily coverage, the two most influential papers in the war coverage, the *New York Times* and *Washington Post*, each saw fit to issue lengthy apologies about their performances in the early days of the Iraq war.

In a piece entitled "The Times and Iraq," the editors of the New York paper wrote on May 26, 2004, that they had examined the war and the failures of those managing it and that it was "past time we turned the same light on ourselves." While there was much reporting of which to be proud, "we have found a number of instances of coverage that was not as rigorous as it should have been. In some cases, information that was controversial then, and seems questionable now, was insufficiently qualified or allowed to stand unchallenged. Looking back, we wish we had been more aggressive in re-examining the claims as new evidence emerged—or failed to emerge."

For example, the editorial highlighted its mistaken reliance on "a circle of Iraqi informants, defectors and exiles bent on 'regime change'"—for example, Ahmad Chalabi—"who were often eagerly confirmed by United States officials convinced of the need to intervene in Iraq. Administration officials now acknowledge that they sometimes fell for misinformation from these exile sources. So did many news organizations—in particular, this one."

Without naming reporters, such as its own Judith Miller, who were clearly used by the Bush administration to press its case about WMDs, the *Times* editors wrote, "Editors at several levels who should have been challenging reporters and pressing for more skepticism were perhaps too intent on rushing scoops into the paper. Accounts of Iraqi defectors were not always weighed against their strong desire to have Saddam Hussein ousted. Articles based on dire claims about Iraq tended to get prominent display, while follow-up articles that called the original ones into question were sometimes buried. In some cases, there was no follow-up at all."

In one such instance, on September 8, 2002, as the Bush administration lobbied Congress for an invasion of Iraq, the *Times'* lead article carried the headline "U.S. Says Hussein Intensified Quest for A-Bomb Parts." Judith Miller reported that "aluminum tubes" used in making nuclear fuel were being obtained by Saddam. "The claim came not from defectors but from the best American intelligence sources available at the time," the *Times'* mea culpa said. "Still, it should have been presented more cautiously."

Five days later, when *Times* reporters learned the tubes were a subject of debate among intelligence agencies, that story about the misgivings was buried deep in an article on page A13, "under a headline that gave no inkling that we were revising our earlier view," the editors said. Other challenges to the aluminum tube story were also buried deep inside the newspaper and thus did not get the attention they deserved by the American public.

Predictably, the *Times'* apology did not satisfy its conservative critics. "Last week, the *New York Times* issued an unusual *mea culpa* about the history of its Iraq coverage," wrote Christopher C. Carson in National Review Online. Calling it a "strange self-flagellation," Carson ridiculed the *Times* for its "healthy dose of self-hugging" and for rushing to judgment about the veracity of some of the Iraqi defectors, especially their accounts of terrorist training camps using a Boeing 707.

The *Washington Post* waited a few months before it assumed its position on the couch of public analysis. Headlined "The Post on WMDs: An Inside Story: Prewar Articles Questioning Threat Often Didn't Make Front Page," the article discussed the paper's own tendency to play down stories that questioned whether the Bush administration had proof that Saddam Hussein was hiding weapons of mass destruction. In the days before the 2003 invasion, veteran national security reporter Walter Pincus encountered resistance from the paper's editors, and his questioning piece ran only after assistant managing editor

Bob Woodward, who was researching a book about the drive toward war, "helped sell the story," Pincus recalled. "Without him, it would have had a tough time getting into the paper." Even so, the *Post* conceded, Pincus's cautionary article was buried on page A17.

"We did our job but we didn't do enough, and I blame myself mightily for not pushing harder," Woodward said. "We should have warned readers we had information that the basis for this was shakier" than widely believed. "Those are exactly the kind of statements that should be published on the front page."

The *Post*'s media critic, Howard Kurtz, later reported a "torrent of e-mails and online posting" after his August 12, 2004, column about the newspaper's confessions. "In interviews that sometimes resembled therapy sessions, other reporters and editors recalled frustrations and acknowledged missteps," Kurtz wrote.

While conservatives liked to use the *Post* as a political punching bag, Kurtz recorded a recent trend: barbs from liberal readers. "The harshest missives I received attribute power to the *Post*, as if the president's decisions hung largely on what journalists thought. It's a newspaper, folks—an influential one, to be sure, and one that could have affected the prewar debate, but no newspaper dictates foreign policy. And as we now know, the Bush administration had been gearing up for war for months, and had all but made the decision to invade even before the U.N. inspectors had finished their work."

One reader declared flatly, "You have blood on your hands." Kurtz observed that such comments tried to make "the war and its violent aftermath . . . our fault." But he added, "The idea that journalists wanted war is, well, ludicrous. Who wouldn't have preferred to see Hussein crawl into a spider hole and turn over the country to the forces of democracy?" Kurtz harkened back to the flag-waving and patriotic fervor of 2003. "With opposition Democrats providing little opposition to the war, antiwar activists were often shut out, especially on the airwaves, unless they happened to be celebrities and then belittled."

He described the underlying problem faced by reporters trying to fairly report the nuances of national intelligence, an area where shades of gray are more likely than black and white. The *Washington Post*'s executive editor, Leonard Downie, told Kurtz he liked "definitive" stories for the front page, like "clear and unambiguous" statements from the president, vice president, or other administration officials, "even if the evidence they cited was anything but." On the other hand, "articles questioning whether the administration had the evidentiary goods on WMDs . . . were tentative, incremental, hedged, pieced together from sources of questionable motivation"—not to mention "enormously difficult" to prove since reporters "have no subpoena power [and] can't compel anyone to talk."[10]

In that tense, hyper-patriotic post-9/11 period, reporters were used by Ahmed Chalabi's band of defectors. They "had a vested interested in blowing WMD smoke to trigger a war," Kurtz wrote. "No one, at least on the outside, really knew what the truth was."

Chapter Eleven

THE BLOG
OF WAR

I n early 2004, Bill Roggio was itching to get over to Iraq. He had solid military credentials, having served as an army signalman and infantryman for four years in the early 1990s and then a two-year stint in the National Guard, but he was in no position to join the fight. At the time, he was working as a computer technician in New Jersey and was simply someone who had an abiding fascination with the media's portrayal of the war.

"I became very frustrated with the coverage of the war," Roggio told me. "I felt it was highly politicized and didn't seem like straight reporting." The 2004 Bush-Kerry race seemed to influence the way networks and papers reported from Iraq, causing Roggio to join in the chorus of conservative media bashers.

"I'd get a lot of questions from friends and family, having served in the military and followed the international situation." At first he started venting his frustrations through e-mails to friends, and he also started reading some of the military-themed blogs popping up around the web, usually written by ex-military or intelligence officers.

Roggio's avocation quickly turned into a kind of obsession as he tracked the news and military reports out of Iraq. With a natural analytical skill, he began devoting more time trying to understand the nuances of the war, and before long, he found himself less interested in working in technical support for a large computer company. One reason was that he'd lost family members in the Twin Towers in New York, and the war became "very personal for me. I had promised to go back in the military, but I couldn't." He had a wife and three children and simply couldn't afford to reenlist.

So he sank his time, energy, and treasure into trying to better understand the war—first, by reading every printed account he could find on the Internet and then by posting comments on some of the blogs. Roggio found he was a natural, displaying knowledge of military tactics and strategy. Friends encouraged him to start his own blog. After a couple of week's work, with help from a program called Blogger—what he called "a blog for dummies"—he launched his blog, which he called *The Fourth Rail*. It was March 2004, and the marines were fighting house to house in Fallujah. Another kind of siege was also taking place in the United States, the presidential race between Bush and Kerry, with its increasingly nasty charges and countercharges about military service, patriotism, and manhood. Though Roggio started his blog to analyze the fighting in Iraq, he soon got sucked into the rhetorical wake of the Swift Boat veterans attacking Democrat Kerry over his Vietnam service in the navy.

"I was guilty as sin as the next guy," Roggio admitted to me about his early partisan enthusiasms. His May 18, 2004, blog post, for instance, used the Bush administration's term for the fighting abroad, the "global war on terror." Roggio's entry easily could have been released by the White House press office: "In order to win the War on Terror, we must fight both at home and abroad. . . . In order to root out terrorists within the United States, the government depends on tools such as the Patriot Act. Members of both the far left and the far right who instinctively oppose the Patriot Act for political reasons are unwittingly playing into the hands of a dangerous and deadly fifth column here in America."

Then, after the June 5, 2004, death of former President Ronald Reagan, Roggio wrote, "President Reagan is my personal hero. I was 10 years old when he was elected, and was inspired by his hope, vision and positive outlook on America and our place in the world. I began to follow politics, history and world events solely because of his leadership and personality, and I suspect I am not alone." Republicans, at least, would surely agree.

If Roggio didn't understand the dangers of mixing journalism and politics, it's understandable. Blogging was still in its infancy, and it was easy for self-declared essayists to be seduced by the global stage of the internet. Blogs were an easy way for people of all political stripes—left, right, and center—to vent about the day's headlines. For the cost of some computer software and the time it took to get online, it was easy to make the leap into cyberspace and join the fray. As Nicholas Lemann, dean of the Columbia University School of Journalism, observed in 2005, "Conservatives love to complain about journalism. Lately, they have been not only complaining more full-throatedly but also devising with more energy than before, their own version of what journalism ought to look like: faster, more opinionated, more multimedia, and less hung up on distancing itself from the practice of politics than the daily-newspaper and network-news versions."[1]

In a 2005 *New Yorker* article on conservative journalist Hugh Hewitt, Lemann wrote: "Things get very media-on-media very quickly in Hewitt's world. His blog, in keeping with the conventions of the form, links to many other blogs (Christian blogs, military blogs, Republican blogs), and he regularly urges his listeners to start blogs of their own."

Indeed, the title of a Hewitt book seems to sum up the rush to cyberspace: *Blog: Understanding the Information Reformation That's Changing Your World.* Hewitt compared bloggers' influence with the reformer of Christianity, Martin Luther, and credits them for bringing down Senate Majority Leader Trent Lott in 2002 and CBS anchorman Dan Rather in 2004. Bloggers also received praise—or blame, depending on one's opinion—for "discrediting a crucial part of John Kerry's account of his service in the Vietnam War," Lemann wrote.

As the war dragged on, many liberals found their own spaces in the cyber-opinion world. Some even called it a refuge from what they viewed as a media controlled by the White House, presumably with Karl Rove at the switch. "Thank God for the Internet, or we wouldn't know anything and we would already be a fascist state," said Gold Star mother Cindy Sheehan, who held a vigil outside President Bush's Texas ranch in 2005. "The mainstream media is propaganda tool for the government."

But as Ron Hutcheson noted in the *Philadelphia Inquirer*, "That's not the view from the right." The Media Research Center, a conservative media-watchdog group, told potential donors, "If you believe the liberal media's reporting of the American military effort in Iraq, you're almost forced to be ashamed of America." In return for a donation, Hutcheson reported in August 2005, the center would send a custom-made military-style dog tag to a soldier in Iraq that said, "Don't believe the liberal media! I'm just one of millions of Americans who realize that powerful elements in the media are undermining the war effort."

The antimedia slant in the military could be found on such mainstream programs as NBC's *Today*, where host Matt Lauer wondered how troop morale could be so high given Iraq's problems, Hutcheson reported. "If I got my news from the newspaper, I'd be pretty depressed as well," Army captain Sherman Powell told Lauer. "Those of us who've actually had a chance to go out and go on patrols and meet the Iraqi army and the Iraqi police and go on patrols with them, we are very satisfied with the way things are going here."[2]

Back in Jersey, Roggio decided he'd made a tactical blunder by jumping into the partisan blogosphere. "After the elections, I looked myself in the mirror and realized this was not why I started blogging," he told me. "I decided to just look at the war, at operations, at counterterrorism." Like a latter-day Jack Webb, the stoic Los Angeles detective of *Dragnet* fame, Roggio adopted a "just the facts" credo. He soon found that "facts" could easily be portrayed as fiction.

Through late 2004 and into 2005, Roggio contented himself with commenting on the accounts of the few embedded reporters still in Iraq and on the dry, but detailed, releases issued by public-affairs units. He found he had a knack for connecting the dots in ways that seemed to defy other reporters and bloggers, often by combining mainstream media reports with the military's own dispatches. For instance, as he followed the marines' movements in western Anbar Province, Roggio noticed one newspaper report about a unit breaking some Iraqis' china in their home. It was a critical story, he recalled, portraying the marines as brutes, but it contained a piece of a puzzle he was trying to solve at the time: the unit in the article was operating in the town of Sadah near the Syrian border. This gave him one piece of a puzzle about what the corps was doing to bring order in Anbar Province, and he became more confident in his predictions of the marines' plans. After they retook Fallujah in late 2004, he told me, "I recognized the Marine Corps and the rest of the military was serious about dealing with Anbar Province. . . . I laid out a map and explained the Anbar Campaign on the Web."

By the spring of 2005, he began to get recognition not only from other bloggers, but from U.S. Marine Corps officers in Iraq. "They thought I had a mole in their operation," Roggio recalled. "Marines would say I get more information at your site than at command briefings." Marine spokesman Jeffrey S. Pool, then a captain working in public affairs in Anbar, said, "Roggio was able to look past the headlines and analyze the operation for its tactical or strategic necessity." This analytical skill gave Roggio an edge on many reporters who were "chasing the headlines that kinetic operations"—that is, clashes with the enemy—"produce in abundance," Pool told me.

Roggio found it gratifying to hear from relatives and friends of the marines in Anbar who thanked him for his detailed dispatches. "They said, 'Thanks for explaining my son is not driving around and getting hit by IEDs.'" Roggio was one of the first commentators to see the importance of the marines' building a new alliance with tribal sheiks who, in the tribal traditions of the Middle East, controlled the fighters mounting the insurgency. And despite his early support of Bush's policies, Roggio maintained that his views were his own, and not necessarily popular within the White House or Pentagon. Bush later would make the "Anbar Awakening" of the sheiks a centerpiece of his continuing crusade to keep U.S. troops in Iraq.

From Roggio's perspective, the marines' efforts at rapprochement made sense. "We're working with people who were killing Americans" in Fallujah, Ramadi, Haditha, and other flashpoints in northwest Iraq. "These are guys who have turned on Al Qaeda. This is why insurgencies are ugly—you don't win by crushing them militarily. You win by fracturing them, by reconciling the moderate elements. . . . In the end, insurgency is won by a political settlement." He compared it to the American Revolution. "We were an insurgency," he said of the American colonies. "At some point we came to a political accommodation with the loyalists. This is what war is really about—it's really nothing new."

Yet there was something new about the way he and other bloggers participated in the war coverage and debate over an exit strategy. Though he lacked formal training as a journalist, Roggio found himself in the middle of a major story. Through the summer of 2005, he predicted the timing and progression of various marine operations in Anbar leading to the December elections. He began interviewing senior commanders by long distance telephone, and coupled with his thorough reading of press and public-affairs accounts, Roggio began to establish a name for himself in predicting the marines' next move. Indeed, he began to worry that he could be revealing critical information that could be used against the marines by any enemy forces reading "The Fourth Rail" on the Internet. "My comfort level wasn't good," Roggio reflected. He worried he was "giving away too much at the time it was happening. This was really at the tactical level."

But he was reassured by officers that "by the time you said that, we were already attacking." Still, Roggio remained keenly aware of the age-old tension faced by front-line correspondents: how much can you report without aiding and abetting the enemy? "There is a fundamental conflict here," he said. "What does the American public need to know and how much can the enemy glean from this information?" He leaned toward reporting as much as possible, along with other military bloggers. "This is not a traditional media world," Roggio explained. "The gatekeepers have been diminished. There are other ways to tell your story."

Finally, as he kept making a name for himself, Roggio came to a crossroads: how could he keep working as a computer technician while still providing first-rate analysis? And should he go to Iraq to see the ground truth for himself? He'd been talking with the marines about embedding with them in Anbar Province. After talking with his wife and gaining her reluctant approval, Roggio asked his readers if they'd be willing to chip in with donations to allow him to take advantage of what he called "a once-in-a-lifetime opportunity." The money began pouring in, and he raised more than $30,000 from readers to cover the expenses of his airfare, body armor, and camera equipment.

By November 2005, he was ready to take a leave of absence from his job, which he left for good four months later. Agreeing to the same rules as any newspaper or TV reporter, Roggio embedded with the marines of Regimental Combat Team 2 in Husaybah on the Syrian border. He also embedded with marines and army soldiers assigned to the 2nd Brigade Combat Team in Ramadi. Using a third-person narrative, Roggio described his experience in the country that had become his professional obsession: "Bill patrolled the streets of Iraq with U.S. Marines and Iraqi soldiers, drove in convoys, rode on the Euphrates River, met with the Azerbaijani Army battalion at Haditha Dam, sat in on meetings with tribal leaders and military officers, went on an IED hunt in the city of Ramadi, and witnessed Iraq's historic Parliamentary election on December 15th, 2005."

His blog sounds like a bit of a travelogue, as he describes his subsequent adventures in Kandahar, Afganistan, "during a series of Canadian operations to sweep the area of the Taliban." Later, he would return to Fallujah to follow the marines and army military police transition teams.

"I got to understand the lay of the land far better," Roggio said of his 2005 travels. "I got to see what I was talking about." Without such firsthand experiences, he said, "I would not have believed [the marines] had been that successful in getting the peace." Going out on patrols, getting to know the young marines serving in the dangerous Sunni Triangle, witnessing the elections, it all was "one of the most amazing events of my life."

His pivotal journey soon hit a pothole, though. The day after Christmas 2005, the *Washington Post* ran a story with the headline, "Bloggers, Money Now Weapons in Information War." The article, by Jonathan Finer and Doug Struck, had this sub-headline: "U.S. Recruits Advocates to the Front, Pays Iraqi TV stations for Coverage."[3]

Roggio was portrayed as a pro-military blogger who was invited by the marines to come to Iraq to provide more favorable coverage. "What is often seen as an attempt at balanced reporting results in underreporting of the military's success and strategy and an overemphasis on the strategically minor success of the jihadists or insurgents," Roggio told the *Post*. The reporters linked Roggio's journey to Iraq with what they called "an increasingly aggressive battle for control over information about the conflict" and noted the heightened "scrutiny of what the Pentagon calls information operations . . . when news reports revealed that the U.S. military was paying Iraqi journalists and news organizations to publish favorable stories written by soldiers, sometimes without disclosing the military's role in producing them."

"Information operations" were now part of the battlefield, one defense expert told them, and the insurgents made their attacks with several audiences in mind, American and Arab alike. Finer and Struck reported the military had a hefty budget to "place favorable coverage on television stations in three Iraqi cities."

Army commanders defended some of their practices as part of a drive to help establish a free press and to counter increasingly media-savvy insurgent groups. For example, in Ramadi, "the violence-plagued capital of Anbar province," Finer and Struck reported, "Some reporters at the scene were told by rifle-toting guerrillas to publish accounts claiming the city had been taken over by insurgents." The marines later claimed the incident "was staged to influence media coverage."

Marine captain Pool told the *Post* that the Ramadi incident became a "propagandist victory for the insurgents," whose words and actions convinced several news organizations that the city had been lost. Pool cited anther incident at Fallujah—in which insurgents claimed a video showed a bomb attack on Marines at a factory in the city—that was a fake event reported by unwitting news organizations. "Pool said he spends a growing portion of his time working to dispel what he calls erroneous tips from insurgents to reporters, including regular reports of Marines taken captive or helicopters downed," the *Post* reported.

"We now take all of these rumors seriously," Pool said. "We also use different [media] to get our messages out." Among those media were the bloggers, who were getting his news releases. Pool praised the work of Michael Yon, an independent author and blogger who embedded for almost a year with the army in the northern city of Mosul.

Roggio reemerges in the *Post* article, which said he managed to get credentials as an embedded reporter only because of help from the American Enterprise Institute, "a conservative-leaning group in Washington." The *Post* contrasted Roggio's coverage of the Ramadi story with other news organizations—in effect, portraying him as a pro-military voice on the internet. "When news organizations began reporting about the insurgent activity in Ramadi on Dec. 1," they wrote, "Roggio posted 'The Ramadi Debacle: The Media Bites on Al Qaeda Propaganda.'" Roggio's blog post cited information from Pool, who was criticizing the media's performance. "The reported 'mini-Tet offensive' in Ramadi has turned out to be less than accurate," Roggio wrote. "In fact it has been anything but."

Roggio's blogs from Iraq took on a more authoritative tone than his earlier commentaries which were written far from the action. But his criticism of the media remained a constant theme of *The Fourth Rail*: "The AP and other media organizations have bought into a sophisticated and clever al Qaeda information operation designed to weaken support for the war in the United States and project an image of strength for the insurgency. After al Qaeda's defeat along the border, there is a dire need for them to do so."

Contrary to the "false reports," he wrote, U.S. and Iraqi forces had engaged the insurgents in a number of operations in Ramadi, leading to a marked decrease in insurgent attacks. His blog, while focusing on the details of the operation, also had a personal tone and openly expressed sympathy for the American fighting men and women. "Thankfully seven of those wounded were able to return immediately to duty. . . . Our thoughts are with the four injured Marines and the families of those ten lost in the attack."

The *Washington Post* article about Roggio noted one of his subsequent posts from Barwana in western Anbar, where voter turnout was heavier than expected. "Barwana, once part of Zarqawi's self-declared 'Islamic Republic of Iraq' is now the scene of al-Qaeda's greatest nightmare: Muslims exercising their constitutional right to chose [*sic*] their destiny." Roggio clearly was thrilled with what he saw and included a photo of a cute Iraqi boy holding up his finger with the purple ink designating a vote. It was clearly too much for the *Post* writers, who implied that Roggio was an ambitious amateur military analyst who, perhaps unwittingly, was being used by the U.S. government.

On January 3, 2006, Roggio penned a blistering rebuttal headlined "Embedded Bias? Why doesn't the *Washington Post* correct some simple facts?" He recounted how "my recent embed in Iraq was the subject of scrutiny as a military-information operation. It is a fact-challenged article that manages to cast an unfair shadow on my reporting from Iraq."

Roggio took the reporters to task first for making a couple of fairly minor errors, including the fact that his military service wasn't long enough to merit using the term "retired soldier" in the first sentence. More significantly, Roggio complained, "The authors report that I was credentialed by the American Enterprise Institute, when in fact this is impossible, as a think tank cannot provide media credentials—this must be done by a recognized news organization. I was credentialed by *The Weekly Standard* and the Canadian talk-radio show *The World Tonight*. And finally, contrary to the report, I was not in Iraq when the article was published. I had been home for nearly a week. Each of these items could have been easily confirmed by a simple inquiry."

Roggio clearly was most upset by the implication that he was a conservative pawn. "The incorrect facts on their own can easily be discounted as trivial, but the suggestion that I was credentialed by the American Enterprise Institute certainly implies that I was part of some kind of orchestrated right-wing ploy (there go those neocon war hawks again!). But couple the *Post*'s fake 'facts' with the misrepresentation of the embed-credentialing process and the blending of my story with military-information operations, and the groundwork has been laid to label me as a tool of the military." The blogger also took issue with the article's implication that he needed special authorization to embed. According to Captain Pool, Roggio wrote, all reporters attempting to embed are subject to the same approval process, and he received no "special consideration. But you would not know any of this by reading the article."

While these errors of fact were bad enough, Roggio took even stronger issue with the article's references to U.S. payments to Iraqi television stations and recruiting "advocates" to report on the war, as well as to the efforts of a contractor, called the Lincoln Group, to pay for positive coverage. This "clearly implies I am a tool of the military," he continued. "I have had a private conversation with Mr. Finer. He can dissemble to me about how there was no intention to equate my embed with a military-information operation. . . . But the fact is that intelligent people from varying political persuasions viewed the article this way."

Roggio went on to describe himself as a "mere blogger" in search of the truth, explaining how he had raised the money and took a leave of absence from his job to do "what many reporters in Iraq admitted to me they do not do: Embed with frontline units to tell the stories of those serving."

I tried to contact Struck and Finer by e-mail in 2007, and Finer responded. Now on leave from the *Post* to attend law school, he said he regretted the factual errors. However, the American Enterprise Institute's sponsorship was on Roggio's blog, so it seemed to be accurate. And the time discrepancy that placed Roggio in Iraq at the time of the article resulted from *Post* editors holding the story for about a month, which is not unusual at any publication. As for Roggio's complaint that he was portrayed as a kind of pawn of the U.S.-backed Lincoln Group—the contractor that disseminated pro-American stories in Iraq—Finer said, "We didn't say he was being paid for what he was doing."

Speaking about the overall theme of the story—the U.S. military's information operations in Iraq—Finer said, "I don't really have any regret about that at all. He's very much on the record that he's pro-war and was hand-picked to embed for that reason. There weren't many embeds getting picked" at that time, "and the fact that Roggio was selected to do this very clearly—though it was not something we stated in the article—was because the tone of his coverage was something they approved of." Finer added that this was "not a critique of bloggers by any stretch of the imagination," since he had covered the trend for some time. While some in the mainstream media denigrated bloggers as neophytes, Finer said he wasn't among them. The *Post* article simply raised questions about the way the military was hand-picking sympathetic bloggers to cover the war, he said.

Pool, for his part, praised both Finer—"one of the best reporters I worked with in 2005"—and Roggio. But he denied giving Roggio preferential treatment to embed in Anbar. "The access for media, mainstream and nontraditional, was the same across the board in 2005. CNN, *Washington Post*, *New York Times*, and BillRoggio.com all were treated equally."

Pool noted his chief concern is accuracy, not editorial slant. "Inaccurate reporting is a violation of trust and can do a great deal of long-term damage. This applics to both positive and negative bias. 'Pro-military' coverage, if not anchored by accuracy, can be extremely damaging because it sets false expectations. I would rather have an accurate but negative *Washington Post* journalist embedded with us than a reporter with rose-colored glasses from National Review Online."

Summing up the Roggio-*Post* flap, Pool said, "Bill wasn't singled out because he had a perceived bias but because he was and is an excellent analyst who knows what is important and what isn't." The marine public-affairs officer concluded, "What I think you are seeing is friction between reporters and bloggers."

Cori Dauber, an associate professor of communications studies at the University of North Carolina, says bloggers like Roggio and Michael Yon created a new form of journalism. "These online essayists have invented this new form of combat reportage, embedding with the troops but doing so independently," she told me. "In many cases, they're going out to areas where the mainstream press is not going . . . filling a vacuum of specific weaknesses in mainline coverage."

Dauber is critical of what she called "the unwillingness of even the largest outlets to cover Afghanistan," which she called "unconscionable," and she noted the inability of smaller outlets to be able to pay, given insurance rates particularly, to cover Iraq or Afghanistan."

Even if the mainstream press did a better job, Dauber thinks " there would still be benefit to what the online authors have brought. It's additive—we're being served when we get good, solid coverage from the mainstream outlets, critiqued by mil-bloggers [military bloggers] writing from their unique perspectives, with gaps filled in by online essayists like Roggio, Yon, [and others]."

As the war dragged on, the friction between the media and the military increased, especially over word choices such as *insurgency, civil war*, and—as the McIntyre-Rumsfeld verbal jousting showed—*guerrilla*.

The disagreement extended to the carnage in Iraq. By late 2006, estimates of the Iraqi war dead ranged from a low of 150,000 from the Iraqi Health Ministry to 655,000 estimated casualties by a team of Johns Hopkins University epidemiologists. As sectarian violence spread in Baghdad, American dead approached 2,000, with thousands more young service members suffering grievous wounds. All the while, the number of embedded journalists from the U.S. continued to drop, along with Americans' once sky-high confidence in a positive outcome. On October 24, 2006, *USA Today* reported only 19 percent of Americans believed America was winning the war. Even President Bush seemed to agree on some level: "No question it's tough," he said in late November

2006. "There's a lot of sectarian violence taking place, fomented, in my opinion, because of these attacks by Al Qaeda, causing people to seek reprisal."

The United Nations reported that fighting between Sunni Muslims and Shia Muslims killed more than 3,700 Iraqis in October 2006 alone. That spike in violence led NBC News and the *Los Angeles Times* to officially refer to the violence as a civil war, a decision that sparked a debate over words and what they meant for U.S. foreign policy.

"It's something that we have a responsibility to ask ourselves as we're reporting and to try to get as close to the truth as possible," Marjorie Miller, foreign editor at the *Los Angeles Times*, told PBS's *NewsHour* on November 29, 2006.

Quoting Nicholas Sambanis, a political science professor at Yale University, PBS reported, "Traditionally, the term 'civil war' refers to an armed conflict between a government and internal challengers that results in the deaths of a large number of people—1,000 over a year is a common benchmark."

However, others noted the confusion in Iraq and the lack of clearly stated issues between the warring parties. Typically, opposing sides "have stated goals that divide the general public." Donald Kagan, a Yale history professor who writes extensively about warfare, told *NewsHour*: "At this point in Iraq, there are still Sunnis and Kurds and Shiites who want to have stability, and they are trying to put down the insurgents. Now it is also purely possible that at some point they will give up. Then it is a civil war."[4]

Some experts also disagreed about the ultimate impact of using the phrase *civil war*, with some believing it was used as propaganda to scare America into removing troops while others thinking it was an accurate characterization of Iraq. "It's inevitable that, in public discussions, things will be simplified," Richard Betts, a political science professor at Columbia University told *NewsHour*. "Probably the most neutral term to use would be 'the war in Iraq,' but then you have to explain what's going on. If you want another shorthand term that does turn people's attention one way or another, 'civil war' does that."

Whatever you called it, Iraq remained a hot potato—or live hand grenade—for anyone who dared to speak, or write, about it in public. Consider the early 2007 proclamation by Democratic presidential hopeful Barack Obama: "We ended up launching a war that should have never been authorized and should have never been waged, and to which we now have spent $400 billion and have seen over 3,000 lives of the bravest young Americans wasted."

After a storm of criticism from Republicans and military families, Obama quickly apologized and said he had misspoken by using the word "wasted." The Illinois senator explained later on the campaign trail in New Hampshire, "What I would say—and meant to say—is that their service hasn't been honored because our civilian strategy has not honored their courage and bravery and we have put them in a situation in which it is hard for them to succeed."

Other words—such as *occupation* and *war on terror*—acquired their own special weight in the complicated periodic table of political elements. In 2006, Democrat Jim Webb narrowly defeated Virginia senator George Allen partly because Webb pounded Bush and Republican allies like Allen on what he called a "chaos that has resulted from the lack of proper political leadership." Webb added, "When people keep talking about the war in Iraq, I, at this point, prefer to call it an occupation. I think we need to start doing that."[5]

In April 2007, the House Armed Services Committee voted to banish the phrase *global war on terror*—which had first been used by President Bush after the September 11, 2001, attacks—from the 2008 defense budget. "This is not because the war has been won, or lost, or even called off, but because the committee's Democratic leadership doesn't like the phrase," Rick Maze wrote in the *Military Times*. A staff memo said the 2008 bill would set defense policy and, in a quest to be specific about military operations, "avoid using colloquialisms."[6]

The House committee also banned the phrase *the long war*, which military officials began using as a way of acknowledging that military operations against terrorist states and organizations would not be wrapped up in a few years. The House memo provided examples of acceptable phrases, such as *the war in Iraq, the war in Afghanistan, operations in the Horn of Africa*, or *ongoing military operations throughout the world*.

One unnamed Democratic aide told *Military Times*: "There was no political intent in doing this. We were just trying to avoid catch phrases." An unnamed Republican aide countered, "This is a philosophical and political question. Republicans generally believe that by fighting the war on terror in Iraq, we are preventing terrorists from spreading elsewhere and are keeping them engaged so they are not attacking us at home."

Sometimes, it seemed, the global war on terror had a way of devolving into a global war on truth.

Chapter Twelve

AS HE
LAY DYING

I f "every soldier's death is a public event," as Rick Atkinson writes, then surely some public deaths are more difficult—and more controversial—than others. A soldier's passing usually receives little more than a cursory notice from military authorities and perhaps a story in the local paper about the loss of a life filled with promise, with the requisite quotes from an old teacher or coach, minister or youth leader. As war deaths mount, news of combat casualties often is shrouded by the background noise of talking heads holding forth about the situation, both at home and abroad. The punditry reaches ridiculous levels in the 24/7 coverage of a presidential election. Sometimes news organizations try to make up for the collective amnesia by running pictures or stories of lost soldiers, marines, airmen, sailors. Such all-American accounts typically leave out any flaws or problems in the life of the fallen, practicing a form of hagiography as old as the scriptures and filled with the same kind of imponderable questions about loss and pain as one finds in the Psalms.

Such was the case after one Texas soldier's death reported on January 25, 2007, in the antiseptic prose of the U.S. Department of Defense. Under the headline "DoD Identifies Army Casualty," the military's news release consisted of two sentences, followed by contact information for an army public-affairs office:

> Staff Sgt. Hector Leija, 27, of Houston, Texas, died Jan.
> 24 in Baghdad, Iraq, of wounds suffered during combat
> operations. Leija was assigned to the 1st Battalion, 23rd
> Infantry Regiment, 3rd Brigade, 2nd Infantry Division
> (Stryker Brigade Combat Team, Fort Lewis, Wash.).

The local newspaper for Leija's hometown, Raymondville, Texas, the *Valley Morning Star* of Harlingen, published several articles filled with images of yellow ribbons, quotes from grieving friends and family, and memories of a fallen hero. One such tribute began, "As a boy, Staff Sgt. Hector Leija's ears perked when his uncle talked about the battles in Vietnam, Domingo Leija Jr. said."

Domingo Leija Jr., the sergeant's older brother, recounted their uncle's war stories and told of how his kid brother "loved to hear the stories about how the smallest difference anyone can make is a difference that can change somebody's life."

Reporter Fernando Del Valle wrote the kind of story people want to read at such times, one that reassures readers that the soldier did not die in vain. "For the community that hails him as a hometown hero, Hector Leija's spirit lives on like the legacy of his triumphs as a young sergeant who grew up as a high school honor student here."

Raymondville is a small farming town of about 10,000 people near the Texas border. Hector's father, Domingo, was a farm foreman, while his mother, Manuela, was a housewife. Upon hearing news of their youngest son's death, they declined to speak to the media and made their eldest son, Domingo Jr., the family spokesman.

"Since he was little he always had a big smile on his face," Domingo Jr. told Del Valle. "That smile never dimmed."

Hector Leija, like his peers, had joined the army to work toward a better future. Reporter Del Valle told me that the army finds plenty of recruits in the area "because of the unemployment rate and the promise of an education and a career" in a town where the median family income is around $24,000. Before Hector graduated from Raymondville High School at age seventeen, he turned down offers for college scholarships to join the army in 1997.

Domingo Jr. told the newspaper that "he always loved the army. He felt like he needed to help [Iraq] so families wouldn't suffer under no tyrant. Like my brother always said, if we don't do it, who will? It's up to us to make it better for everyone."

Hector had returned home in 2006 before leaving for a second tour of Iraq, as the specter of soldiers dying from IEDs and other insurgent tactics kept taking their toll. When he left for Iraq again, "it surprised friends who didn't know his dedication to trying to make a difference," Domingo Jr. told the *Valley Star*. "It made my father proud."

Hector planned to finish another tour of duty, then get out of the army and find a job with a security firm. But returning to Baghdad was his duty, Domingo Jr. said. "If they leave now, all the brothers and sisters who gave their lives [would have] died in vain."

A week after his January 24, 2007, death, a military jet carried Hector Leija's body into Harlingen Valley International Airport before an honor guard escorted it into a private family ceremony. Then, according to Del Valle's account, a line of police and sheriff's cars led a procession of fire engines and U.S. Border Patrol Jeeps, followed by a white limousine that carried the Leija's family and the hearse bearing the fallen solder to Raymondville's Duddlesten Funeral Home.

Residents lined the streets waving tiny American flags. Normally, this would have been the end of the story, at least that part concerning the public side of the life and death of Hector Leija. But when the Leijas arrived at the funeral home and cemetery, they had to pass through a gauntlet of TV cameramen, newspaper photographers, and reporters craning their necks for a look at the family.

Hector Leija had become, quite by chance, the subject of a *New York Times* article and photos. The controversy surrounding the newspaper's coverage illustrates the often conflicting perceptions of a soldier's family and the journalists covering combat. It also became a flashpoint in the ongoing friction between the media and military in Iraq. But mostly it's the story of men doing their jobs even in the face of extreme danger and extremely hard choices.

On paper, Damien Cave seems an unlikely candidate to become a top combat correspondent and one of the most prominent military observers of his generation. In his mid-twenties, Cave joined Salon.com in 1999 to cover the heady days of the dot-com boom. After the 9/11 attacks on New York and Arlington, his beat expanded to energy and national affairs, and he found his own outlook becoming more international.

"Like a lot of people at that point," he told me by e-mail, "I was eager to contribute, to somehow do something about a world that seemed destined to become more violent and deadly for me and the people I loved." His father had avoided military service during Vietnam, "and it was always his life's regret, something I swore I would never repeat. Eventually, though, I started to feel I could do more good with a notebook than with a gun."

He volunteered to go to Afghanistan, but Salon.com, one of the first online magazines, lacked the resources to send him. Instead, he wound up accepting a fellowship to study in Cuba, a fitting assignment since Cave's wife is Cuban-American.

He joined the *New York Times* in 2004 and immediately worked to get a piece of the Iraq story. He impressed his editors by writing a series about military recruiting and subsequently volunteered to report from Iraq. "At first the foreign editor hesitated since I didn't have prior war experience," he explained, "but about a year later, she asked me to come for a six-to-eight-week tryout."

After landing in Baghdad in the summer of 2006, he expected to stay about two months. "But instead I found myself hooked on the story. I felt that I could learn more with a year in Baghdad—about myself, about the world, about journalism—than I could with five years any-where else. And that's pretty much been the case."

In January 2007, Cave accepted the army's invitation for a *Times* reporter to embed with the 3rd Stryker Brigade Combat Team of the 2nd Infantry Division. They would be part of a joint American-Iraqi force trying to clear a part of Baghdad, Haifa Street, plagued by fighting between Sunni insurgents and Shiite militias.

"It was my second embed," Cave recalled. "I had been embedded in Dora [in the summer of 2006] on a clearing mission that I thought was similar to what I'd encounter on Haifa Street. I thought it would be pretty uneventful, especially since we were invited, like my last embed, in which most of the 'bad guys' had fled in advance of the operation."

Cave hooked up with Bob Nickelsberg, an experienced combat photographer working as an independent contractor for the *Times*. He didn't know Nickelsberg well but heard he could be trusted and had seen his share of combat—"which was a relief to me," Cave noted, "as someone who had seen very little."

Nickelsberg, fifty-seven, had been a conflict photographer since the early 1980s, when he was based in El Salvador for *Time* magazine, covering that country's insurgency and the U.S. military involvement. He also covered fighting in Guatemala. In 2001 and 2002, he spent five months covering the American-led invasion and toppling of the Taliban in Afghanistan and Pakistan.

The morning of January 24, they met a group of U.S. Army soldiers from the 3rd Stryker Brigade who were riding in the back of a Stryker vehicle. Sgt. Hector Leija was among them. "I could tell right away that I liked him," Cave said of Leija. "He had a calm, easy-going style of command and it was clear that his men respected him. When he asked them to do something, it was with just a few words and the guys always moved immediately."

Nickelsberg remembered Leija as a big man who could have played lineman on a college football team. "He was certainly photogenic and didn't mind the camera" being close by. The Strykers, like the marines, were used to having media around, including a recent CNN crew. "They opened up for the press," Nickelsberg observed. "They're not shy."

A commander had told Cave that the combat team would be securing a hospital near Haifa Street in central Baghdad, but when they rolled out for the early morning operation, he learned this was no longer the mission. "We'd be heading to the center of the neighborhood where we were almost guaranteed to see fighting."

Cave set the scene in a January 25 article based on notes and impressions he called in to James Glanz, the *Times'* acting bureau chief in Baghdad. "In the battle for Baghdad, Haifa Street has changed hands so often that it has taken on the feel of a no man's land, the deadly space between opposing trenches," they wrote. "On Wednesday, as American and Iraqi troops poured in, the street showed why it is such a sensitive gauge of an urban conflict marked by front lines that melt into confusion, enemies with no clear identity and allies who disappear or do not show up at all."[1]

The article was written in the context of the American command's "surge" of 20,000 more troops to try to stabilize Baghdad. "Just how those extra troops will be used is not yet known," Cave and Glanz reported, "but it is likely to mirror at least broadly the Haifa Street strategy of working with Iraqi forces to take on unruly groups from both sides of the Sunni-Shiite sectarian divide."

The combat team's commander, Lt. Col. Avanulas Smiley, "conceded the cost of letting the Iraqi forces learn on the job was to add to the risk involved in the operation. It can be organized chaos."

Cave experienced the chaos, and loss, in a way he could never have imagined as they entered the no-man's-land of Haifa Street, "a stretch of ragged slums and mostly abandoned high rises." Accompanying Leija's squad, they hustled from the Stryker vehicle and ran into a high rise in search of insurgents. "Many of the Iraqi Army units who were supposed to do the actual searches of the buildings did not arrive on time, forcing the Americans to start the job on their own."

Despite the tension of moving from apartment to apartment, Leija's calm demeanor helped keep his men focused on the dangerous mission. "For several hours before dawn," Cave told me, "when the fighting started, the squad and me and Bob were in a room on the top floor of the building. It was a weird place—there was a skateboard on the floor, if I remember correctly, and the wall had English all over it. It looked like a hang-out for a bunch of teenagers. Me and Bob and the guys engaged in the usual chatter, about sports, food, hometowns.

"I talked mostly to Leija, who would go out on the roof and check things out, bravely without much tension, and then return to a perch in a doorway near the top of the stairs. He had a sense of humor, he told me he was from Texas, and I could tell he'd been in Iraq for a while—long enough for him not to worry about getting in trouble for saying what he really thought. At some point before dawn, I decided that he would be someone worth following through the day. I had decided before I went that I wanted to profile one soldier during the operation and I figured he was the logical choice."

Cave never got a chance to write that profile, though. The empty apartments had become "lairs for gunmen who flitted from window to window." The firing after dawn became intense and seemed like it would never stop. But time seemed to slow for Cave as he ran up the street with the Stryker platoon, scribbling as many notes as he could in his notebook. "I didn't know what I'd do with it but it just felt good to do something, anything" amid the mortar booms and machine gun fire. He also shot video with a small Sony camera, alongside Nickelsberg who had two Canon cameras around his neck.

In Cave's first article on January 25, he noted that the enemy snipers "killed at least one American soldier, with a shot to the head." The soldier was not named in that report because his family had not been notified, and the rules of embedding with the army prohibited reporting his name until that took place. That soldier was Sgt. Hector Leija.

In his first report on Haifa Street, Cave captured bits of the chaos of the urban combat, as Sgt. First Class Marc Biletski shouted, "Who the hell is shooting at us? Do we know who they are?"

Even before they ran into the apartment building, "It was difficult not being able to pinpoint where firing was at any one time," Nickelsberg recalled. With helicopters chopping through the air above, and the mortar blasts bouncing off walls, and the racket of machine-gun and semiautomatic fire, Haifa Street became a huge "echo chamber" where it was hard to distinguish between friendly and enemy fire, the veteran photographer said.

Haifa Street, especially his abbreviated time with Sergeant Leija, taught Cave hard lessons he would not soon forget. "One thing I learned that day is that, in combat, there are waves of danger and the movements are slow. For a while we waited in an empty apartment, as they tried to find their Iraqi counterparts who had rushed ahead. We just talked small talk as gunfire and mortars popped all around. I remember Leija talking about how much he wanted to go home, and what he'd do when he got there. Then we'd moved, and it would be stomach-tightening time (or as the soldiers would say, time to pucker your ass). The clock just moved so damn slowly. I remember being amazed at that. Just how slowly time seemed to pass when you were out in the open or in a place close to gunfire.

"There was also a point," Cave said, "when the team was moving from the building where Leija was shot. [Sergeant First Class] Biletski offered me a chance to leave, to get in a Stryker and go. But at that point, I felt like it would be unfair. They couldn't leave. Why should I? So we kept going."

Cave pushed on, though it could be hard to tell friend from foe. "One Iraqi soldier in the alley pointed his rifle at an American reporter and pulled the trigger," he wrote. "There was only a click: the weapon had no ammunition. The soldier laughed at his joke."

It took several days before the *Times* correspondent finished writing a more thorough article about the Haifa Street fighting. In a gripping front-page account, Cave retold the story from a more intimate, detailed point of view, one that captured more of the squad's sense of loss and shock at losing its beloved leader. The headline was "'Man Down': When One Bullet Alters Everything."[2] Above the article, one of Nickelsberg's action-packed photos showed the soldiers dashing down Haifa Street, with figures emerging from a yellow cloud created by protective smoke bombs. His photograph of the medical evacuation ran on an inside page, below the fold.

The joint operation involved more than 1,000 American and Iraqi troops who had come to "this warren of high rises and hovels to disrupt the growing nest of Sunni and Shiite fighters battling for control of the area." Cave carefully explained the messiness of the army's attempts to turn over security to the Iraqis. "That promise seemed distant," he wrote. "What was close, and painfully real, was the cost of an escalating street fight that had trapped American soldiers and Iraqi bystanders between warring sects.

"And as with so many days here, a bullet changed everything.

"It started at 9:15 A.M.," when the soldiers started shouting: "Help! Man down. Sergeant Leija got hit in the head."

Next door, Cave wrote, "In the narrow kitchen a single bullet hole could be seen in a tinted glass window facing north."

The soldiers reacted quickly, with platoon leader Sgt. First Class Marc Biletski ordering his men to get down, away from every window, and to pull Sergeant Leija out of the kitchen and into the living room.

"O.K., everybody, let's relax," Sergeant Biletski said.

The platoon leader "was shaking from his shoulder to his hand. Relaxing was just not possible. Fifteen feet of floor, and a three-inch-high metal doorjamb stood between where Sergeant Leija fell and the living room, out of the line of fire. Gunshots popped in bursts, their source obscured by echoes off the concrete buildings."

In the shooting's frantic aftermath, Biletski kept trying to keep his men calm: "Don't freak out on me, Doc," he shouted to medic PFC Aaron Barnum, "who was frantically yanking at Sergeant Leija's flak jacket to take the weight off his chest."

Leija's comrades risked their lives to drag him from the kitchen as a medevac team quickly arrived on the scene; the medics carried him downstairs to a Stryker armored vehicle waiting outside. "He moaned as they carried him down the stairs on a stretcher."

Nickelsberg's photograph of the medical evacuation ran on an inside page of the Times, below the fold. It was a vivid photograph, showing much of the length of Leija's body, and most poignantly, his blood-spattered head. A stretcher-bearer seems to be comforting him and tending his wound, keeping a gloved hand over Leija's forehead, covering his eyes. Nickelsberg shot a series of frames in the very low light while he followed the stretcher through a narrow hallway. The medics took Leija outside to the Stryker, whose hatch was open. The photographer hung back, though, because no one knew if snipers still lingered—or even if it was a sniper who had shot the sergeant.

By then, the soldiers and journalists alike hoped Sergeant Leija might survive his head wound. And as they dealt with the trauma of seeing Leija go down, the soldiers dealt with the vexing problem of recovering his weapons and gear. "We had enough time to calm down and slow the breathing to solve this calamity," Nickelsberg said. "You knew the soldiers were going to solve this—they cannot leave weapons and gear behind."

Cave captured the scene in his article: "The men of the platoon remained in the living room, frozen in shock. They had a problem. Sergeant Leija's helmet, flak jacket, gear and weapon, along with that of at least one other soldier, were still in the exposed area of the kitchen. They needed to be recovered. But how?"

First Sergeant Biletski ordered them to wait and called for another unit to search and clear the building next door. Cave described the agonizingly slow period before the top sergeant finally gave the OK for a soldier to dash into the kitchen and retrieve the gear. While they waited, the soldiers speculated about the source of the single bullet that felled Leija. Was it a sniper who saw Leija standing in the kitchen, his "silent silhouette in the window," looking out on Haifa Street and the joint force moving along below? Or "maybe the shot was accidental . . . fired from below by Iraqi Army soldiers who had been moving behind the buildings." The available evidence—"an entrance wound just below the helmet with an exit wound above"—indicated the bullet was fired from the ground by the supposedly friendly Iraqis. This led to grumbling about their allies' overall performance and the lack of communications between the American and Iraqi forces.

After Biletski asked how his shaken men were doing, PFC Aaron Barnum then stood up and volunteered to retrieve Leija's gear.

Biletski balked, saying, "I can't lose another man. If I did, I failed. I already failed once. I'm not going to fail again."

The room fell quiet and faces turned away, Cave wrote. "You didn't fail, sir," one soldier said as he fought back tears. "You didn't fail."

Later, Cave would describe what he was doing: "I sat against the wall trying to listen and scribbling everything I heard in my notebook. I didn't know what I'd do with it but it just felt good to do something, anything. Biletski was really shaken. But he asked each one of his guys individually if they were OK, and he did the same for me—a small act of kindness I will never forget and which, at the time, nearly brought me to tears. I was moved by the love and camaraderie these guys felt and by the horror of the loss. I still am, every time I think about it."

Finally, after more than an hour elapsed with no signs of another shot through the kitchen window, Biletski relented and "let Private Barnum make a mad dash for the equipment." After pausing in the doorway, Barnum dove for the kitchen. A single gunshot cracked outside, but it didn't appear to be aimed at the kitchen. The private gathered Leija's gear, finally picking up the fallen sergeant's helmet. He "cradled it in his arms, then made the final dangerous move back to the living room, his fatigues indelibly stained with his friend's blood. There were no cheers to greet him. It was a brave act borne of horror, and the men seemed eager to go. As Private Barnum gingerly wrapped the helmet in a towel, it tipped and blood spilled out."

Alongside Cave's reportage was Nickelsberg's equally dramatic picture taken from the living room showing Barnum's dash out of the kitchen: The courageous soldier is caught mid-stride, with one leg up and his left arm pumping. In his right hand, Barnum bears the blood-stained helmet. His right boot touches a trail of red that can clearly be seen along the floor from the kitchen into the living room.

Nickelsberg, asked about the blood-stained floor captured in the photo, said, "It's American blood on foreign soil" and showed the readers, "These are the risks involved" when soldiers are in combat. "It's not pretty," he said, but it served as a "symbol of something gone wrong—as often is the case with bullets flying around."

After returning to Camp Victory, where they shared a trailer, Cave and Nickelsberg worked furiously through the night, operating on pure adrenalin as they'd now gone without sleep for nearly twenty-four hours. Nickelsberg called the *New York Times'* photo desk. "They just said send us your four best," he recalled.

Still, it remained a monumental task as he had to sort through hundreds of pictures taken over many hours as the Strykers, a rapid deployment division, scoured the treacherous urban terrain. Despite the drama of the Leija episode, the photographer noted, "there were a lot of other parts of the day" when they had run down the streets of the slums and ducked for cover as mortar, machine-gun, and rifle fire exploded all about. Elements from Al Qaeda and the sectarian militias jumped into the fray, joined by "looters, whackos—a real area of bad boys," Nickelsberg said. After hours of editing his work, he set up his laptop computer to transmit via B-GAN, the Broadband Global Area Network, a satellite internet connection aimed up into the dark sky. He sent his best pictures into space, then collapsed on his bed.

Nearby, Cave kept working into the early-morning hours to file his first article, along with acting bureau chief Glanz. When he was done with the first article—which reported only that an unnamed soldier had been shot in the head—Cave dropped in to see the Stryker battalion commander to let him know he planned to write a second, more thorough account of what happened to Sergeant Leija's platoon. "I asked him about contacting the family," Cave told me. "It was among my first thoughts. I just felt they should know I was there, should know that a story would be coming, and should know that I had footage of him alive." Besides the stories and photographs, Cave planned to assemble a short video report about the Haifa Street operation, with help from his wife, Diana Oliva Cave, a professional film producer who had joined him in Baghdad. "I thought they'd want to see it," he said of the video, "and I wanted to make it available to them."

Cave said he was told by the commander not to contact the family, that he would take care of it. "He said this again and again when I contacted him via e-mail over the next few days to get details on people's names and other issues. I made him aware of what I planned to write and when it would be published, but to this day, I don't know if he ever contacted the Leijas."

Working on the story and the video, Cave said, "I was extremely careful. I thought a lot about the family, and there were things, particularly in the video, that were edited out because I didn't want it to go too far." Watching the saga of the sergeant's death was hard to do over and over as he labored on the video with his wife. "It was an awful experience to watch it over and over again, and there were times when we both came to tears."

They pushed forward, though, eager to complete both the story and video because they "showed the loyalty of the soldiers to each other and to Leija. It was a moving story of combat camaraderie in the face of horror, and the cost of war. Our main concern was staying true to the substance and feeling of what happened. With the video, we didn't feel it was right to edit out the emotion that the soldiers expressed, or too much of the details because then the viewer wouldn't fully understand the realties of war and the courage and emotions felt by those who fight."

Cave was so concerned about getting the video right that he did something he called "very unorthodox—something I would not do with a print story. We let a military public-affairs officer see the video before it ran. I did this because it was one of the first videos we'd done out of Iraq and since the subject was obviously sensitive. I didn't want the video to come as a shock." He said this was not something he would do again. "But I did it in this case specifically to be sensitive to the family and because of the nature of the footage."

The public-affairs officer raised no complaints about the graphic nature of the video, only taking issue with the fact that Cave did not acknowledge that the Iraqis were part of the operation. Cave addressed that concern by adding a line to the video. The army didn't ask for it, but the Caves also added a disclaimer saying the video contained graphic images.

Cave tried taking the same tack to writing his second article, the one that ran on January 29, 2007. "I approached it with a similar level of sensitivity, but also with a determination to tell the story minute by minute as the soldiers in the unit experienced it. My word choice was centered on being descriptive and accurate—nothing more. I felt close to these guys, and I wanted them to read it and feel that I captured the day as they experienced it." He tried not to overplay the drama or exploit it, at times "dialing back a bit" on the descriptive language, especially when it came to the details of Leija's wounds. Some things were "unnecessarily graphic," he said. If they bothered him that much, "it would bother his family even more."

Cave felt a special bond with the Leija family because of his own recent experience. Only two months earlier, his mother was hit by a car and killed. "That was in the back of my mind as I wrote. In that case, I found myself wanting to know what happened, wanting to know most of the details, because somehow it comforted me, but also recognizing that certain facts were particularly bothersome. My mother's death was covered in the local paper so I knew what it felt like to read about a loved one written by a stranger." It was an awful experience, but one that Cave tried to learn from and apply to his own difficult assignment in Baghdad. "People respond in different ways to the death of a loved one," he told me. "Some want lots of information, some want a little. Some of my relatives needed to know gruesome details . . . others did not."

As he did the hard work on Leija's story, he said, "I didn't feel particularly able to guess, so I just tried to write what I saw."

The reaction to the story, photos, and video was swift: Cave and Nickelsberg received an e-mail from the battalion commander saying he

was unhappy with the package. Then other military officials notified
Glanz that Cave and Nickelsberg had been disembedded—that is, lost
their status as embedded journalists with the Stryker battalion.

Cave was baffled, since he'd scrupulously followed the rules about
waiting until a family has been notified before reporting the name of a
soldier killed in action. But the military cited another clause in the fifteen ground rules for media. This one had been added after the 2003
invasion: "Names, video, identifiable written/oral descriptions, or identifiable photographs of wounded service members will not be released
without service member's prior written consent." Clause 11(a) in the
embed rules was a classic Catch 22, since it would require getting written approval to run a photograph or video of a soldier who might be
dead. "The only thing the military said was a violation was the single
picture of Leija on the stretcher," Cave told me. "At the time, he was
wounded so it's not clear if the alleged violation was that we didn't get
him to sign a release or because we simply showed him—a KIA—and
[identified] him in the caption."

Once again, as in the case of Bush's "Mission Accomplished"
banner and the gruesome pictures from Abu Ghraib, images—more
than words—showed their power to stir up emotions and controversy.
On January 31, *Editor & Publisher* reported, "The intimate portrayal
of a sergeant's death during Army efforts to clear a Baghdad neighborhood has caused friction between the military and the *New York Times*,
while sparking larger questions about war coverage and media-military relations."

In the *Houston Chronicle*, Michael Hedges and James Pinkerton
reported the dispute, which the Texas newspaper said "triggered anger
from his relatives and army colleagues and revived a long-standing
debate about which images of war are proper to show."[3] According to
the *Chronicle*, *New York Times* foreign editor Susan Chira said the newspaper initially did not contact the family of Sgt. Hector Leija "because
of a specific request from the army to avoid such a direct contact."

The *Chronicle* reported that Cave and Nickelsberg had their status
as embedded journalists suspended "because they violated a signed

agreement not to publish photos or video of any wounded soldiers without official consent." Hedges, a veteran combat correspondent, told me later that he understood the tough situation Cave and Nickelsberg faced, balancing the army's rules with their need to tell the story. "This was a great piece of journalism—a compelling read that almost never happens when you see exactly what's happening to these guys [the soldiers] close up. My feeling is the public interest was served by having that story out there, including the picture. But you can't agree to a set of conditions and act like the agreement doesn't bind you."

Cave's and Nickelsberg's embedded status remained up in the air, and *Times* executives said they had not received any official word of losing that privilege. "Press advocates were concerned about distrust between military leaders and the media," *Editor & Publisher* reported, "and other observers noted the power of the video that accompanied the story, capturing the day's mix of confusion, fear and heroics."

Nickelsberg was a contractor and let *Times* officials handle the situation. But speaking for himself, he said he believes the decision to "disembed" the pair stemmed from too many military officials getting into the act, especially those in the army public-affairs office inside the Green Zone. "It took on a life of its own. I don't know where the real nerve was hit, but certainly within the Strykers, they wouldn't calm down until the other side calms down. That's the way it is with the military. We have to cut through all this confusion in journalism and keep working. I saw this continuing on well beyond [the Haifa Street story], as the military went to unnecessary lengths to keep us away from something they'd benefit from in the end. They were covering for themselves in a bureaucratic way."

The irony, he said, was that Gen. David Petreaus had recently taken command of U.S. forces in Iraq and was trying to mend any broken fences with the media. Haifa Street was one of the early operations in the "troop surge" of American forces, "but in this case, there were fewer and fewer journalists covering a very important plan," Nickelsberg said. "Speaking as an independent person here, in this case I feel the army didn't make the effort to contact the family properly when they said they would. They let us down in not trying to resolve the situation as pain-lessly as possible," he said, adding, "And no death will be painless."

There were "too many chefs in the kitchen," Nickelsberg said, "too many public-affairs people working active combat commanders who are under a lot of pressure." The controversy had a chilling effect on other news operations in early 2007, making it harder for all journalists to cover the start of America's troop surge.

Cave noted that anyone reporting in Iraq must sign the embed-ding rules. But if a disagreement such as the Haifa Street incident arises, "There's no way to disagree with the rules. . . . [The military] holds all the cards." There's also no process for appealing the mili-tary's decisions.

Adding to the angst, Nickelsberg and Cave were disinvited from a memorial service in Baghdad for Leija. "Press are sometimes invited to the services," where the soldier's rifle and dog tags are put up front, and prayers and testimonials are offered. "It would have been interesting for me, because you get close to these guys because of the intensity of the encounters," Nickelsberg said. Indeed, before the service, he had e-mailed some of the pictures to members of the platoon and heard back from soldiers who said their family members appreciated the pictures showing them in action. "They don't often have a chance to see them-selves except when they're mugging for the camera," he said.

Back in Texas, the shock of learning of Hector's death, along with the in-depth print, photographic, and video coverage was simply too much for one family to bear, much less to endorse. Domingo Leija Jr., the older brother who spoke for the family, described his reactions to me in a telephone interview on March 27, 2007, and in a subsequent e-mail.

When he saw the video and the picture of Hector on a stretcher, Domingo Leija said he felt "basically anger because there was no proof of documentation that gave him permission to post that. . . . The permission falls on the father after [the son's] death. They never got permission."

The *Times'* coverage of Haifa Street, Leija said, was "all about sensationalism. . . . They don't care as long as it's a 'big' story that can bring in more advertising, more money, sell more papers. That's the bottom-line issue here. It's not about being honest. It's about being greedy, nothing else."

He criticized some of the language in the video, including Cave's voice-over conclusions about the long-term impact of the Strykers' Haifa Street operation. "It negatively affected morale in the U.S. as well as the soldiers themselves. They do not need this shit. It's enough to have their friends die for them and vice versa in order to [realize] that war is war. It's all a part of protecting your loved ones. Someone has to choose to do it. It's not the Sixties anymore. This is a volunteer army. People choose to do this for a living in order for their families to have a future."

Leija said his brother never liked the media coverage of the war. "My brother felt, as well as some other soldiers, that there should be some sort of media blackout because, one, it makes things worse when you see your son or brother or father or mother or sister or daughter on TV, dead or dying. It is a moment that only the soldiers and their families should know about—no one else. It should be dignified and not disrespected." Otherwise, the families will continue to face "the glorification of death in order to sell papers."

Cave and the *New York Times'* editors said they tried to reach the Leija family, but this created its own problems. Cathy Travis, press secretary for Rep. Solomon Ortiz, the Leijas' congressman, denied a report that Ortiz was acting as an intermediary to alert the family about the controversial video. "Whoa, that isn't what happened," Travis told the *Houston Chronicle.* "The reporter [Cave] called me late Monday afternoon and said he understood the family was upset and that they wanted us to know he had the utmost respect for the soldier and wanted us to let the family know that."

Travis later told me that she had to keep Ortiz from being portrayed as a kind of surrogate for the *New York Times*. "My boss's place is to comfort the family," she said. In a series of e-mails with Cave, the reporter's eagerness to reach the Leijas comes through.

But Travis distanced the congressman from the *Times*, e-mailing Cave on January 30: "Hey, what the hell's going on? I just got a call from *Houston Chronicle*—they said the *New York Times* has Mr. Ortiz blessing the picture and video on NYT site. Don't do that. Don't put us in that except as intermediary with family after story ran. . . . Your editors are welcome to reach out, but my advice is gonna be do not try to contact the family right now. That's a remarkably bad idea. I know the stakes are high for all y'all. . . . But don't bring the family into it, even to ask their true reaction. For the record, Mr. Ortiz thought the pic was incredibly thoughtless; and neither of us has seen the video."

Cave categorically denies that he or anyone from the *Times* ever sought the congressman's approval for the article or video. Ultimately, the paper expressed regret for hurting the Leijas in a letter that reportedly was part of an agreement to keep Cave and Nickelsberg embedded with the Strykers. "The *New York Times* agreed to write a letter to Sgt. Leija's family explaining the process we go through to notify families and why we run the articles and photographs we do, and expressing regret that the family suffered distress," the newspaper said in a statement.

The photograph of Leija on a stretcher was taken off the paper's website, but the video remained—a gripping five minute and fifty-two second piece, which includes an interview with Sergeant Leija before he was hit. Cave introduces him as "squad leader Hector Leija, an easy going but direct twenty-seven-year-old from Raymondville, Texas."

The big sergeant wore a helmet and goggles and told Cave, "What we're doing today is securing one area of the house." When they encounter a family of squatters in the apartment building, Leija said, "I feel bad for these people." The exploratory mission soon turned tragic, however, starting with a cry for help heard on the video.

"What?" a soldier replies.

"Somebody f—ing talk to me!"

"Sergeant Leija got f—ing hit in the head. Is he f—ing dead?'"

"Is he dead? Is he f—ing breathing?"

The squad is distraught as they struggle to help their fallen leader. "He got hit in front of the window," a soldier says. "Right there, sarge."

Amid the scramble to help Leija, a soldier can be heard gently imploring him, "Come on, sarge. Come on, sarge."

After the medics arrive, Cave narrates the surreally slow process of trying to get into the kitchen to retrieve Leija's weapon and gear. Red streaks of blood are clearly and chillingly visible on the floor. As Private First Class Barnum retrieves Leija's helmet, Cave says in the video voiceover, "The last thing he grabs is Sergeant Leija's helmet, but leaving, he wraps it in a towel."

Cave sums things up with a comment that would infuriate Leija's brother: "At the end of the day, it's unclear what the lasting impact would be. . . . There's no telling whether this week's effort would bring a more lasting peace."

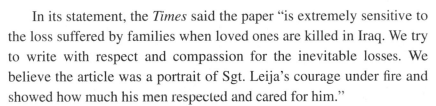

In its statement, the *Times* said the paper "is extremely sensitive to the loss suffered by families when loved ones are killed in Iraq. We try to write with respect and compassion for the inevitable losses. We believe the article was a portrait of Sgt. Leija's courage under fire and showed how much his men respected and cared for him."

The paper's apology and explanation did nothing to soothe the pain felt by Leija's brother, parents, or other family members. It didn't help that the funeral turned into a media circus, with satellite trucks parked outside the funeral home and cemetery in tiny Raymondville. TV crews began staking out the Leija home the day they learned of Hector's death. "With one reporter, a state trooper had to show up and asked them to leave," Domingo Leija told me. "They were sitting outside our home at midnight" with TV lights on, "waiting for someone to come out. There was no respect for privacy whatsoever. . . . The only one who was polite was Fernando [Del Valle, of the *Valley Morning Star*], who asked if it was all right to speak with us."

Manners only went so far, though. For when Del Valle slipped into a church service at the funeral home, the reporter said, "Someone must have pointed me out" to the funeral director. "I was sitting in a pew trying to be inconspicuous about the note taking. He just came up to me and said, 'There's no photos or notes here,' or they'd kick us out." Del Valle kept taking notes and covered the story. When the service came to the point of offering one another peace, he happened to be next to Domingo Leija. "I said, 'Peace be with you.' He said the same thing. He and I never had a problem."

Del Valle witnessed the problems caused by visiting TV reporters trying to interview reluctant family members out on the street and the spectacle of trailing the funeral procession to the cemetery. The media was ordered to keep 500 feet away from the grave site. "I guess they may think what other people think—that the media preys on tragedy," Del Valle said. But he noted he has seen the other side of the equation as well: families of fallen soldiers who actually want to talk about their feelings against the war. "It seems to me that families that are patriotic or want to put on a patriotic face are the ones who tend to be a little more hostile toward the media," Del Valle said. "However, the ones who are protesting the war and are upset about what happened to their son, those families seem to be more open."

The pain of war and loss can follow soldiers to their graves. Certainly, that was the case in Sergeant Leija's death, as his older brother never forgave Cave and Nickelsberg for their coverage of Haifa Street. He dismissed Cave's effort to reach him as "an attempt to save his job" and "portray himself in a good light. But if you see the video . . . it basically promotes his own political view instead of just reporting the news."

Asked if he would ever talk with Damien Cave, Leija's older brother replied, "To be honest, I would not want to. My brother used to say there is a consequence to everything you do. This guy is trying to backtrack from what he did. He needs to face up to his actions because everything comes with a consequence."

Cave, for his part, seems keenly aware of the consequences of his multimedia reporting from Baghdad, both during and after Haifa Street, as he has continued to provide dramatic front-line accounts of soldiers under fire. "My main effort to contact the Leijas was through the commander. I did try to call them the night before the story ran but no one answered the phone. This was the case the following day as well. I was calling because I wanted them to know that the story was there so they could avoid it if they wanted to, and to let them know that I would do anything else I could to comfort them—by explaining more of what happened or answering questions.

"Looking back, I should have done more to reach them. I probably should have called the unit's American base. What I didn't know at the time was the casualty-assistance officer is based at home and often has little contact with the unit commanders. I should have called to make sure that the casualty-assistance guys knew it was coming."

Asked about Domingo Leija's contention that his brother disliked the media, Cave said, "All I can say is that I never got the impression from Hector Leija that he didn't appreciate the media. He was friendly, open, and honest with me up until when he died. We did not discuss how something like that should be covered, obviously, but he was not hostile—as some soldiers can be when it comes to this issue."

Cave noted that the picture selection was out of his hands. "I didn't know that picture would be used until I saw it on the *Times* website," he said of Nickelsberg's photo of Leija in the stretcher. "I had absolutely no role in choosing the image, which is something that tends to be overlooked. That's not a criticism of the choice. I believe we should have been able to use it, and that it was tasteful because of the distance it was taken from and because it illustrated how hard the soldiers worked to try and save Leija's life. But the fact remains that the one element in violation of the embed rules had nothing to do with me."

Asked about Domingo Leija's accusations about his motives, Cave replied, "As for my political views, I can understand how he would say that, but he's incorrect. I wrote what I saw. There was no political agenda involved whatsoever. I'm not able to discuss my broad political views because of *Times*' policy, but when it comes to this war, I'm completely conflicted about what to do, what's best, and how it's going. The more time I spend here, the more I feel completely humbled by it all and more confounded. I couldn't insert a political agenda, in other words, because I really don't have one when it comes to this issue."

He cited the thematic paragraph of his story, known as a "nut graph" because it provides the nut, or heart, of the article: *What was close, and painfully real, was the cost of an escalating street fight that had trapped American soldiers and Iraqi bystanders between warring sects.* "There is nothing in there saying that it was all for nothing. In the video, I ended with the apartments being empty because that's what they were, and it was not clear whether they would be filled with families or with gunmen. It was a valid journalistic question, not an attempt to opine."

Cave added in his December 2007 e-mail: "I actually went back to Haifa Street the other day, unembedded, which is a sign of things improving here. I did a few interviews nearby, and people offered mixed reviews. An American commander had told me earlier that the area is coming back, but still not completely. In the high rises, no one lives above the fourth floor, he said, because they can't get electricity or water up there. It is, however, more peaceful. For now, the snipers appear to have gone, though some in Baghdad fear they'll return as soon as the Americans leave."

Looking back, Cave repeated that he had no regrets about his coverage, only about his inability to reach Leija's family before the story ran. "I should have had one of our stringers from the national desk knock on the Leijas' door. I should have done everything possible to reach them, instead of listening to the military, and trusting the military to get in touch with them. That's what I regret. Immensely. Because from what you're saying Domingo said, it's pretty clear that they have some serious misconceptions about who I am as a person and as a reporter, and it breaks my heart that they thought I intended to hurt them or didn't think about it. . . . Someday I'd like to meet them, to talk to them myself. Hopefully then they'd see that I'm not the insensitive monster they think I am. I'd like to tell them I'm sorry Hector died. That I'm sorry that what I wrote caused them additional pain."

Lost in the controversy, Cave told me, is the importance of such front-line journalism. "There's one other issue that you haven't directly asked about—the potential value of a story like the Haifa Street story, for readers. Part of the reason I don't regret what we published is because I believe it accurately portrayed a single day of a long war— that it gave readers information they would not have had, information that could help them understand the war and connect with it and the soldiers who fight it."

In a democracy, he continued, "in a country at war that relies on a free press to inform it about the policies of its taxpayer-paid leaders, it's possible that there was a lot of good that came of it. I received quite a few e-mails from people telling me just that—from soldiers who thanked me for telling the public what combat is really like; from military wives saying the video helped them understand what their husbands go through.

"And as I try to make sense of what happened, as I feel pain for the Leijas and because of how my story and work affected them, this is what I think of. I try to remember that I was hired to do a job—a job I care about, a job I believe in. And I believe I did it honestly and did it well."

Chapter Thirteen

"GOING TO BAGHDAD! WOOHOO!"

Sitting in the waiting room at Washington's Dulles International Airport, I was surrounded by soldiers and military contractors chatting amiably like a bunch of morning commuters waiting to catch a ride to the office. They were headed to work, but it was 6,575 miles away on a United Airlines flight to Kuwait City. The Boeing 777 had an estimated flight time of twelve hours and ten minutes, with two meals and movies thrown in. My ticket for a round trip on June 16, 2007, with travel insurance and my friendly travel agent's fee thrown in, cost $1,750.50.

Listening to this group of seasoned travelers, I heard them bitch about the travel connections they would make on their way to Iraq and Afghanistan. "I shouldn't have let the Corps of Engineers buy my ticket," said a trim man with a blond buzz cut, wearing a "Go Red" T-shirt. "I had a ticket to Afghanistan, one to Iraq . . ." he said, his voice trailing away.

A hulking man with razor-cut red hair strolled past. With wide shoulders and cordlike forearms, the six-foot-five-inch guy looked like a Navy SEAL or Army Ranger—a warrior heading back to the fray. He wore a dark blue tropical shirt, cargo pants, running shoes, and a back-

pack. Everything about him said *seasoned traveler*. By contrast, everything about me said *rookie*. I was still trying to determine the where-
abouts of my body armor and helmet, the two key items that I needed to
wear for a military flight into Iraq. I'd checked them when I caught my
first flight of the day back in Richmond, Virginia (inexplicably flying
west to Chicago, then back east again to Dulles—a net gain of about
100 miles from home, all for a day's worth of flying). My helmet and
body armor filled an entire suitcase that barely made the fifty-pound
weight limit. My clothes and other items were in a second large suitcase. On top of that, I had my notebooks, pens, tape recorders, and other
reporting material in a backpack. With my travel orders and passport
strapped awkwardly in a pouch on my waist, I was the antithesis of the
seasoned traveler. I felt like a human moving van. I was relieved when
my suitcase with the helmet and body armor arrived in Washington in
time for my night flight to Kuwait.

The government contractors and warriors had a rough-hewn quality
about them, with intense expressions that didn't encourage easy banter
with an interloper such as me. As the flight time neared, I watched this
parade—mostly men ranging from around twenty years old up to
around sixty—in casual shirts and cargo pants, some sporting running
shoes, others wearing the rubber soled boots of the army or marines.
Most of us wore cargo pants because they have so many pockets. (I had
recently purchased my first pair of cargo pants at a sporting goods store,
along with a variety of other gear, including flashlights, mosquito repel-
lent, sunscreen, and a military-style, camouflaged New York Yankees
cap to cover my oversized head.) These seasoned travelers carried neck
pillows tied to the top of their green or tan camouflaged travel bags.
One young man—a Kuwaiti, perhaps—carried a guitar case. With the
exception of some of the foreign workers who joined the group for the
half-day flight, this could have been a line for happy hour drinks at a
base club at Camp Lejeune or Fort Bragg. The stray comments were
filled with the acronyms of military culture and other details of the lives
of the military alumni who joined the massive contracting industry serv-
icing the war.

One traveler said he was "TDY," the term for "temporary duty" assignments for military workers or federal contractors.

"How long were you over?"

"Nine months," he replied.

"I went over fourteen days after they invaded Kuwait."

Amid the old salts were greener soldiers and marines, including one young man who wore an Atlantic Beach, North Carolina, shirt and who looked nervous as he sat near me, rocking in the vinyl chair. The latest news from Iraq was enough to set anyone's nerves on edge. A TV above the waiting area was turned to CNN. Lou Dobbs droned on about the "possibility of a regional war" breaking out following the June 13 bombing of the revered Shiite Askariya shrine in Samarra. The story fueled ongoing fears by American authorities that the mosque explosion could unleash more sectarian violence, or what *USA Today* called "a new wave of sectarian bloodletting. An early 2006 bombing of the shrine triggered months of fighting between Sunnis and Shiites, leaving thousands dead."[1]

Gen. David Petraeus said violence between the factions in Baghdad was "trending down" after a brief jump in May, partly because of increased U.S. patrols. "But, candidly, we're going to have to see what the impact of this tragedy in Samarra is on that," he told *USA Today*.

The article was part of a file that had been growing as thick as my baggage since April 2007 when I reluctantly decided that the only way to better understand the media's coverage of the war was actually to go to Iraq. As Lou Dobbs grimly reported the possibility of a regional firestorm, I sat at Dulles and mentally flipped back through the rapid-fire events that led to this trip, one I had to squeeze into my two weeks of available summer vacation from the *Richmond Times-Dispatch*, my former employer.

In late April, I began e-mailing the U.S. Central Command in Tampa, Florida, to apply for embedded journalist status. U.S. CentCom is the entry point for embedding because it oversees all military operations in the region of Iraq and Afghanistan. I filled out a form listing my professional experience, along with some newspaper clippings, including some dealing with the U.S. Marines. I was encouraged when I soon received a reply from a distant soldier in Baghdad, from something called CPIC:

"Hello, Charles," it began. "Thank you for inquiring about covering Operation Iraqi Freedom. We look forward to helping you get your stories out. We will need to get some information from you to process your request." The e-mail included instructions to submit an accreditation letter on company letterhead, signed by my "publisher or network." This led to an immediate concern: was I going to travel as a *Times-Dispatch* reporter or as an author of military books for Stackpole, the publisher of my first book?

It made sense to start with my own newspaper, since the *Times-Dispatch* had not had an embedded reporter in the region for some time, and it seemed like a good opportunity to match my book research with the newspaper's continuing coverage in the war. I also had discovered a Virginia connection that I thought would make the perfect story for Memorial Day in late May. So I wrote CPIC, the Combined Press Information Center, in late April: "I would like to start the ball rolling to get embed credentials for a reporting visit to Baghdad either in late May or late June. I am a reporter at the *Richmond Times-Dispatch* and am currently trying to convince management to allow me to come to report on a Virginia pastor, Col. Joel Jenkins, a reserve army chaplain with the Multi-National Security Command." I explained I was getting in touch with Jenkins, a friend of my wife's parents who pastored their church, First Baptist, in Charlottesville. The *Charlottesville Daily Progress* had covered his return for a visit at Thanksgiving and detailed his duties, which ranged from conducting services for the troops to marriage counseling and suicide-awareness education. In addition, Jenkins recently had received a Bronze Star for making more than 100 air sorties across Iraq, and by all accounts, he was a gregarious, interesting man who put his soldiers' welfare above his own. His son, Jay Jenkins, was a sportswriter at the *Daily Progress* and helped me reach his dad, who, much to my amazement, called me one morning from Baghdad.

"Come on over!" Reverend Jenkins said. "Love to have you."

I hastily typed a story proposal, complete with what I thought was a catchy headline: "The Preacher of Baghdad." I pitched a story to the *Times-Dispatch* editors about a dedicated Baptist pastor "who can't carry a weapon but has a body guard, has put his life on the line ministering to soldiers and Marines facing increasing mental and emotional strains as tours of duty kept getting extended." Jenkins, I told my editors, had recently been featured in the *Christian Science Monitor* for his work helping the burned-out soldiers. "My intent is to put a human face on what is too often just another headline about bombs blowing up in a distant land."

I would file my first story from Baghdad on Memorial Day as Jenkins conducted church services and then follow him back to Charlottesville two weeks later, when he was scheduled to return to his flock and deliver a stemwinder of a sermon on Father's Day. It seemed like everything was lining up for me to put a human face on the war, one with a local angle. It seemed like the perfect story pitch and a way for me to get to Iraq for my book.

But my pitch struck out. I was soon turned down by a senior editor who told me the news managers wanted to hold a meeting about the paper's future war coverage. I was invited to come to that meeting, which, as far I know, never happened. The *Times-Dispatch*, Virginia's capital-city newspaper, had taken a path followed lately by other mid-to-small-size dailies as they coped with declining circulation. In response, the paper's editors zealously followed a marketing plan that stressed local news—known as "hyper local" coverage—to leverage dwindling resources and create linkages with the paper's uneven web offerings. The corporate-owned newspaper was hardly unique: 2007 saw plunging stock prices for such prestigious companies as *Times-Mirror*, Knight Ridder, the *Washington Post*, and the *New York Times*. Even the *Wall Street Journal* was selling out to Rupert Murdoch's News Corp. The media was a messy business as bean-counting executives were only too willing to slash staff and shrink their papers' reach. It was not a good time for aspiring war correspondents.

Even as the web created instant access to readers and bloggers alike in the late 1990s and into the new millennium, it had created a downward spiral on the print side of the business—with daily newspaper circulation and advertising dollars sinking faster than George Bush's poll numbers. As Paul Steiger put it when he retired as managing editor of the *Wall Street Journal* in late 2007, "The cornucopia of national, international and business news, sports, and especially opinion available free on the web is rich beyond historical parallel. Anyone with a fact, a comment, a snapshot or a video clip can self-publish and instantly compete with the professionals. At the same time, the vast array of investigative reporting and foreign correspondence assembled at American newspapers over the past several decades is being cut back at all but a few publications, as papers succumb to the pressure to cut costs."[2]

As papers struggled to redefine themselves, most retrenched into community news—often under the feel-good banner of "public journalism." In some ways, Steiger wrote, "what's happening to the newspaper industry is a return to the past. Less than fifty years ago, American newspapers were in the main relatively small, narrowly profitable, family-owned, locally focused and hotly competitive."

Someday, no doubt, this too would pass and capital city papers (or whatever they morph into) would once again have the resources to finance foreign reporting trips such as the one I proposed. Indeed, the *Times-Dispatch* had sent Rex Bowman to embed with the marines in 2003 and financed two subsequent trips of reporters and photographers to Iraq and Afghanistan.

But for me, the clock was ticking. According to military intelligence reports, Iraq could explode into more violence in August, the month before Petraeus was scheduled to testify before Congress about the results of the "troop surge." Fueled by arms and money from Iran, the argument went, Iraq might see its own Tet offensive in August. With my limited window of opportunity, I had to get to Iraq quickly or risk not going at all.

Reluctantly, I e-mailed Colonel Jenkins that I would not be able to join him in Baghdad for Memorial Day. What now? April was the deadliest month of the year, with 100 soldiers killed and increasing mortar attacks on the Green Zone. The once-impregnable fortress was an easy target for anyone trained in mortar or rocket attacks. Those accounts gave me pause, since one former United Nations worker had told me in April not to worry about visiting the security zone. Downtown Washington is more dangerous than the Green Zone, he told me.

Since my goal was to better understand the dynamics of the military's media operations, it seemed logical to spend time in the Green Zone and perhaps try to get to know the top public-affairs officer at that time, U.S. Army major general William Caldwell. I duly revised my embed application to the distant sergeant in Baghdad, asking to attach with the public-affairs branch in Baghdad. Time passed. More mortar shells hit the Green Zone. There was more alarming news of a potential late summer offensive to influence the U.S. Congress to pull out the troops.

I was still working as a *Times-Dispatch* business reporter, so there was only so much I could do to break through the military bureaucracy. Every morning, I'd check my home e-mail, looking for any signs of progress. Though various sergeants sent me reassuring e-mails from CPIC, I couldn't seem to get anyone to say, as Reverend Jenkins had done earlier, "Sure, yes, come on over!"

In mid-May, I received an e-mail from yet another sergeant at CPIC who was understandably confused: was I coming on Memorial Day to see the chaplain, or did I want to see General Caldwell? To my horror, I realized that my story ideas had blended together in the army bureaucracy, making it even more unlikely that I would ever succeed in planning a productive trip to Iraq. Soon after that, I reached General Caldwell's public-affairs officer, Lt. Matt Breedlove, by telephone. He had some bad news: General Caldwell was leaving Iraq the following week and would be stationed at Fort Leavenworth, Kansas. Perhaps I could interview him there?

Flying to Kansas to conduct an interview looked like a step in the wrong direction. What to do? I had already booked the cheapest flight I could find to Kuwait City for June 17—Father's Day—and had gotten the required or recommended shots and other inoculations for travel in this region: malaria, Hepatitis B, and tetanus.

Finally, I decided to play my wild card: I called the marines. During my earlier research about the fledgling U.S. Marine Corps Special Operations Command at Camp Lejeune, North Carolina, I had gotten to know its bright, media-savvy public-relations officer, Maj. Cliff Gilmore. Maybe he could figure out a way to untangle the trail of red tape I had created.

I called Gilmore's cell phone and found him in San Francisco, where, in typical marine fashion, he was getting ready to dive into the bay to swim from Alcatraz to the city. When I explained my situation, he told me he would send the e-mail address for his friend, Maj. Jeff Pool, at Camp Fallujah. If anyone can get you over there, Pool can, his friend said.

On June 2, 2007, I e-mailed Pool and pleaded my case. Was there any way to embed with Pool's public-relations unit in Fallujah? The next day, I got home from church and checked my e-mail and read:

Chip,

I will personally call CPIC tomorrow. I will tell them that you are authorized to embed anywhere with MNF-W.

One of my pet peeves is PAOs being the story. We have 32,808 stories that are more worthy of paper and ink, but we're willing to help out if possible.

Let me talk to CPIC and square the approval process away and we'll go from there. If you send me any of the documents that you've previously sent them, I could work this quicker.

SF [Semper Fidelis],
Jeff

A chill went down my spine as I read this because now going to Iraq was not just an abstract plan—it was a reality. I was going to the war zone, though I still didn't really know what I'd do when I got there. Pool had authorized my visit to Fallujah, and we'd work out the details

As we approached Ali Al Salem, we stopped at the first guard post. We had to get out of the vehicle and wait while American military police conducted a bomb search. As we waited, I pondered the first signs of the sheer magnitude of my country's presence in this sandy land: We had made a Faustian bargain with the Kuwaitis, guarding their oil reserves in return for a military base. But they had pushed us farther away from sight, far out in the Arabian wilderness. I was told this was to reduce the American "footprint" in the country, which explained why the army majors wore civilian clothes to pick me up at the airport (they wore side arms but kept them hidden from view). But looking at the golden lights of an airport runway nearby and hearing the first sound of jet engines roaring in the night, it was clear the U.S. military had all the subtlety of King Kong in this nervous neck of the woods.

We bumped along a rutted gravel road, navigating past a labyrinth of Jersey barriers and more armed guards, and finally arrived at a huge village, with buses taking troops out to aircraft and row upon row of tents for offices and sleeping. Ali Al Salem was the nexus for anyone entering or leaving Iraq and Afghanistan.

Before they entered the base, the majors walked up to a sand-filled barrel and opened the chambers of their revolvers to ensure they were empty—a safety precaution to avoid accidental discharges. Major Russo handed me a two-page set of "invitational travel orders for public-affairs travel." When I read the first line, I had to smile: it called me "an accredited member of the news media . . . employed by *Richmond Times-Dispatch*." Somehow, in the stream of e-mails the army didn't get it that my paper wouldn't send me here. It should have read Stackpole Books, which wound up providing the needed sponsorship for my research—on their company letterhead, in triplicate.

"Transportation shall be furnished at DOD [Department of Defense] expense when said travel is in the interest of improving the public's understanding of DOD operations." Hmm, I wondered whether I was going to fit the bill there as well. There were other details listed, such as the requirement that I must wear body armor and an approved army combat helmet (ACH). The orders were filled with acronyms, some of which mystified me.

One thing I did understand, though, was the importance of NOT LOSING THESE ORDERS. Major Russo repeated this over and over as she took me into the administrative processing center. She also informed me that one of the embed rules was not to interview troops here because I was not yet assigned to a public-affairs officer, and so I was not yet officially embedded. Photos were also prohibited. And, I learned, I was not to name this base, Ali Al Salem. I wasn't sure why and decided not to ask. It seemed like a formality she had to explain, if not enforce.

The processing tent was filled with soldiers and other members of the military I couldn't readily identify; there were plenty of marines and sailors, who wear their own kinds of camouflaged uniforms. The tent was run by gregarious civilians who were clearly ex-military. These were employees of KBR, a subsidiary of Halliburton, the Texas-based engineering conglomerate once headed by Dick Cheney.

I had to hand over my passport and pay $12 for an entry visa. This would take at least a day to process, and it suddenly dawned on me that my plans to get to Baghdad—where I had to go to receive official press credentials before going on to Fallujah—already had been dealt an unexpected twenty-four-hour delay. With only two weeks of vacation—and two days already spent traveling—I could hear the clock ticking.

Major Russo led me over to a building marked, appropriately enough, Theater Gateway. In my jet-lagged state of mind, I first thought this was a movie theater—like the base theaters I'd grown up with on marine bases. Indeed, it had the feel—and sounds—of a theater as one video after another played on a flat-screen TV in front of the main counter. Little did I know how this building would morph into my own theater of the absurd.

With Major Russo's help, I was put on an administrative list and given precise instructions on what to do when I got my passport back the next night. The goal, she explained, was to get on the list for space available on outgoing flights. This involved a series of check-ins that

started precisely at 6:30 each morning. I nodded, pretending to understand the complex procedure for getting a seat on a flight to Baghdad.

Then I was assigned a place to sleep for the night—in something
called Q-5—and after helping me get my bags to the tent, the army
majors bid me farewell, with one final caution from Major Russo:
"Don't lose your orders."

If I needed something to eat, she advised heading to a familiar sight
glowing in the distance. "There's a McDonald's over there," she said,
plus a Pizza Hut and some other food joints.

I thanked her and entered the tent. I was more tired than hungry. As
I dragged my bulky bags inside, I was surprised at how chilly it was, in
stark contrast to the warm desert night. Each tent had a powerful air
conditioner powered by a generator. With hundreds, perhaps thousands,
of generators running on the base, the area hummed like an industrial-
strength beehive.

The tent was dimly illuminated by the light of someone's laptop
computer. A thirty-something man glanced over at me and nodded, but
he didn't speak. This seemed to be the norm in these temporary sleeping
facilities. No one traded war stories or asked where you were from. This
seemed like an extension of the manners from Dulles airport—everyone
was on a professional journey, all in a day's work. Journalists and contractors slept in one set of air-conditioned tents, with military units in
another. Some tents were reserved for women, as were the nearby showers and restrooms.

I found an empty bunk above someone sleeping and tried to climb up
as quietly as possible. I had brought along only one thin blanket, and after
setting my alarm for 6 A.M., I curled up for the night. I regretted not bringing a sleeping bag. Who would have thought Kuwait could feel so cold?

Monday, June 18, 6:15 A.M. I groggily take a seat back at the Theater Gateway, awaiting the "accountability roll call." The wide building,
with concrete floors, is set up like a big meeting or theater hall, with

padded chairs. Off to the side is a huge refrigerator with signs reminding you to drink bottled water and replace any you take. Even at this early hour, there are about 200 military personnel in various states of lounging and sleep, some on the floor snoozing on their duffle bags. In the row in front of me, a young man who doesn't look a day over nineteen sits holding his rifle, with the stock against his face. I wonder what's going through his mind, but recalling Major Russo's stricture against interviews, I resist the urge to ask.

A movie drones on the flat screen TV—some kind of urban action flick, perhaps with the nineteen-year-old shoot-'em-up sensibility in mind. At 6:30 on the dot, the movie is paused, and one of the KBR employees behind the counter barks into a microphone: "OK, this is the 6:30 A.M. accountability roll call. Listen for your name and let me know you're here."

I strain to hear my name and am relieved when it is called out. After responding, "Here," I feel a little bit more like one of the troops. Yet I also know I'm not one of them; I'm just a visitor—a green one at that—and I'm not even supposed to talk to them. Since it would be another twelve hours before my passport with the entry visa could be returned to me, I knew I was about to embark on that age-old practice for GIs: Hurry up and wait. The next roll call would be at 9 P.M. By then, I hoped to have my passport and visa, and maybe—just maybe—get a seat on a flight to Baghdad. The sooner I got my credentials, the sooner I would reach Fallujah, Major Pool, and the marines in Anbar Province.

I trudge across the paths between the tents toward the golden arches. By 7 A.M., the heat is already stifling, despite a slight breeze. I pass civilian contractors, some of whom remind me of cowboys from the Wild West: bearded men, some with wild hair, carrying towels and dop kits toward the shower trailers. A group of men wearing shorts walk by with M-16s slung casually on their shoulders. Women contractors look more groomed and perkier as they walk along, talking to each other on the way to bathrooms or showers or to coffee and breakfast. The base seems like a hybrid of a frontier town and a beach boardwalk.

As I head to the golden arches about a quarter mile away, I begin to grasp the size of Ali Al Salem and the scope of the base's amenities. There are basketball courts, recreation halls, Internet cafes, AT&T calling centers, Pizza Huts—all powered by that constant hum of Caterpillar generators and cooled by air conditioners. And in the faces of the young men and women I pass, there is the forlorn look of kids thousands of miles from home. I am also struck by how easily the contractors and soldiers and marines mixed in this foreign base in a way one doesn't always see back in the States. "Yo!" one soldier calls out to another, reminding me of the banter back at my local YMCA.

I pass the McDonald's, which has its name written in flowing Arabic script beneath the English and decide to seek the base chow hall. I can eat here for free and follow the line of soldiers and marines. *No bags allowed in DFAC*, a sign warns, and I think of a friend, Dean Hoffmeyer, a photographer at the *Richmond Times-Dispatch*, who was in the mess hall in Mosul in late 2003 when a suicide bomber blew himself up and killed twenty-two troops, civilian contractors, and Iraqis. The explosion was in the early days of what Rumsfeld never wanted to call an "insurgency," and Dean, who was sitting down to eat when the bomb exploded, managed to shoot a series of images broadcast on CNN around the world. I wonder if this sign restricting bags in the dining hall was a result of that bombing.

On the way into the hall, every service member stops in front of a pair of sand-filled barrels and inserts their weapons, emptying their barrels to protect against accidental discharge. The hall is huge and loud, with flat screen TVs on the ends and to the sides. I go down the line and hand my plate to Kuwaiti servers, wondering what they think of this huge American caloric intake of pancakes, waffles, scrambled eggs, biscuits, bacon, and sausage. And those were just main courses. To the side are coolers with yogurt and milk, a variety of cereals, and enough coffee to keep you awake for a year.

I slide to a random table and eat by myself, remembering the stricture not to interview the soldiers (though by now I doubted anyone knew I was a reporter). There was plenty to watch on the big screen TVs: a mix of CNN, Fox, and the military's own Armed Forces Network. The AFN draws me in with various public-service announcements, designed, it appears, mostly for service members in Europe.

One such spot shows a soldier typing an e-mail home, "We are ready for our next deployment." A headline flashes onscreen: "The enemy is watching." Was Al Qaeda reading our soldiers' e-mails? It seems far-fetched, but then again, I knew that cyberspace was a new battleground. Maybe the old World War II stricture "loose lips sink ships" applies to the age of Yahoo and Google as well.

Watching the TV shows from home, I think of Marshal McLuhan's prediction of a global village. A *60 Minutes* rerun is on, with an interview of a former Iraqi minister of defense about stealing funds. And at the commercial breaks, there are promises of upcoming coverage of the day's hot story: will Paris Hilton report for jail in Hollywood?

A civilian contractor sits beside me. I'd met him in the tent that morning, a former cop from Kentucky who said he was on his way to Iraq to train policemen. "CNN," he informs me, "we refer to as that Communist News Network." The Kentucky cop regales me with stories about the Iraqis and claims that working with them "is like herding cats." He complains about the American military's approach to the training, which he says isn't done well because it stresses the number, not quality, of Iraqis getting training for police work. The point is for military officials to be able to meet their quotas and make reports to superiors. "We call it death by Power Point," he joked. Jamie McIntyre of that "Communist News Network" had used the same line about the briefings at the Pentagon.

The Kentucky cop proceeds to tells me more than I really want to know about himself, including this, "I'm a mean person—I know that. But I learned to control it." As I prepare to enter Iraq, he offers this caution: wear your helmet at all times because if a sniper sees you with it off, "he'll shoot you for being stupid." This gives me pause as I watch Paris Hilton being whisked away to jail in a black SUV.

With so much time to kill, I wander around the base, checking out the goods at the PX. Do I need another hat, or a flashlight, or powder to guard against heat rash? I buy some powder, because even by mid-morning, the heat is extreme. I walk outside to desert's edge to look about. I put my notebook down on a Jersey barrier. How hot is it? I wonder, thinking of the old Johnny Carson–Ed McMahon routine. It's so hot that when I try to prop my notebook on the Jersey barrier, I feel a stinging heat on my hand. How hot is it? "One hundred zillion degrees," I write. Strangely, there are no thermometers around the base, and nobody seems to keep track. Perhaps it's better not knowing.

I gaze past the barbed wire perimeter, taking in a terrain as flat and barren as anything I've seen since . . . Nevada? Death Valley, California? There are a few trees here and there, and a guard tower, perhaps from an earlier war. But why would anyone fight over this unappealing real estate, unless it was to drill for the oil beneath the rock and sand?

The heat drives me inside again, into one of the large tents marked MWR (Morale, Welfare, Recreation), with couches, high-definition TVs, books, chess and pool tables, and various other amenities. I sit in an easy chair, pick up a copy of *Stars and Stripes*, and scan the headline from June 18, 2007: "Baghdad lifts curfew set off by Shrine blast. Al-Sadr calls for Shiites to gather at Samarra next month." The newspaper report sends a small chill down my spine. This is the country I'm going to visit, perhaps within a day. I read more bad news from the other destinations of soldiers and contractors: "Bus bombing kills 35 in Afghanistan. Attack represents leap in scale, prompting worries of Iraq-style blasts."

Here in Kuwait, war news takes on a new poignancy, as though it's happening next door, which, in a sense, it is. Yet there's a constant soundtrack and Hollywood imagery in the MWR tent, and The Who's anthem plays in the background: "We won't get fooled again!" I idly wonder if I'm a fool for choosing to enter a war zone.

I trudge next door to the gym. Maybe a little time on the treadmill will dispel my dark thoughts and help me sleep later on. At the front of the gym, the ubiquitous big-screen TV shows a rerun of ESPN's *Sunday*

Night Baseball. If I shut my eyes, I could be back at the Richmond YMCA. When I open them, I see the Armed Forces Network offering a pep talk to the troops from country singer Lee Ann Womack, followed by AFN's warning to troops traveling around Europe not to travel alone because of terrorist threats. What would Marshall McLuhan make of the violence in his global village? How could he have predicted the strange juxtaposition of information broadcast from the U.S. to Europe to the Middle East: "*Access Hollywood* covers the Paris Hilton saga," the TV blares. Three soldiers near me walk on a cross-trainer, a device perhaps first envisioned on *The Jetsons* in the mid-1960s as George Jetson walked his dog, Elmo, in midair. McLuhan surely would have scratched his head over another public-service announcement reminding soldiers leaving for combat to protect their last will and testaments in fireproof boxes. The global village had become less like *The Jetsons* and more like *Combat.*

By Tuesday morning—a full day and a half since I was left out in the Kuwaiti desert—I'm starting to think I'm seeing mirages. Getting to BIAP—Baghdad International Airport—becomes a kind of unreach-able, almost metaphysical goal—*Waiting for Godot* in a tent.

By 9:45 A.M. on Tuesday, June 19, I have it made to the fourth slot on the waiting list for the next flight to BIAP. Since I have to spend at least a day in Baghdad getting my credentials, I am starting to get nerv-ous about accomplishing my goal of spending at least a week at Camp Fallujah with the marines. Major Pool and I hadn't settled on any par-ticular course of action, but I knew I needed to get "outside the wire" to see more of Iraq than the marine base. I also knew now that I would have to factor in an extra day to return to Ali Al Salem, turn in my passport, and hope to get an exit visa from the Kuwaitis. This was a relatively new requirement, which meant that if I wanted to make my return flight to the States, I was going to have to leave Iraq a day sooner than expected.

With the heat and the boredom and the uncertainty of my travel plans, I began to feel like I was in prison, waiting for parole, with the air force enlisted men who maintain the list serving as prison guards. KBR, the Halliburton subsidiary, is like the warden running this halfway house for errant journalists, contractors, and soldiers. And the waiting area, the Theater Gateway, seems increasingly like a theater of the absurd.

I'd been around prisons, so I knew that escapes were usually inside jobs. It was time to call Major Russo, the army major who'd left me her number in case I had any problems. The prospect of being stuck for another day, through Wednesday, meant I wouldn't get into Baghdad until Thursday. My grand scheme for reporting during my summer vacation was falling apart as surely as Saddam Hussein's regime.

I went to the front desk and asked to use a phone. After explaining my plight to Major Russo, she was noncommittal but said she'd see what she could do. "One of those guys owes me a favor."

I sat down and waited, watching the TV broadcast of *We Were Soldiers*. Mel Gibson as U.S. Army colonel Hal Moore talked to his daughter before he went off to the Vietnam War.

"Daddy," she asked, "what is war?"

"It's stuff that shouldn't happen, but does."

As several dozen soldiers lounge near me with gear and weaponry waiting for a flight into the war zone, this Hollywood version of an earlier war—perhaps their grandfather's war—plays out with images of fighting, thoughts of home, fear, courage, God. Iraq, it seems from this perspective, is just another reel on a long-running movie—one that long ago started tanking at the box office. General Petraeus's surge continues, and these fresh-faced kids are the new players on the block. Looking around the room, it occurs to me that some of them could be working on Capitol Hill in Washington for the very same senators and representatives who are arguing the merits of this war everyday. They could be working those cushy staff jobs, then going down to Georgetown or over to Rosslyn or Alexandria to meet their friends for drinks and dinner, or maybe take in the new Major League Baseball attraction, the Washington Nationals. Or they could be in New York working as bond traders or stockbrokers, amassing small fortunes and taking summer trips to the south of France.

"Charles Jones, report to the front counter." A young man with dreadlocks said to me matter-of-factly. "You'll be going out tonight." Major Russo, it seems, has cashed in one of her chips. Come back at 1500, he says, using military-speak for 3 P.M. The bus will load at 1630 to take us to the plane. "Wheels up will be 1800," he says.

I thank him profusely, saying how great he's been. He shrugs and, turning away, says, "I ain't nothin' special."

Leaving the Theater Gateway, I blink in the daylight like a waking possum. The heat takes my breath away for a moment, but I collect myself and return to the tent to organize my bags. The Kentucky cop has long since gone, replaced by other contractors who don't bother to introduce themselves. Most have laptop computers and wear headphones to watch DVDs. I organize my clothes and try to decide on the right apparel to wear to Baghdad. I've been wearing shorts on the base to keep cool but know I had better don cargo pants and a short-sleeved shirt to look halfway professional once I reach the Green Zone.

After packing, I eat yet another meal at DFAC and take in some more Paris Hilton and baseball news, and on the way back to get my gear, I decide to stop by a tent I'd noticed near the PX, the chapel. It has a small waiting lounge, where a few guys are reading or talking quietly. Inside the chapel, a man in a navy T-shirt stands with his back to the door, saxophone in hand. He wears a headset and looks ready to practice. I slide into a back row, pull down a kneeler, and bow my head.

After a while, the sax-playing sailor turns and bids me good morning. He proceeds to play a sweet, soothing melody that sounds vaguely familiar.

Theater Gateway, 3 P.M. I stand with Bravo Battery, 1/10 of FA 3rd Infantry Division awaiting further orders. I'm already drenched in sweat from dragging my two suitcases several hundreds yards across the gravel and dirt to the staging area. My bags are dumped among duffel bags and rucksacks and gear from civilian contractors who also plan to ride with this army unit on the six o'clock flight to Baghdad on a C-130 transport plane.

The first order of business is getting all the gear together to put on pallets that will be moved by forklift onto the four-engine aircraft, one of the workhorses for transporting people and supplies. As we deliver our gear, I overhear a fresh-faced soldier who declares, "Going to Baghdad! Woohoo!" He looks to be about my son's age, with blue eyes and rosy cheeks.

I'd like to interview the young soldier but nervously recall the restrictions on my embed orders: "Media are not permitted to conduct interviews, gather information or images or any news reporting while unescorted by an authorized public-affairs representative." Here in the bright lights of Theater Gateway, what if I start interviewing this soldier, only to get booted from the flight into Baghdad, thus scuttling my research? I resist the urge to report.

We're moved into another waiting room, with yet another TV where some soldiers, marines, and sailors are watching a cop movie with Matt Damon and Leonardo DiCaprio. I observe the range of emotions and body language of the troops. One soldier adjusts the straps to his helmet with a screwdriver; several lie on the floor, able to nap in the broad daylight; one navy logistics officer starts talking to me, looking around at the fatigued troops. "It's sad," he says. "They've been through so much."

Baghdad, I learn, is one hour ahead of Kuwait, because it operates on Daylight Savings Time. Shortly before we board the bus to be taken out to the flight line, I decide I can risk chatting with the pumped-up soldier. Still, just to be on the safe side, I don't take notes to remain inconspicuous. Later, I note that he is Matthew MacLean, an artillery specialist with Bravo Battery. He's twenty-two years old and a 2006 graduate of the University of Dayton. At age seventeen, he had joined the army reserves after graduating from high school in Fairborn, Ohio.

A thoughtful warrior, I would learn that he's planning to write his own book about his experiences. As he put it later in an e-mail to me:

> All that I have to say right now about the media is that I'm completely pissed off right now. So much is going on in this war, so many people are losing their lives and losing their minds over here. The media has exploited soldiers' lives in a way to make money. I'm not saying you're doing this. I'm pointing the finger at such media as television and Internet media. The week I return to the U.S., I plan on going to the CNN HQ in Atlanta and painting "Soldiers' blood of ratings" on every single building they own.
>
> I know this is what America wants, they want to know about the war, they want to know about who is screwing up on Capitol Hill (In my opinion, EVERYONE). I agree the American people deserve to know what is going on. As do I, when I was home I was glued to the TUBE watching CNN, completely enthralled by the war. But being over here, and seeing death and personally causing the death of other human beings with your own hands, it makes you understand this war, understand the nature of the beast.
>
> In Iraq, we see the war, we live the war, we are in the middle of a war. And as a soldier I understand what is expected of me. But I don't understand why. And the media (most) makes us out to be killers and pawns. Talking about how many of us die each day, telling the enemy how much closer to victory they are.

When the time comes to load up, one of the air force flight technicians announces, "You will have a bottle of water on you or you won't be allowed on board." I stick a bottle in the side of my backpack and wonder how long it will last. Then I put on my protective vest—marked "O" to show my blood type—and pull on the helmet. I'm still trying to snap it into place when I climb onto the bus and try not to look too dorky around these professional warriors and contractors.

On the flight line at Ali Al Salem, 5:20 P.M. The late-afternoon sun beats down on us as we wait to march up the ramp to the C-130, a gray, rather chubby looking airplane with camouflaged exterior. Nearby sits a gargantuan C-17, a hulking elephant of a plane with four jet engines compared to the C-130's four propellers. The C-17 makes our C-130 look like a pack mule.

Finally, the order comes to march on board our flying mule. We walk up the rear ramp and enter its belly; its hydraulic lines and electrical wires are exposed in a way a commercial plane never is. It's both fascinating and a bit nerve-wracking as you see how many pieces of machinery could fail. The soldiers and random guys like me fill the rows of red web seats along each side.

We cram elbow to elbow and butt to butt, with our body armor and helmets on. Matthew MacLean is across from me. He gives me a thumbs-up, then pulls a digital camera out of his pack. Smiling, he snaps my picture. Soon enough, no one is smiling. The plane starts heating up in the 120-degree late afternoon, and we start stewing in our gear. I take my required bottle of water and pour some on my head and quickly drink its lukewarm dregs. I have another water bottle, but it's stuck in the side of my backpack, which I foolishly stowed on a hook that's now out of reach. Since I'm already belted in, I don't want to upset the jigsaw-puzzle arrangement of our seating. I longingly look up at the overhanging water, wondering how long it will be before takeoff. Surely this oven will cool down once we get off the ground, maybe even when the engines start. After what seemed like an interminable wait, the engines start with a steady *weeee*, creating a cacophony. The smell of fuel adds to the overall discomfort. The only relief comes from the rear of the plane, which remains open as the flight crew secures palletized luggage and gear. The sky is a pale blue but seems as distant as my water bottle.

I'm not the only one hurting. Next to Matthew is a burly sergeant who tells me later he has a knee injury from college football, one he never seems to get enough time off to get repaired. The 260-pound former lineman keeps shifting in his seat, trying to find some new position to bring relief from the cramped conditions and the growing heat. He pulls out a white handkerchief and pours water on it. It looks like a shroud on his gleaming face.

After spending twenty minutes like this, at 5:30 P.M. the plane lurches forward. The technicians leave the rear hatch open for a while, and I feel a bit of air stirring. This is a cruel hoax, though, as they quickly shut the hatch, putting us in dim light. I feel like I'm in a huge oven. A skinny airman straps himself in to a side seat, rather like a trapeze artist since there must be a thousand straps to swing from in this cargo hold. As it gains speed, the C-130 creates a huge racket, and two minutes ahead of schedule, it takes off at 5:58 P.M. Kuwait time. The fuselage rattles like a million hangars, and we're soon over a brown landscape as desolate as the moon.

Too late, I remember to put in a pair of earplugs stashed in the front of my armored vest. The relentless high-pitched sound strangely reminds me of a loud rock concert, sort of like "Free Bird" meets "Stairway to Heaven." Maybe the heat is just getting to me.

There's no way to talk and little to say anyway. After being airborne for about an hour, I start regretting taking those last sips of water. The fear of flying into combat is replaced by another fear. I pray a simple, if completely prosaic, prayer: "Dear God, please don't let my bladder burst." I also wonder if the rest of my body, including my heart, can survive this heat. I touch my brow, trying to remember the first sign of heat stroke. Coolness? No, sweat? I look down at my legs and, much to my horror, see both my thighs are dark from dampness. Has it happened—have I wet my pants from sheer fear? No, it's just perspiration from the more than two-hour-long ordeal of boarding and waiting and then waiting again on the tarmac.

After exactly an hour in the air, I see the first view of Iraq's rugged terrain, with some streams, but little else is visible in the evening haze.

There are few announcements on air force flights, so no one told us when we began the approach to Baghdad. But then again, no one has to. It became obvious that we were nearing BIAP when, without warning, the plane started a series of roller-coaster-like dips, tilts, and drops. The engines protest with a high-pitched whine. Matthew makes a hand motion, but I don't understand what he's trying to tell me. I offer another mundane prayer: "Dear God, don't let me throw up over these guys' boots." I had forgotten to take the Dramamine my wife sent with me, knowing I could no longer stomach roller-coaster rides.

After about ten minutes of protective maneuvers, I see a river flowing below—either the Tigris or the Euphrates—and hear the hydraulics of the airplane flaps lowering, followed by the landing gear. Farmland sweeps into view, the Fertile Crescent. Then Baghdad International Airport, with hangars, helicopters, and warehouses. It's a bumpy landing, but short of a crash, anything would beat sitting in hot, suspended animation any longer. My prayer is answered: I manage not to vomit.

More physical tests await, though. After we march down the rear ramp, we are told to get our gear. I find my two huge bags and drag them along the black-hot tarmac, even as I try to keep my backpack over my shoulder and my errant helmet on my head. We are herded into a processing center, where a young female soldier barks orders. In my dehydrated, stewed state of mind and body, I have no idea what she's talking about. All I know is I have to find some kind of shuttle to something called "Stryker Stables." I am helped along the way by a gregarious man named Mohammed Mohammed, an Arabic translator from Chicago who somehow attaches himself to me. "Be careful," he warns, "wear your body armor." It doesn't take much convincing.

We find our way to a shuttle stop, and I take in some of the landscape in the distance. At first glance, Iraq looks like Kuwait, except it has a ridge line and many more Jersey barriers. Dragging my luggage to find the shuttle, I feel like a rat winding through a maze.

The airport is a busy, dirty, cheerless mess. A Saudi medical truck whips by, as well as other trucks and jeeps. At 9:10 P.M., standing at the shuttle stop, I hear a boom in the distance. "Probably Camp Victory," a contractor laconically remarks, "where I'm going."

A second boom follows. "That's closer," he comments. "It's always bad when it gets closer."

I check my watch. Not quite 9:15 P.M. Then a third boom. Three in five minutes. This can't be good. No one seems too worried, though.

"You'll get used to it," the contractor says. I doubt it.

A shuttle bus arrives, and we hop on. I eavesdrop on the driver, a thirty-something Filipino. "I'm stuck here," he's saying, "good money. I can save a lot of money here."

At Stryker Stables, I follow Mohammed into the waiting room. I check at the desk and am told it will be a while, but no one will give a precise time for the arrival of the Rhino, an armored bus that will make the late-night run from the airport into the Green Zone. We leave our bags in a pile to await its arrival

"Nothing is clear here," Mohammed comments. "Everyone has his own agenda." We are walking under camouflaged netting in a dimly lit area near Stryker Stables.

It's true of the media, too, he tells me. "The problem here is different than Fox," he tells me. Fox is "100 percent Republican," Mohammed tells me. He considers CNN more objective.

A small man with expressive hands, Mohammed tells me he's a former stockbroker and insurance agent in Chicago. A native Egyptian, he came to work as an Arabic translator at the American embassy here after his wife died. In Baghdad, "someone fixes your room and gives you food. Here you are in the news—part of the news."

We find a Subway, where I order a sandwich. Looking about at all the fast-food signs, it seems the only winners here are American corporations—retailers, military hardware, and contracting. I ask Mohammed: what are the prospects for peace?

"I hope the people get tired of the war," he says, "and it just stops suddenly. It's possible." Sitting in the dim light, Mohammed doesn't sound very convinced. Again he offers cautionary advice: "Don't leave the Presidential Palace. They hit [around the Green Zone]."

We return to Stryker Stables and await the Rhino. Illinois senator Barack Obama, who had recently declared he was running for the Democratic presidential nomination, is on CNN. "We knew back then this war was a mistake," he says. CNN's John King and Candy Crowley appear, rattling on about Iraq and a truck bombing that killed seventy-eight people earlier in the day in Baghdad. I stand in line for some coffee and overhear a strapping air force mechanic: "The heroes are those guys fighting outside the wire."

Before we leave, Fox reports, "The army is considering extending tours in Iraq." I watch two soldiers with airborne patches on their sleeves, but they don't seem interested in the news.

Around 3 A.M., we are led outside to make the ride downtown into the Green Zone. The Rhino pulls up, and a team of bomb-sniffing dogs inspects our luggage, duffel bags, and backpacks. I was told by army public affairs that the Rhino was last attacked earlier in the year, wounding two journalists.

It's the only way to get down to the Green Zone, though. The Rhino is a custom-made vehicle that looks like a cross between a large RV and a stodgy bus. Climbing on board, I notice a thirty-something contactor with a goatee posted in the front with an M-16; he looks like a former ranger or SEAL now working as a civilian contractor. Beside him sits the driver, a young black man with a pistol in a side holster. They chat as though it's another day at the office, which for them it probably is. In front, serving as an escort, is a Humvee with a soldier behind a mounted machine gun. (Later, I learn that an Apache escort helicopter probably flew overhead.)

Where to sit? I'd like to hide in the Rhino's midriff, but the middle seats are taken. I wind up behind the driver's seat and feel very exposed. If we're attacked, won't I be one of the first passengers in the line of fire? Only later do I read that the thirteen-ton Rhino has bullet-resistant windows, as well as special armor to protect against IEDs.

The driver turns off the lights, puts on his helmet, and off we go. It's hard to make out anything through the windows—palm trees and shadows, mostly. There's little conversation among the passengers, and I wonder if anyone else is quietly praying for a safe arrival.

After twenty minutes or so, we enter the bright lights of what must be the Green Zone. It's a dizzying sight: more Jersey barriers, Saddam's old Republican Palace, now the American embassy, and dominolike trailers everywhere. As I try and fail to get a sense of place, I find myself left alone in another waiting room (I'm not even sure what building I'm in). I pick up a phone and dial the number I'd been given for a ride to CPIC.

Somehow in all the confusion, I'd lost track of my new friend Mohammed. I wonder where he's gone in this dizzying palace, filled with shadow and light.

Chapter Fourteen

NEXT STOP: THE GREEN ZONE

After a few hours of much-needed sleep, I woke up and tried to get my bearings. A soldier picked me up at the Rhino stop and drove me over to the Combined Press Information Center. CPIC is more modest than it sounds; it's a warren of offices in one of the many makeshift trailers used by the Americans since the creation of the Green Zone in 2003. The press center was quiet around 3 A.M. as the soldier showed me where I could grab one remaining spot atop a bunk bed. CPIC looked more like a college dorm room than the center of international press activity in Iraq. Someone was dozing on an old brown couch, and a young woman draped in a Budweiser beach blanket checked e-mails on a computer. She registered little interest in the dusty interloper looking for a place to sleep.

Despite the many press accounts of the lavish living by Americans in the Green Zone—or what the military liked to called the IZ, or International Zone—CPIC lacked even the basic cleanliness or comfort of a Motel 6. My host soldier cheerfully explained that water pressure had been low lately, so perhaps I should consider taking what he called a "combat shower"—that is, grab some water bottles, stand in the shower stall, and pour. To my surprise, it was a simple, yet effective way of cleaning off the day's dust and grime.

After I dried off, I put on fresh clothes and climbed up on the upper bunk to pass out. Around 8 A.M., I sat up, freezing from the air conditioning. After getting my bearings, I pondered my next move, though I hadn't a clue what that might be. I knew I would get my press credentials, but I wasn't sure how or exactly whom to ask for. I also wasn't sure how I would get out of Baghdad once I did get my papers. How would I hook up with Major Pool and reach Fallujah?

It was Wednesday, June 21, but it seemed like a dream, albeit a stressful one. The clock was ticking on my visit inside Iraq. Because of the delays in departing Kuwait, I felt pressed to get out of Baghdad. I did want to talk to some senior army public-relations officials here, including Col. Steve Boylan, General Petreaus's chief spokesman, but I had no idea if or when this had been arranged. E-mails had been exchanged, but nothing had been nailed down. The more information I got, the less I knew.

So I did what comes naturally to a reporter: I snooped around. Two old cards were stuck on a bulletin board, evidently sent by American school kids. "Happy Valentine's Day," one declared in a child's scrawl. Even here, cynical journalists didn't mind the corny touches. As I prowled the premises, I was surprised to see a familiar face out in the hallway: Joe Klein. I remembered the movie based on his 1996 novel, *Primary Colors*, about Bill Clinton's run for president. Klein had a salt-and-pepper beard, green jacket, and cargo pants. He was chatting with an army officer, and in my disheveled state, I hesitated to approach him.

But reporting is not about following protocols or worrying about making a fashion statement. It's about seizing opportunities, and this was my one shot to interview a media star. Overcoming my doubts, I approached Klein, introduced myself, and, no doubt babbling, tried to introduce my research. He graciously granted me a twenty-minute interview, in which he explained his reasons for being here, his interest in the Middle East, and the blame he put on President Bush for not doing the necessary work of educating the American public about the strategic importance of Iraq before launching the invasion.

Klein told me why staying home simply had not been option. The war's back story had a personal dimension that became clear in the passionate way he told the story of September 11, 2001, when his suburban New York town lost nine men in the terrorist attacks on the World Trade Centers. "In my town that night," Klein said, "I saw the forces of social capital—which is a euphemism for women—set up a feeding schedule for the nine families, so the widows wouldn't have to cook. Then we heard they needed shovels and gloves down at Ground Zero, and we bought out Home Depot. People were scared. We didn't know what was going to happen next. But there was also exhilaration about being citizens again and caring about each other. That was the point that I, personally, was starting from."

The word "passion" is overused these days, but sitting in the dim lights of the hallway, operating on little sleep, Klein clearly was passionate about following a story that had many human faces. Too soon, it was time for him to have his eyes biometrically scanned, which was part of the process of receiving press credentials to report in Iraq. Klein was sure of many things, but there was one question he couldn't answer for his army handlers. "What's your blood type?" one asked. "Unknown," he told them.

As I waited to get my credentials, I met another reporter, a bright young woman who worked for the Associated Press. At twenty-nine, Lauren Frayer had been in Baghdad since November 2006, about eight months at the time we met. She started with AP in Washington, DC, and parlayed her Arabic language skills to gain an editing job at AP's Cairo bureau. She also managed to travel around the Middle East, including coverage of the Palestinian-Israeli conflict.

That morning in Baghdad, we went outside to sit in the shade of a camouflage net. It was good to get away from the hum and clutter and stale air of the press center. Frayer described some of the frustrations of trying to get straight answers from the U.S. military command, which was why many veteran reporters were skipping out on routine press briefings. The chief military spokesman, Rear Adm. Mark I. Fox, "isn't terribly forthcoming with any kind of information, and a lot of the western reporters decided it's not worth it to come to these things. Increasingly over the past few months there have been more and more Iraqis, and less and less westerners, at these briefings."

She explained how the American reporters—whether from AP, the *Washington Post*, *New York Times*, or other major outlets—often watch the briefings on TV. It's not unlike Washington reporters who watch C-SPAN to follow congressional hearings or press conferences. "I don't even have to be here" because AP has direct TV feed to her office across the Tigris River. "Normally I just sit and watch it," Frayer said. "But you know, it sets a dangerous precedent, and one of the plans for security in the IZ is to shrink it, and eventually have it just be a security zone around the U.S. embassy. It's unclear whether these kinds of briefings will be here, or at Camp Victory [the Baghdad army base where General Petreaus has his command headquarters]. We're talking a year out into the future. It worries me because fewer and fewer reporters are going to these things. OK, they're watching them on TV, but they're not here to ask questions, they're not here to confront, which is dangerous for us."

Her concern reminded me of Josh Rushing's complaints about the compliant press at CentCom headquarters in Qatar during the invasion. Keeping reporters at arm's length, Frayer said, "allows the U.S military to spout out information to the television cameras without the give and take with reporters." And unlike other high-level briefings, such as those at the White House or Pentagon, there was no preliminary briefing, or "gaggle," with reporters before the cameras turned on and the official posturing began.

Frayer noted that more Iraqi media were getting involved and asking questions at the military press conference, "which is great to participate more." She sighed. "Maybe I'm cynical, but I get the sense that the U.S. military is a little more comfortable handling questions from the Iraqis than from a more cynical or confrontational western reporter who might be writing a story about the U.S. military rather than the Iraq situation on the ground."

There was a different dynamic between the Iraqi military spokes-men and the Iraqi reporters, some of whom were women. "They think if the information comes from the ministry of defense, it's a 'fact,'" Frayer noted. "That's how it always was here." The newly minted reporters find it hard to challenge the "facts" presented by the generals, she said, and the press conferences often devolve into lovefests with an American general or admiral "saying what good friends we are and how they're working together. Then you have the Iraqi general rattle off a long list of accomplishments the Iraqis have made in the past week." Meanwhile, the Green Zone was getting to be more dangerous every day. "Mortars are flying next door, and you have things blowing up all over the place. The juxtapositions of these kinds of briefings, and the reality on the ground, sometimes I wonder if they really matter."

Frayer hoped General Petraeus would change this dynamic and help bring more balance to the briefings, but she hadn't seen it yet. Though still in her twenties, Frayer said, "I find myself getting pretty cynical. I call these guys the 'good news boys.' They spend their whole time in the IZ, and aside from the mortars that are now falling here everyday, most of the guys who speak to the media here, and control the media message, don't ever go out into Iraq. I mean, I don't even consider this Iraq," she said, gesturing to the scene around us. "The Green Zone is more Washington than it is Iraq, in some ways more connected with Washington than with Iraq, and caring more about the hearts and minds in Washington than about the hearts and minds in Iraq."

She did her best reporting out in the field with company command-ers, she said, usually with "the guy who's been on the ground, who has read Petraeus's counterinsurgency manual and has an idea of the chang-ing nature of warfare. Those are the most reality-based, revealing inter-views I've had."

Our interview was interrupted by a loud *boom*. It was hard to say how far away the explosion was, or what created it, but it was likely another mortar from the insurgents. Frayer coolly took us into one of the concrete "duck and cover bunkers" placed around American bases for moments like this. We sat below the concrete roof, and trying not to sound too concerned, I asked where she thought this latest mortar had hit. It was hard to tell from the sound, but Frayer guessed it wasn't close by. The day before had been a different story.

"I was in an area at the PX [post exchange] that's frequently pretty packed with people around dinner time. I was just reading my book, and I decided to get a sandwich at the Subway sandwich shop maybe fifty meters away. And two minutes after I got up to get over to the sandwich place, a mortar hit just where I'd been sitting—literally just behind the table where I'd been sitting."

She was matter-of-fact about this near miss—more so than I would have been under the same circumstances. "It toppled the wall. Thankfully, the area was clear. There was one man who was sitting a couple of tables away from me who was thrown a good amount of distance from the blast. He had some shrapnel [wounds], but I think otherwise he was OK."

Was that her closest call? "That's the only close call I've had in the Green Zone, which they think of as a safe zone, but it's not." As we waited for a few minutes in the bunker, she described "a couple of close calls" she had out in the field, including one in Diyala province northeast of Baghdad, which stretches to the border with Iran. In one incident, she witnessed an explosion from an IED that struck an Iraqi Army Humvee and lifted it off the ground. The blast destroyed the vehicle and killed four Iraqi soldiers. "There was so much RPG [rocket-propelled grenade] and so much gunfire that we were looking out the window of our Humvee, but we couldn't get out and help. So we literally watched these guys writhing around in the wreckage, dying . . ."

She paused, thinking back on a scene that obviously was etched in her mind forever. "It always seems to happen in Diyala," she continued. "Diyala's just a really, really violent place." A Russian photographer for *Newsweek* had recently perished there.

With so much danger and death—and its mounting toll on journalists—I asked her why she volunteered to cover the war for the Associated Press. "I really wonder," she replied with a laugh. "No, well, I do it because I think the story will define my generation as an American, it will change the world forever," including, she said, "the idea of America in people's minds around the world." Professionally, "I think I'm an OK journalist and able to tell good stories, and able to inform people back home about what's going on. And it's not completely selfless. It's exhilarating to see the story firsthand."

A female journalist in the Middle East faces special challenges, but Frayer said she also can see some interesting advantages. "I find people are more surprised that I'm an American who speaks Arabic and lives among Arabs" than they are surprised that she's a woman journalist. Speaking Arabic often surprises American soldiers, who, for some reason, also think she's Australian or British. Often, the young soldiers—the nineteen- and twenty-year-olds—"have never left their home states, and are perplexed by the idea that an American woman has chosen to come here."

The mortar attacks on the Green Zone were likely to continue, since the insurgents had been helped by Iran, had plenty of funding for mortars and rockets, and recently nearly hit U.S. ambassador John Negroponte. "They had a rocket hit on the road just as his convoy passed. I don't think it's a coincidence," Frayer said. "I think they have ways of getting intelligence on top-level U.S. officials' movements." And, she noted, Iraqi prime minister Nouri Maliki's "office gets mortared a lot."

Would the U.S. ultimately succeed in Iraq? "I don't know who's winning," Frayer said. All she knew for sure was the disparity between the hard truths of warfare she saw in the field—and the openness of the soldiers who talked to her—and the spin zone at CPIC. "I'm shocked by how much soldiers will tell me and trust me with," she said. "Then you have to sit through these briefings and they try to put a good news spin on everything—it's almost insulting, or not grounded in reality."

Was the military creating yet another credibility gap? "Yeah, a little bit," she said. "I think it's been a little bit worse recently. Right around now there's a lot of pressure on these top guys to show some real progress here—four months into the Baghdad security plan. For the past four months they've said we can't gauge progress yet, not all of the surge troops are here. Well, now they're here and they're under a lot of pressure this summer to show some progress. I'm going to try to weed through the spin and figure out whether there's real progress."

How? "It's really hard," Frayer conceded. "For me, it's getting out in the field and seeing it firsthand, which can be incredibly dangerous." She reflected on the impact on her family back home and on herself. It didn't help matters that her friends back home seemed to have lost interest in her news coverage or *any* coverage of the war, for that matter. "I really think about what I put my poor mother through, worrying about me here. But I decided that this is the time in my life to do an assignment like this. I'm not married, I don't have children, but yeah, it's an incredible sacrifice just in terms of missing weddings and everything that goes on back home, and worrying everybody."

The workload in Iraq is heavy compared to the hardest reporting job back in the States, where, even after the most challenging day, "you get to go home and sleep in your own bed. We don't get to do that." Plus, she said, back in the States, a reporter normally gets to see her family, even for half an hour, and get rid of some of the day's stress. This never happened in Baghdad.

The thoughtful reporter with long, curly hair, wearing an athletic shirt and black slacks was not a complainer. But she did sound tired of the story that would define her generation. She lived in AP's fortified compound in the Red Zone of Baghdad, outside the military enclave of the Green Zone. Though she liked getting out with the military, the long days and nights could be grueling. How did she cope? Did she have any kind of support group? "It's hard," Frayer replied, "because I try not telling my friends and family the scary stuff. But we talk to each other—reporters.

"I actually got sick recently," she continued, "and I really think it was fueled by my being here; it sort of affected my immune system." But her workload, she added, pales in comparison to the average soldier's day. "I see these soldiers, who are in incredibly trying circumstances, and do a fifteen-month stint and get just a two-week break to see their families. . . . They work eighteen-hour days, seven days a week."

Most of this is lost on her friends back home, even some in the media whose priorities seem driven by the latest celebrity news. "My peers who are in their thirties are young, professional, just starting families," Frayer observed. "They're well-educated, most of them watch cable news, they get their headlines over their cell phones, but they don't really read a newspaper, and they have a good friend over here writing for a newspaper. It really worries me. I feel I'm here strolling among a diminishing group of reporters and news organizations who are footing the bill, and the insurance cost of sending their people here. And, frankly, not a lot of reporters want to come here because of the danger, and the personal sacrifice it takes."

The disconnect between Iraq and the U.S. includes her own profession, she noted. "I do these interviews with radio stations, and AP members get me on the air. One day, there was rioting in Kufah in the south, and I was asked, 'What is it like for you, an American woman, to be standing in that riot?' I said I'm in Baghdad. The roads aren't even safe enough for me to drive here, let alone being an American woman standing in the middle of Kufah. I'd last for thirty seconds."

She shook her head and laughed at the ignorance of what it's like to live, and report, in this dangerous clash of cultures. "It's too dangerous for me to go out in the neighborhood where our house is. I have to be fully covered, head to toe, and I have to have security guys who are disguised trailing behind me. It's incredible. Picking me up at the airport takes two armored cars, with three armed guys in each car. . . . Any westerner is just such a target."

Yet most of the feedback on her reporting arrives through cyberspace from people she termed right-wing bloggers, who skewer her via e-mail for any perceived wrongs, including having the audacity to report the obvious fact that the Green Zone was under an increasing number of mortar attacks. The near-miss of the previous day was testimony to that fact. Yet she said, "I get these people who write about me and e-mail me and call me an unloyal American. . . . It's another thing that makes me think, what am I doing this for? It makes me wonder whether those voices are representative of the American public now."

Shortly before 3 P.M., I went with Frayer and a few other American reporters to attend one of the regular press briefings. The small room was crammed with TV cameras and bright lights in the rear, including two cameras run by the military. Iraqi or other Arab cameramen were ready for the event, but there didn't appear to be any major U.S. networks on hand, confirming Frayer's observation about the scant coverage of these tightly scripted events.

Headphones at each seat were marked for Arab or English translations. In walked the chief American spokesman, Rear Adm. Mark I. Fox, along with his Iraqi counterpart, Brig. Gen. Qassim Atta, a slight man with a black mustache and black beret who reminded me of Peter Sellers in *The Pink Panther*.

Before questions were taken, the military spokesmen paid respects to each other. Then Atta began a statement while pictures flashed on a screen behind showing an attack that had killed or wounded children near a mosque. Fox began his statement with a traditional Arab greeting, then talked about taking the fight to the extremists and "taking back neighborhoods." He described a night air assault involving 10,000 soldiers from a joint Iraqi-American force against elements from Al Qaeda, and said he "shared the outrage" with the Iraqi people over the bombing of the Askarirya mosque in Samarra.

Most of the questions came from Iraqi and Iranian reporters. One Iraqi asked about reports of the taunting of civilians by U.S. forces that led to some casualties. The reporter seemed quite worked up as he leveled his charges. Fox kept a steady gaze and denied the charge, saying he knew of "no reports whatsoever" along those lines. After seeming so exercised, the Iraqi reporter nodded, took notes, and seemed to calm down.

Some posed questions about the Americans' security checkpoints, and Fox explained the goal was to open as many streets in Baghdad as possible. At that point, eighty-eight streets in the city had security barriers stopping traffic. When someone asked why more barriers had not been in place around mosques, Fox said, "We want to make it easier for the people to get on with their lives. Adding cement will create a traffic jam." The admiral seemed cheery, despite the serious topics and occasional accusation. Atta, on the other hand, exhibited the air of an authority figure not accustomed to being questioned and seemed impatient with any doubts shown by Iraqi reporters. "These are the facts," he said. "We must get away from any kind of exaggeration."

As the discussion of the attack in Samarra continued, Atta said, "We went into every single part of that mosque and actually prayed inside that mosque. The imam himself said there was no targeting of the mosque. So where are the facts?" he asked, scanning the faces of his interrogators. "We have to separate between the truth and bad intentions. We don't work on analysis and suggestion. That is the job of the media." He gave one reporter a hard look and stern lecture.

Fox was no more helpful, but he kept a more upbeat tone. When he declined to give numbers on the mortar attacks on the Green Zone, he said, "Yes, we do keep very close tabs. But I'm not going to give those doing the shooting" any details about whether they hit their targets. He did acknowledge an "increasing pattern of attacks on the Green Zone," calling this a "clear attempt to get lucky shots."

After the press conference, a friendly army major took me for my second meal of the day at the well-stocked dining room of the American embassy. The former conference room for Saddam Hussein in his Republic Palace had been converted by the latest conquerors of Mesopotamia who gave it a distinctly all-American, slightly kitschy look—with green and yellow Christmas lights, flags of nations hanging from the ceiling, and more ice cream than you could shake a drumstick at.

Before I could sink my teeth into the chocolate fudge delight, I was interrupted by Maj. Jeff Pool, who strode over to our table. I'd met Pool, my marine contact, earlier at the press conference, and he'd told me to stand by. But I was surprised we were leaving so soon.

"Get your gear. It's time to go," he said. As we hustled back to CPIC, he explained that a general doing a briefing in the Green Zone had given permission for me to fly with him back to Camp Fallujah. There was no time to waste. The chopper was waiting. As I retrieved my two rolling bags and backpack—once again feeling like I had ridiculously overpacked—I felt a sense of relief. If I had stayed another night, I would have had to ride the Rhino one more time back to the airport to catch a helicopter to Fallujah.

Pool grabbed one of my bags as though it weighed nothing. I followed behind him, sweating profusely in my body armor and helmet. He walked out onto a parade field behind the embassy where the chopper was warmed up and ready to go. Two other helicopters would fly as escorts.

I blinked in the late-afternoon light like a rat let out of a cage. What next? My question was answered when the general who had approved my trip with him walked up and introduced himself.

"Hi Chip, John Allen. Follow me." With those few words, I was reintroduced to Brig. Gen. John Allen and gladly followed him over to the chopper and up the ramp, where I took a seat and tried to stay out of the way. I couldn't believe my good luck: I'd met then-Col. John Allen in 1999 when he was the commanding officer of The Basic School, the U.S. Marine Corps' officer training program in Quantico, Virginia, and I was researching my first book on the marines. Allen had been generous with his time and insights.

Now, much to my amazement, I was airlifted out of the Green Zone by Allen, who was now the deputy commanding general of the 35,000-strong II Marine Expeditionary Force. This was doubly enjoyable because, unlike the hot ride on the C-130 into BIAP, this ride was pleasant and cool. And it was above ground, with none of the tension of riding along waiting for an IED to explode.

The transport chopper lifted off gently, and the marines left the rear hatch open. We skirted over Baghdad, which unfolded below in all its beauty, grit, and splendor. There were huge statues I couldn't readily identify, except for the garish Monument to the Unknown Soldier, with its massive shield from a fallen Iraqi; from the air, it looks like a big clam armed with a cannon. Smokestacks spewed smoke over high-rise apartments and the city's jumble of slums.

Just as the city looked beaten and haggard, something lovely would appear—a turquoise mosque and minaret, and then another, bigger mosque. I saw a bend in either the Tigris or Euphrates (I couldn't be sure which, and there was no way to ask over the din of the chopper's engines), and the land opened up to large palatial estates on a lake. I was surprised by how quickly the urban terrain became rural. We banked toward the sun, which reflected off the two escort gunships. Below, the landscape turned to lush green farmland that was divided into squares of fruit groves. From about 1,000 feet, it finally became evident why people had been fighting to own this fertile landscape for so many thousands of years.

Even with ear plugs, the chopper created a high-decibel drumbeat as we flew over rural villages, housing compounds, and rugged desert. By now, I knew we must be in Anbar Province, which was the gateway to the desert kingdoms of Syria and Saudi Arabia.

I watched two young gunners on either side of the chopper, peering out the windows for any dangers below. Fallujah came into view, and we began our descent. The gunners clicked rounds into their .50-caliber machine guns. No one was firing from the ground, so we made an uneventful landing at Camp Fallujah, about twenty miles northwest of Baghdad.

Chapter Fifteen

"IF IT BLEEDS, IT LEADS"

The next morning I woke up with a start to the rumbling sound of cannon fire, which shook the room in a trailer I'd been given. *What the hell was that?*

But the mysterious sounds ended as quickly as they began, and I put them on the list of things to ask about on this, my first full day at Camp Fallujah. I cleaned up at the nearby showers, then followed the gravel path back to the sand-bagged offices of Major Pool and his public-affairs group. It was only 9 A.M., but the heat was already stifling. I walked along an asphalt road and turned at the palm trees near Pool's office. I was met by a pair of pleasant, but firm guards, young men from Uganda who worked twelve-hour shifts despite the furnacelike conditions. I handed them my paperwork, and they read over my embed orders, showing no emotion. They let me through this time, but this would not always be the case. Sometimes, they would question me; other times they would call their supervisor. It was life on a military base, where Catch 22 still ruled. But whenever they made me wait, the young Ugandans were always exceedingly polite.

Pool's offices were in a plywood building built behind a sandbagged wall, under some sickly-looking palms. The trailer had a wooden door that sometimes latched and sometimes didn't, letting out the cool air and letting in flies. Tacked on the door was an internet photo of Rosie O'Donnell's face on the chunky body of captured Al Qaeda terrorist Kalid Sheik Mohammed. When I walked in, Pool was sitting at his desk with his combat boots up, bantering with his two lieutenants. The first was 2nd Lt. Roger Hollenbeck, a rangy newcomer to the p.a. shack who was given the unenviable task of getting embeds like me settled into place. Hollenbeck, like Pool, was a big Texan. Pool had been trying to fine-tune the lieutenant's approach to conflict resolution, whether it was with the enlisted men and women working on stories in the office or someone giving him grief on the phone. Whatever the cause, Hollenbeck sometimes looked ready to crush the receiver and throw it at the wall. Pool had a calming, almost zenlike effect on his young charge, uttering aphorisms like, "Sometimes doing nothing is an option."

His second in command was Lt. Shawn Mercer, an easy-going New Yorker who kept a picture of his wife and little girl on his desk. Master Gunnery Sgt. Phil Mehringer was gone on leave during my first few days at the camp; when he returned, the veteran "Master Guns"—as Mehringer was called—served as the listening board and liaison for the enlisted men and women out in the field, a process of story, photo, and video assignments not unlike a typical newsroom back in the States. Some tension between the officers and enlisted marines was inevitable, and Master Guns served as the intermediary to defuse it. In some ways, his role was comparable to a city editor in a newsroom, like Lou Grant on the old TV show. Pool was more like the managing editor of this press operation. His public-affairs unit had eight full-time members, a small number considering the size of their area of responsibility and the scope of American military operations.

Anbar Province is roughly the size of North Carolina, making it the largest of Iraq's eighteen provinces. Anbar means "granaries" in Arabic, which seems appropriate when one views the orchards and fields along the Euphrates River, which flows from Syria in the north to the southeast, where it meets the Tigris River near Basra in southern Iraq. The region resembles the Old West in the United States, with a history of outlaws and now terrorists sticking up convoys running across the desert roads linking Syria and Iraq.

With so much ground to cover and history to understand, it seemed remarkable that the occupants of this cramped press shack served as the clearinghouse for any reporter, editor, or TV correspondent who e-mailed or called about the military situation for Multinational Force West. An ace in the hole for Pool was a precocious corporal, Christopher Stankiewicz, the son of a Massachusetts school superintendent who had left college to join the marines. Stanky, or Stank, as he was known, was a dynamo on a variety of media, from the Internet to the latest episodes of *The Office* and *The Colbert Report*. Stanky also provided an eclectic blend of music worthy of a satellite radio producer. He'd grown up near Arlo Guthrie and knew most of the words to his Sixties antiwar anthem "Alice's Restaurant."

Pool laughs when I tell him about my rude awakening that morning, Friday, June 22. "We need to tell embeds about that," he remarks dryly. The rounds, he explains, were outgoing, not incoming, as the marines periodically fire illumination shells above the base's perimeter as a security precaution to ensure no one's crawling up on them.

Pool perches atop a large workout ball, something Mercer recently introduced to prevent back pain from sitting for hours at a desk. "I used to make fun of him," Pool said, nodding at the first lieutenant, who sits a spitball's toss away, "but the floor slants, and I started sitting on it."

Pool's leadership style is to keep things loose in his shack, but amidst the fun, there's a strong work ethic and focus on thinking of public affairs as something new and evolving, an integral part of the marines' battle plan. He disdains old-school thinking about the public-affairs specialist's role, saving his most pointed barbs for the kind of "stunts" that sometimes find soldiers waving happily from Iraq while they watch NFL football on a big screen TV. That happened during a Super Bowl game before he came to Fallujah in 2005, and he vowed never to repeat such foolishness on his watch.

"I think the best kind of public affairs is when you show people what we're actually doing," he explains. "You can't go wrong when you're showing marines doing their jobs. These silly stories that show Chuck Norris or the Denver Broncos' cheerleaders . . ." Pool shakes his head in disgust. "If I was a parent back home, I'd say, 'Why is my kid over there?' If you're at war, and you're kid is hanging out with Chuck Norris or watching cheerleaders, it's not a very good thing."

Pool quickly pulled the plug on such feel-good offerings, including one called "Fallujah Two Minute" that kept Chuck Norris and other stars on the Multinational Force West website. In its place, Pool's crew developed *The Anbar Report*, named after *The Colbert Report* on Comedy Central. They found a hipper and smarter way of looking at the news and developed a creative edge for the work of young combat marines in their twenties and early thirties. The emphasis is on getting out in the field and showing what the marines actually do around western Iraq.

"I think we've banned any inside-the-base reporting," Pool says. He wants his marines to stick to the old rule of good reporting—write about others, not yourself. It's important to get outside the camp, "because not everyone lives in this sort of nice base with air conditioning, computers, ice cream."

Gunnery Sgt. Brenda Varnadore, a native of south Boston, was working on a video report on the marines' training of the Iraqi army and police. Such coverage can lure the mainstream media out to Anbar to do their own stories. But the immediate audience is the U.S. Marine Corps and its families and friends. "The families are the ones who really want information on what's going on out here," Pool says. They're often not pleased with the scant coverage in the mainstream media.

That's not surprising: Media coverage of Anbar Province saw a precipitous drop in attention as attacks plummeted in 2007. In the capital city of Ramadi, for example, attacks dropped from about 100 per week in 2005–06 to fewer than five per week in June 2007. In Fallujah, only about 200 marines were patrolling, down from the thousands who fought there in 2004 and 2005.

"Really there are no insurgents left in the major cities," Pool says. "It's small pockets in outlying areas, mostly closer to Baghdad," such as Diyala Province, where the AP's Frayer witnessed the deadly attack.

In late June 2007, I was one of only four embedded journalists assigned to units in Anbar, and one of only thirty-nine embeds in the whole nation. "I've seen it as low as nine embeds throughout all of Iraq in 2006," Pool says. That number doesn't include reporters who aren't embedded with troops (known as "unilaterals") and news agency, newspaper, or television reporters.

Faced with this interest void, Pool says he makes it a point *not* to help Al Qaeda in Iraq's continuing propaganda machine, a bloody operation best known for the macabre videos of Abu Musab al-Zarqawi, the terrorist organizer notorious for videotaping beheadings of American contractors. Zarqawi was eventually tracked down in Diyala and killed by a U.S. air strike in June 2006. His legacy of Internet-driven propaganda continues.

"They don't teach you anything about counterpropaganda," Pool says of the training program at Fort Meade, Maryland. "Lieutenant Mercer and I are probably the two marines who are best educated in countering propaganda because we had to do it so much in 2005." At that time, he said, Zarqawi was beating the Americans on the information battlefield, issuing "news releases" about supposedly huge setbacks for American and Iraqi forces and great victories for his terrorist group, Al Qaeda in Iraq (AQI).

In a lighter moment, Pool put himself in the role of his counterpart at AQI. It couldn't be that hard to issue such lurid material, probably while sipping coffee at a Starbucks somewhere in the Middle East or Europe. "You could make it up if you want—you kind of loosely base it on the truth that a bomb went off," inflicting "mass casualties," even if there was no proof. Pool sips his own cup of home-brewed coffee and mulls over the strange battle he wages in cyberspace. "It would be so easy to be an insurgent propagandist. You just go, 'Huh, I think I feel like a tank was destroyed today. An IED blew up a tank, and oh, when the people were rushing to help the marines out of the tank, it blew up and killed more people. And the local villagers watched the marines burn and didn't help. Good to go—thank you, Allah!'"

Pool knows this game well, since he is sometimes vilified by name in AQI's reports. The terrorists' creative-writing classes wouldn't matter, he says, except that frequently these fantastic reports receive credence from mainstream media outlets who should know better. In that sense, the media in Iraq was mirroring the world back in the States, where major newspapers had tried for years to ignore the political rumor mill on the Internet, but in the late 1990s, during the scandals of the Clinton Administration, eventually caved in and began running gossipy stories based solely on online speculation.

Now, all too often, the mainstream media does a lousy job of fact-checking before running a story planted by AQI. And even when Pool or his counterparts can prove the stories were wrong, the damage is done. In this first American war of the new millennium, perception warfare is as real as the battles fought on the ground.

"You know, there's no AQI left in Anbar, and they haven't told us where their new capital is because it's not in Ramadi anymore—because they lost Ramadi. It could be Diyala, and they'll say, 'We never wanted Al Anbar anyway.' God only knows what they'd say. Their press releases will say, 'A truly faithful man, by the grace of God, oh Allah so merciful, shot a bullet in the air and it hit an F-16 fighter jet and caused it to crash.' Or they'll say, 'It caused the cross-worshipping infidel to crash his plane.'" Pool rose from the exercise ball and stretched. "Their hope is that people will believe if you're really faithful, you can kill a jet flying at 10,000 feet."

Unlike the scrutiny given the U.S. military's press releases or the stories in the *New York Times* or *Washington Post*, Pool says it's rare for Al Qaeda to face tough scrutiny of its claims. "It's like episodes of 'Jihad Combat,'" Pool says. "You just make something up. Nobody's ever going to check, as long as they keep it within the realm of possibility. Nobody in Jordan is going to check, it just has to have the hint of truth . . . this is not an Islamic website; this is an *extremist* website, so the people who would go here are already believers. They trust their source. They drank the Kool-Aid. And they think automatically that we're lying and covering things up."

Pool developed his ideas of working with the media starting with his own battlefield experiences in 2002 during Operation Anaconda in Afghanistan. He worked with more than eighty reporters at Bagram Air Base, forming relationships with journalists that carried over into Iraq. A native of Abilene, Texas, Pool knows the good, the bad, and the ugly about reporters and the news business. It reminds him of the news coverage back home, where reporters chase tornadoes and floods.

"They'd cover it almost like a sporting event," says Pool, a graduate of the University of North Texas. "Disaster sells. This is the same thing. I don't really blame the media for covering death, because if no one wrote the story, the military would be just as upset." He knows this from recent experience: As fewer TV and major newspaper reporters were taking time to embed or visit in Anbar, he noticed a steady stream of queries and ideas from senior officers in Baghdad pitching ways to, in effect, prime the pump of news coverage. For example, one senior officer kept bugging Pool to invite reporters in to witness the turnaround in Anbar's security situation on the eve of the anniversary of a story by the *Post*'s Tom Ricks that cited intelligence officials who had written off Anbar as a terrorist haven. Dumb idea, Pool told the officer. Going after reporters always backfires and turns into a pissing match. His willingness to say "no" to a bad idea comes from his knowledge of how the news professionals do their jobs. Pool knows that improving Anbar's municipal utilities probably is "not a front-page story."

On the other hand, he tired of seeing the kind of sloppy journalism that occurs when reporters followed the predictable, if tragic, story of soldiers and marines getting blown up by IEDs. Repeating the military public-affairs mantra, Pool says, "If it bleeds, it leads." Put another way: death sells.

Pool could relate to the quandary faced by Frayer of the AP's Baghdad bureau. Iraq was too dangerous for most western journalists to travel about. "Western journalists can't go out and can't go everywhere, and it's just not safe for them to live in a town," such as Ramadi. "So they hire a local who's a journalist, he's just a guy who gives some information, and he gets paid by the month, or by the story, depending on which agency you work for.

"So," Pool continues, "the information they provide could be hearsay—'I heard that ten people were killed.' How do you know that? 'Oh, I asked my brother, he drove by and asked someone who said the police said . . . so it could be fourth- or fifth-hand information they're passing along. It's extremely poor journalism. Before, wire services used to make a concerted effort to verify the facts. Now, with the rise of the Iraqi police and the Iraqi army, someone will call them and say, 'I'm an Iraqi policeman, and we just had ten people killed,' and they [the wire services] will run with that."

This happens all the time in Iraq, Pool says, and he faults the major wire services for not verifying information and also not correcting it once they see it's wrong. The American military runs the medical evacuations (medevacs), and it's easy enough to verify the number of killed and wounded.

Pool says he hears all sorts of explanations for this shoddy work, mostly justifying it because of competitive pressures. "They have to get it fast. Reuters will say AP is running this, so we have to run it." Sometimes reporters say, "We're in a war zone. It doesn't have to be perfect. They rationalize, I think, how they do business."

For military commanders from General Petraeus on down the chain of command, this creates an ongoing problem of sorting fact from politically motivated fantasy. Car bombs were detonating almost daily shortly before my visit. Coupled with phony reports generated by AQI—one even used a toy action figure to create a video showing a "soldier" held hostage—it doesn't matter if the news is slightly wrong or a complete fabrication. "For a few hours, they control the news cycle, and if you can control the news cycle and continually put what you want out into the press, that's your main job."

As we spoke, Lieutenant Mercer was dealing with something along those lines. A suicide bomber and two other attackers had been shot by Iraqi units as a group of insurgents drove toward an observation post.

"We saw it as two suicide bombers and the vest bomber killed," Pool said. "But the website for the Islamic State of Iraq said the Iraqi troops wounded dozens and killed scores when the vehicle drove into a compound and it exploded—that it was extreme mass casualty."

A major newspaper kept calling Mercer because of the report on the Al Qaeda website. "They wanted us to double-check because on the Islamic State of Iraq website, they clearly said they killed dozens of soldiers." Because of the wild claim by the extremists, the western newspaper "was questioning Shawn's accuracy." In other words, the reporter believed the terrorist more than he believed the marine.

Based on his experiences as a kind of buffer between journalists and the media—perhaps racking up the most time abroad in a combat zone of any marine public-affairs officer serving in both Afghanistan and Iraq—Pool has developed four rules of media engagement:

1. *Tell the truth.* "I don't want them to lie—lies of omission or lies of commission. I don't want them to mislead reporters."

2. *Don't be the enemy's public-affairs officer.* In other words, don't issue press releases about attacks that no one asks about. "It just hit me around 2005 that it seems like we keep doing their [Al Qaeda's] work for them. . . . They want to stay in the news and stay relevant. It's probably upset them that I don't always issue press releases." Pool wears it as a badge of honor that he's sometimes vilified by the Islamic State of Iraq. "I know we're doing good when he [the extremists' propaganda chief] starts talking about me."

3. *Don't get anyone killed or fired.* As Pool put it, "I don't want to get anyone whacked or sacked." This applies to Iraqi soldiers, who are put at risk if they're pictured on the marines' website.

Similarly, Pool tries to protect American commanders from the media's line of fire. "I'd never put a general up at a press conference before an angry mob" of reporters. "That's my job. I get paid to do the bad news. It's the general's job to get up and do the good news, so to speak. I get paid . . . to catch a few spears from the media now and then." In that role, Pool's job is reminiscent of Tom Wolfe's memorable description of the public-relations professional of the 1970s: the Flak

Catcher who would tell angry citizens, "We're hacking our way through the red tape as fast as we can."[1] The difference for Pool is that he usually deals with angry reporters. And with higher-ranking officers breathing down his neck, Pool and his staff operate in a unique nether-world between the civilian and military spheres. In many ways, the public-affairs pro is on his or her own and must exhibit a unique set of skills—part officer, part media expert, part mediator, even part anthro-pologist and translator trying to negotiate the conflicting expectation and languages of two different tribes. On the media side, there's the tribe of clamoring reporters who want confirmation of one disaster or another; on the military side, there are defensive, deeply suspicious commanders who want Pool and his colleagues to simple "handle" the unruly media mob.

4. *No P.R. stunts*, such as having Chuck Norris visit the troops. Sen. John McCain's stroll through a town market in Baghdad became an instant case study in what not to do for military flak catchers. As McCain tried to illustrate progress in the Iraqi capital, he and other vis-iting lawmakers were protected by more than 100 American soldiers, three Black Hawk helicopters, and two Apache gunships. The image of the senator under siege sent the exact opposite message McCain intended, particularly since it came on a day when six American soldiers had been killed by roadside bombs in Baghdad.

"I don't want stunts," Pool said, almost spitting out the word. "I've banned doing stunts. I've heard from [public affairs in] Baghdad, 'If it's safe out there in Anbar, why don't you do a stroll through Haditha or through one of these cities without body armor on? That would make for big news to show how safe it is.'" Pool leaned back at his desk, shaking his head at the obvious stupidity of some of the sugges-tions that came from on high. "It would make even bigger news if someone was killed!"

Within the small circle of public-affairs specialists, the push to think in a more holistic fashion has been called "effects-based public affairs." Thus, instead of providing information for the sake of providing infor-mation or approving a publicity stunt for the sake of a stunt, "we're providing information to get a certain effect, like firing artillery to get a certain effect." Pool knows, however, that his views aren't always shared by his bosses. "They just think, 'Send out all the press releases and the American public can decide.' That's traditional old school" among senior officers. "From the rank of major and below, the ones out here who see the war and how it actually is, believe the same things I do."

Not everyone likes Pool's philosophy or counterpropaganda methods. One senior army officer in Baghdad described the difference in the army's approach and Pool's way in less than flattering terms. "Typically, you'll find the Marine Corps will be fast on the ball when it's good for them," the officer said, speaking on a not-for-attribution basis. "If it doesn't look good for them, the tendency is not to do anything. They're very parochial. It creates problems. Things happen in a war zone that you have to provide information on, and *not* doing that is not a good thing. You frustrate your command, you frustrate the media, and you have a tendency to lose credibility and transparency. You're made to look like you're hiding things. Jeff [Pool] is a fairly good example of that philosophy."

Pool knows he has detractors but is unconcerned. The goal is to help the marines, he says, not to win popularity contests. He never intended to work as a public-affairs specialist anyway. After joining the corps in the late 1990s, he shared the same goal as most of the second lieutenants who graduated from The Basic School—to command an infantry platoon. "I loved walking through the woods," he says, almost wistfully. "There's nothing better than going on patrol with your buddies."

His post-graduation orders told him otherwise: "I was ordered to be a naval flight officer, stuck in the back seat of a fighter, like Goose in *Top Gun*." So he reported to Naval Flight Officer School in Pensacola, Florida. He was thrown for a loop when he was told by a doctor that he had an unknown allergy that automatically disqualified him from the aviators' ranks.

The next thing he knew he found himself in the public-affairs training program—again, not his first preference. He was dismayed to see the lethargy around him when he worked in New Orleans at a Marine Reserve station, which he called "a retirement home for public-affairs officers." He managed to escape the institutional inertia by volunteering to serve in Afghanistan in December 2001. While at Bagram Air Base, he met dozens of reporters and photographers and established himself as a straight shooter willing to go to bat for a reporter or photographer if the situation warranted. But his allegiance is always to the corps. "I epitomize doing public affairs for the Marine Corps. I'm not just doing it for the media."

Working in public affairs is a career-ender, he says, and there seems to be a hint of sadness when he explains what it means to be on this track. "I will never be a battalion commander. I'll never get a company. It's the life of a staff officer. I'll never be a colonel."

Even in a war zone, the public-affairs shop handles routine assignments, such as photographing and interviewing medal recipients and trying to get their local newspapers interested in the coverage. Corporal Stankiewicz grabbed his camera and notebook to attend a medal ceremony at the nearby Marine Airport Support Squadron, the unit that maintains planes and helicopters at Camp Fallujah. It was a routine event, but Stankiewicz took it seriously, worrying about the lighting of the makeshift parade deck for the medal ceremony. "It's going to be tricky because of the shadows," Stank commented.

There was little time to worry, though, because the general soon arrived and everyone snapped to attention. Standing in the front of the formation was Staff Sgt. Christopher R. Taylor of Choctaw, Oklahoma. He was being recognized for heroism exhibited back in the States the previous summer. While on vacation at Atlantic Beach, North Carolina, Taylor, who was on leave from nearby Camp Lejeune, saved the lives of two Canadian tourists, a father and son, who were swept out to sea in a rip current.

Brig. Gen. T. C. Hanifen, a lanky man in a tan flight suit, began the ceremony by speaking quietly with the diminutive Taylor, like a father talking with his son. Then, turning to the marines, Hanifen said, "We're proud to have someone who exhibited true courage and heroism. It's an honor to shake his hand." The general delivered a pep talk about the role this support unit plays in keeping the choppers and planes aloft for the mission in Anbar. He concluded with "God bless the marines" and strode off as the unit hollered "Hoorah!"

Once the general was gone, Taylor was asked to say a few words to his buddies. Though he didn't look a day over eighteen, the freckle-faced staff sergeant delivered a stemwinder of a speech that explored the responsibility of being a marine. By swearing to uphold the Constitution, he said, "That means you have a responsibility to act. . . . I could not have lived with myself if I'd watched two people die."

He described the incident, watching the father and son thrashing in the water in distress and how he rescued them. And Taylor explained how he almost didn't make it and "puked up the ocean" afterward. Yet, he said somberly, "I got a chance to prove who I was." His message for the marines: "Just be who you are. That's what takes heart . . . to step up every day takes courage."

Stankiewicz dutifully took notes and interviewed the sergeant, hoping to write a story that might run in Taylor's hometown paper.

The following day, Saturday, June 23, Brigadier General Allen, who had rescued me from the Green Zone, invited me to ride along for a day-long visit to Haditha, a city about 140 miles northwest of Baghdad where the Euphrates River supplies two hydroelectric dams and irrigation water for the region's farmers. When U.S. Army Rangers seized the Haditha Dam and hydropower complex on April 1, 2003, this eliminated what could have been a kind of nontraditional weapon of mass destruction from Saddam's arsenal—that is, blowing up the dam could have flooded the entire region and killed thousands of Iraqis and Americans, according to Globalsecurity.org. Since 2004, the U.S. Marine Corps patrolled the area, trying to stave off sabotage to the dams and limit damage to key rail links and bridges.

Haditha became synonymous with wartime atrocities after the deaths of civilian men, women, and children. Initially, the marines charged eight men from the 3rd Battalion, 1st Marines, with crimes related to the November 19, 2005, killings. Four infantrymen were accused of murder, while four officers, including the battalion commander, were charged with dereliction of duty and other crimes related to failing to investigate the episode completely. Subsequently, two infantrymen were scheduled to be tried in courts-martial for wrongful killings; two officers also faced courts-martial.

Allen's visit was unrelated to the ongoing Haditha cases. It was about continuing to build good will with the Sunni sheiks and city and provincial officials. Operating more as an ambassador than as a warfighter, the cerebral general was on a diplomatic mission.

Before taking off, Allen's staff gathers in his office in an aging complex that had been a training base for Iranian dissidents during Saddam's regime. It was yet another reminder of the fleeting nature of power in the Middle East. The marines review the mission to improve municipal operations across Anbar one city at a time. "This is not our meeting," explains Capt. Sherif Aziz, "this is their meeting." Born in Egypt, Aziz serves as a foreign-affairs officer in the corps. He understands the customs of the Sunni Arabs and manages to cross the cultural bridges needed to gain trust in a world where centuries-old tribal allegiances trump any card in the government's hand.

During his time in Iraq, Allen has studied its multifaceted history and culture, and before we board a chopper, he pulls me aside to explain the intent of this day's trip. "The success out here is going to come from our ability to connect Baghdad to the provincial capital," he says over the din of helicopters warming up. "Unless we can do that," Allen says, "there will never be governance that will be enduring out there. It will always end up being something ad hoc or improvised. It's got to be permanent. It's got to be something that survives us when we go."

Anbar's provincial government, based in Ramadi, needs to establish a new system of local governments to achieve any kind of lasting peace in this sprawling territory with a history of violence and lawlessness, a Wild West ravaged by RPGs, roadside bombs, and AK-47s instead of six-shooters. Still, Allen says, the mid-2007 security situation has seen steady improvements for more than a year. "Many of these municipalities are starting to spring up with their own governments. And that's a really good thing."

Today's sojourn is one of a series of visits in which the marines provide the transportation and security for the provincial governor, Ma'moun Sami Rashid, to meet with the city officials to tackle the tedious work of democracy one action item at a time. "We want the governor, the provincial council, and the provincial chief of police to make it to every major population center in the province every other month. That's connectivity. The governor already has been to some places where there's no memory of a governor ever showing up before."

Repeating the day's main talking point—"this is not about us, it's about them"—Allen is asked about his role in this. "All I'm doing is driving the bus, so to speak, to get them there," he says, downplaying his part in this political drama. The "bus" fleet consists of two CH-46 helicopters warming up nearby with all the subtlety of old washing machines. Two Cobra and Huey attack helicopters are whirring into action as well, ready to fly alongside to protect the troop transports.

Before we lift off, Allen continues giving me a kind of primer about what I'll see but, with the language differences, may not understand. Since the players speak Arabic, it's easy to misinterpret their interactions. "They have a big meeting, and everybody yells at each other for a while. It's just typical Arab negotiation for power." He also alerted me to watch the governor exercise his authority and build good will as he "spreads a little money around" to the Hadithans to prove he means business and to show that "the provincial capital isn't this remote city across the desert."

On cue, Governor Ma'Moun arrives with his small entourage of men in suits. They walk up the ramp of the other chopper, and we board ours, and soon we're zooming over the sprawling base, with its seemingly endless stacks of container boxes and high fences and walls. A marine gunner in our CH-46 clicks a round into the chamber of his .50-caliber machine gun, ready to fire from the open hatch.

From our bird's-eye view, Fallujah was a brown mass of buildings, the enclaves that once gave refuge to insurgents and Sunni fighters in some of the most deadly urban warfighting of the war. Yet from a distance, the city seems sleepy and safe. It's a routine day on Highway 10 as a truck convoy slowly rolls along. I see a bridge over the river and wonder if this is the notorious "Brooklyn Bridge," scene of the atrocities against Blackwater contractors that prompted Bush's order for the marines to retake the outlaw city in 2004.

Soon we're soaring about 1,000 feet above villages and green fields and settlements along the Euphrates. In America, this could be south Texas, home of so many army and marine fighters. The green river slowly winds its way northwest, with streams slicing off like veins from an artery, providing lifegiving irrigation to farms and orchards.

After about an hour, we reach Haditha, where sandy bluffs and fruit groves hug the river for life support. General Allen's jaw is clenched as he looks out the window of the chopper, scanning the scene like a hawk. We swoop over low-slung homes, where a few kids ride bikes, and a smattering of cars poke along its outer streets.

The chopper lands at an air base on the edge of the city, where the mayor waits to greet the governor with a hug and peck on either cheek. Blue-clad Iraqi police stand by, along with a number of marine security forces carrying M16s. The joint security force surrounds us as we stroll to a nearby building.

We are shepherded into the mayor's office, cramped quarters that quickly become stifling in the mid-morning heat. A ceiling fan and a wheezing air conditioner offer little relief to the rising temperature. An old travel poster on the wall advertises scenes from Switzerland, which seems like a distant dream in this place where sandbags fill the office windows.

Haditha mayor Hakiem, a fifty-ish businessman with a gray crew cut, dark sports coat, and open-collared shirt, gives up his place behind his desk to Governor Ma'moun as a sign of respect. Shame and honor, I am told, are the two sides of the cultural coin of the realm in this Arab territory. And on the wall behind the mayor's desk is a photo of a respected sheik, Baria, who died in 2005 after killing four members of Al Qaeda who attacked his home. Eight marines, along with provincial and state department personnel, sit on old mustard-colored sofas as the meeting begins. General Allen stays in the back of the room, listening attentively to a translator and taking notes.

Governor Ma'Moun is a broad-shouldered, middle-aged man who has outgrown his tan business suit. He is clearly suited to his leadership task, quickly taking charge of the room. A trained civil engineer, Ma'Moun worked during Saddam's regime for various government ministries as an engineer, including stints in Haditha. His knowledge of the city's hydroelectric power dam and electric utilities and his ties with municipal officials help him understand the city's infrastructure—something the mayor obviously relishes. Ma'Moun also is known for standing up to the terrorists and is said to have survived more than thirty attacks on his life since his 2005 appointment (his predecessor was kidnapped and killed). These close calls may explain the governor's toughness and charm as a kind of Sunni Godfather.

Speaking in Arabic translated into English by several interpreters around the room, Ma'Moun begins by praising the mayor and his staff. He lauds their continuing efforts to improve Haditha, which he calls an important gateway in western Anbar. Under Saddam Hussein, most of the central government's improvement plans for Haditha were "just ink on the paper." He's "sorry the old regime didn't take care of this wealthy town . . . even though the old mayor, he ran away from Iraq."

Mayor Hakiem laughs at this inside joke and takes his cue to speak up. "In the name of Haditha, we have big hope that you'll support our projects and the Haditha people," noting that the national government in Baghdad has ignored Haditha "since Iraq got established in the 1920s." Opening a notebook, the smiling mayor continues, "We need more budget because it's not enough to support our projects. I know you're honest," he reassures Ma'Moun, "But the problem is the people of Haditha don't care—they need services."

They then reviewed a list of pressing issues, starting with people who are siphoning off much-needed funding, those who "cheat on their jobs" and get paid for doing nothing. Iraq and the United States clearly have more in common than they realize. The governor agrees that Anbar Province, which administers national reconstruction funds to civil servants, should check to see who's qualified and who's not. "We're going to send you a list of all the people, some of whom have two salaries . . . even sometimes we find some terrorist people on the list." Ma'Moun returns to the topic of corruption under Saddam, estimating that 10,000 terrorists may still be pocketing government checks.

Then Ma'Moun takes a break in the discussion to sign decrees financing Haditha's utility and electrical rebuilding projects. The opening of Anbar's funding spigot has the desired effect, as the mayor sees Ma'Moun is putting dinars where his mouth is. "We need to establish a center for a water facility and give them more authority," Mayor Hakiem says.

Ma'Moun listens attentively, and they continue talking through the fine points of paying contractors and subcontractors, some of whom are corrupt. One contractor was charging 80 percent of the total cost of a project as his fee. "I told him no," the mayor says, with a dismissive wave of his hand, "you get 35 percent."

The meeting drags on, interrupted only by the ritual serving of hot tea in tiny concave glasses on crystal saucers. The tea is ultrasweet and, despite the heat, remarkably refreshing. Oil production, tankers, security for gas stations—the list of needs seems as long as the Euphrates.

Around the room, American and Iraqi officials scribble furiously. The importance of repairing this broken city is evident as Mayor Hakiem says that if the repairs are done, "the rest [of the populace] will follow us."

Occasionally, the leaders share a joke that comes through even in translation. As they considered the problems of keeping up phone service, the mayor observes, "The phone center [employees] need punishment. I'm going to dig in the ground and hide them." This gets a big laugh.

Sometimes they discover creative solutions to problems such as attacking the vulnerability of cell phone towers—easy targets for insurgents still lingering in Anbar—by putting the telephone towers on trucks, which then could be driven to secure locations such as police stations. And in a plan reminiscent of America's Depression-era Civilian Conservation Corps, they discuss hiring the unemployed to "to give a chance for 500 people to work, besides clean the town," Hakiem says. With a 60 percent unemployment rate and 100,000 men needing jobs, this is a small bit of progress.

Women get short shrift in this male-dominated discussion (there are no females anywhere in sight). They do discuss contracting to build a cultural center for women to learn to sew and provide for health needs in what sounds like a municipal home economics class.

Gradually, Ma'Moun draws the Americans into the discussion. General Allen takes this as an opportunity to announce that he's just signed an order to begin a long-awaited road-paving project for Haditha. He gives all the credit to his Iraqi friends. "It's their friendship that has made this happen," he says through a translator and speaks about the importance of Haditha to Anbar's overall infrastructure. "We need to continue to be close partners on this."

Ma'Moun then presses Mayor Hakiem to provide supporting data to back his funding requests to the provincial and national government. "I really, really need the numbers," says the ex-engineer. "This is important." As they discuss fixing Haditha's damaged water system, he doesn't just want a report, he wants "a deep study—from now and ten years from now."

The morning-long talks seem fruitful, with the seeds sewn for a number of new projects and planning for still more. And so it is time for lunch, not just a bag lunch of the American variety, but rather an elaborate spread out in the main meeting room. Allen briefed me earlier on the etiquette of this Sunni ritual: Eat with your right hand, since the left hand is used for personal hygiene. Don't act surprised if they serve goat—even if the goat's head is on the platter and its eyes are looking up at you. If you're lucky, Allen said, they'll serve lamb. Whatever they serve, accept it and eat it with the bread that comes with the meat. Then offer some back. This is a sign of honor and welcoming for an honored guest. If you get confused, the general said, just follow my lead.

We enter a large room filled with sheiks in white or tan shirts, with loose-fitting pants. Some wear headdresses that show tribal allegiances. The air is filled with pungent cigarette smoke as the sheiks mill about. I follow General Allen to the head of the food-and-drink-filled table. I hope I don't commit a gaffe that hurts the spirit of good will.

Ma'Moun, true to the general's prediction, tears off a chunk of the steaming heap of lamb, along with a sliver of flat bread. The ritual reminds me of a Jewish Seder meal, and it occurs to me that these Arabs and Jews share more than they usually realize. I accept the governor's food with a bow of the head and return the favor.

That's the easy part. Not so easy, though, is trying to interview the governor and mayor as we keep eating and chatting. I hold a tape recorder in my left hand, while eating with my right, and ask questions through an interpreter. Each man compliments the other, with Ma'Moun declaring, "I met a lot of directors from government services here, and it looks like the departments are starting to serve the town. And that comes from the mayor. You feel happy to see Haditha, and now they have their government and kick terrorists from their town . . . Haditha has a very good location for the economy and the roads."

Hakiem says how much he appreciates the governor's backing and the support of the coalition troops. "I thank everybody," he says, toasting them with a Pepsi. The sheiks seem happy, especially when they come to eat the free food.

Allen takes me aside and offers more commentary. "What we've done here is so successful because we have such good relations with the Iraqis. We treat them with respect; we have a genuine bond of friendship. We fought shoulder to shoulder against the enemy out here, with a lot of bleeding on both sides."

But, he adds, he's letting them know the clock is ticking. "We're not going to be here forever," Allen tells the Sunni leaders, "and you've got to take advantage of every minute we're here and consolidate the forward progress of the province." This is not a welcome message by any means. "They don't like to hear we're leaving, they really don't. But they understand that time is coming and there is a sense of urgency with them to get on with these projects."

After lunch, the governor and mayor reconvene in a larger meeting hall, surrounded by sheiks and city officials who pummel them with queries and complaints. Listening to the Arabic—with no translator nearby—it sounds like a town hall meeting with angry citizens. Jim Soriano, a veteran state department official who is the provincial reconstruction team leader in Anbar Province, watches from the rear. "These meetings go in rhythms," he says in a whisper. "You'll hear voices move to a crescendo and come back down and up again. They walk in as friends and go out as friends. They argue because in this culture there's a push and shove for authority. It's about honor and shame. You want to preserve your honor, and [when necessary] you'll shame someone else to do that."

For much of the year, Soriano and his marine counterparts have arranged these talks in key cities such as Fallujah, Ramadi, and now Haditha. "They've never come to blows," Soriano says, "but there's some yelling. Some sheiks' supporters have feigned walkouts . . . but it's all posturing. It's how they communicate and do politics—the words and actions and back-and-forth negotiations. It's wonderful to watch."

Only six months ago, in early 2007, there were only one or two city councils in Anbar. "Today, almost every city and town has a functioning local council and a mayor," about twenty councils in all, according to the American official.

Soriano planned to import North Carolina–based consultants to help build on this progress in government-building. The goal was to train provincial and local officials in the techniques it takes to govern and reach consensus—skills that simply have never been taught in a land accustomed to either colonial rulers or shotgun-toting dictators. They would start by writing an economic development vision statement for Anbar Province.

"For decades, this has been a socialist, centrally planned economy," Soriano explains. "A five-year plan has been part of that approach to planning." Now the goal is to let each local government write their own plans, their own vision statements, and set their own priorities—that is, to begin the hard work of give and take of a democracy. "That's new," he says, "That's one of the foreigners' gifts."

I ask him if, as IEDs kept fracturing the tenuous peace in Baghdad, Diyala, and Mosul, this "Anbar Model" can work elsewhere in Iraq? "There are good days and bad days," Soriano admits. "I'm not going to paint a rosy picture. There are a lot of brave Iraqis who just want to get ahead with life."

What is the most discouraging possibility? "A precipitous withdrawal [of U.S. forces] would be discouraging." In Soriano's view, the U.S. should turn over more of the daily governance and security to the Iraqis, "and then go home. They're adults. There's a lot of talent in Iraq. They know what to do."

As the meeting progresses, the heat and smoke and rising level of rhetoric seems to reach a kind of peak. Finally, one young man stands up and starts shouting. Is he about to attack them? No, I quickly learn, the young Hadithan is pledging his allegiance to "The Awakening" among Sunni tribal leaders battling terrorists in Anbar. Using a form of Arabic poetry, he is damning Al Qaeda and swearing his vengeance. "They hurt everyone! They hurt the families of the mayor! They hurt the police; they hurt the family of the sheik! We are coming together!" The young man's father and brother were killed by Al Qaeda in Iraq, I learn later.

By mid-afternoon, the meetings are done, the hands are shaken, the cheeks are kissed (which is the common practice among Arab men and, to my surprise, culturally sensitive marines such as Captain Aziz). A trip to a local hospital and the town's marketplace, known as a *souk*, is planned. We board a convoy of trucks and SUVs, including a seven-ton truck where I wind up with Soriano. We're sweating in our protective vests and helmets as the heat easily tops 110 degrees. Somehow Governor Ma'Moun manages to maintain his cool, professional appearance in his tan suit—reminding me of the time I saw Bill Clinton speaking in the Rose Garden on a sweltering August day in Washington. Clinton didn't seem fazed by the heat, either, and I wonder if an ability to withstand the elements is a required trait for leaders.

The truck bounces down the rough road, and we pass an abandoned outpost with a sign on a guard tower that speaks of the bloody fighting here the year before: "HiDeatha," it reads.

We pass a jail where prisoners wearing robes and sandals plod outside in a long line. They are blindfolded, and I wonder what awaits them. Passing through a foreign city like this—especially when there's no way to stop and ask questions—can be frustrating for a reporter, as military correspondent George Wilson said about his experiences with the marines. You see things such as these prisoners—a scene that seems right out of Guantanamo Bay—but you can't stop the convoy to ask questions about what you're seeing. And by the time I want to ask Soriano for his thoughts, we've turned the corner, and the prisoners are gone.

So I put down my notebook and just take in the local sights, such as the black metal grills on the windows of the stucco or brick buildings that resemble cheap hotels in California or Mexico. Haditha has other buildings in mint condition, including a two-story villa with a yellow balustrade. There seems to be tons of construction material strewn about the sidewalks and lots, but not that much activity in the mid-afternoon heat. A little boy waves in front of a general goods store, and I wonder what life must be like for him in this broken place.

The convoy stops at Haditha General Hospital, once the scene of fierce fighting between the marines and insurgents. Its walls are pockmarked, and broken glass is scattered along its halls. Ma'Moun seems cheery amid the ruins, though, and quickly begins visiting patients in their rooms—often surprising patients and families alike. He talks to the parents of a young woman who stares with a questioning look from her bed. She's wrapped in a pink blanket and hooked to an IV. The family appears respectful of the governor and his entourage, although one wonders how much their deference stems from the men standing with rifles outside their door. A little girl in a crisp white dress looks at me and the other Americans impassively. What could she be thinking about these intruders?

The governor moves to another room where a young man has a chest wound that's covered by a blood-specked bandage. He was shot earlier in the day by one of the rogue members of Al Qaeda still operating in the area, according to the marines. The governor pulls out a wad of bills, Iraqi dinars, and drops them in the crook of the wounded man's arm.

"That's what you do," Allen whispers to me. "You take care of them." Ma'Moun, it seems, is spreading good will one dinar at a time.

After we got back outside, I notice Allen studying the specifications of an electrical generator. When I asked him what he's doing, he laughs. "My whole life is about generators and water pumps." Asked how many generators the U.S. has bought for Anbar Province, Allen replies, "Thousands, thousands! The national [power] grid was never very efficient, and when the war hit, people just went to self-generation. So we have no idea what the total power [need] is."

The governor cancels his planned tour of the *souk* because its stores and restaurants have closed for the day. He pulls the city and provincial officials together for one final photograph, and around 4 P.M.—six hours after we landed—we climb back aboard the marine choppers. They lift off and fly over the Haditha Dam and its wide, shimmering blue lake. Something's missing from this picture, I realize: there are no boats out on the water, no swimmers, no fishermen. Like so much of Iraq, the waters of the Euphrates appear beautiful from a distance, but up close, they are deeply damaged.

That night, back at the public-affairs shack, Pool and Stank are watching a CNN report about an Iraqi child helping foil a terrorist plot. Pool is curious about the story because he recalls a request from Baghdad several weeks ago to get this kind of story told. They were looking for coverage about kids or women being used by Al Qaeda in Iraq. Watching a military spokesman on TV spinning that exact narrative, Pool seems suspicious.

"Trickery, tomfoolery, jackassery," he observes.

"At least it's not Paris Hilton, sir," Stank says.

"You should feel bad, Stanky," Pool says. "Is that winning the Information Operations War just because CNN picked it up?"

They agree that is not winning much at all. Support for the war is falling as fast the president's poll numbers. As the commander in chief's popularity plummets, the questions and stories about the war increase with a near-mathematic certainty. The major media doubted the U.S. could ever get out of Iraq—short of a permanent presence there such as in Germany or Korea. "It's already agreed we lost," Pool says. "Now the question is: How can we lose gracefully. How can we lose *less*?" This puts him, and other public-affairs specialists, in a tight corner, one with ethical dimensions. "How can you combat against that and *not* be the propagandist?" Pool asks. "I'm not sure you can."

The major and the corporal discussed their dilemma, observed coverage, and told bad jokes well into the night while drinking coffee, eating junk food, and monitoring computers and TV screens. They fielded phone calls and e-mails from the media and military around the world. The Internet has made this tiny sandbagged shack the epicenter for any news out of Anbar Province.

"America got used to the first Gulf War and Grenada, thinking technology was the answer for all problems," Pool says. "We, as a nation, must reexamine what is winning, what is victory, and ask whether just being here is a victory." Whatever happens in Iraq, he says, "The next time we venture onto foreign soil, there will be massive debates on whether we should or not. Before we commit our troops, should we think this out?" If Iraq ends badly, Pool thinks many in the military will blame the media for losing the war, as they did after Vietnam. He also thinks that would be a mistake. "Hating the media, instead of hating the insurgents that manipulated the media—I don't think that's good."

After spending Sunday and Monday at Camp Fallujah, I'm told I can get interviews with some of the top army public-affairs staff in Baghdad, but that means flying back to Baghdad International. I'm not eager to leave, since I've come to enjoy the banter in Pool's shop, the colorful personalities, and the debates over the rights and wrongs of getting the military's story out into the public sphere. And, truth be told, I have no desire to ride the Rhino along the airport road again.

But to get the rest of the story and hear from some of Petraeus's top public-affairs advisors, I agree to return to the capital whenever Lieutenant Hollenbeck can book a flight out on Tuesday. I start plotting my escape once I get to Baghdad and back to Ali Al Salem in Kuwait. Because of visa restrictions, I have to factor in an entire day to ensure I don't miss my United flight back on Friday night.

After bidding farewell to Pool and his crew—with promises to send some Starbucks coffee their way—I'm driven out to the plywood waiting room at the air base at Camp Fallujah. Over the course of the day on Tuesday, June 26, Hollenbeck cautiously updates increasingly bad news about Iraq's weather. When high winds pick up, the resulting sandstorms turn the sky a kind of muddy brown and blue. They remind me of the swirling, blood-red skies painted by the Norwegian expressionist, Edvard Munch. At times I feel like the man in "The Scream," slowly going nuts as I wonder if the sky will ever clear.

After two full days of waiting out the sandstorms—first in Fallujah, then, after a helicopter ride, over at the air base at Taqaddam (TQ)—I have to scratch my trip to Baghdad. Then I start sweating the timing of simply making it back to Kuwait. At TQ, my mood wasn't helped by the fact that I felt obliged to stay near the air force's desk for standby flights and managed to secure only a chocolate frosty for nutrition over a period of twenty-four hours. At one point, we were marched out onto the runway at TQ and expected to board a nearby C-17, the mammoth cargo plane whose illuminated storage bay looks large enough to play a football game.

It's a mirage, though, and the flight is cancelled. It's well after midnight, and I doze off on the rocky ground by the tarmac. When a marine sergeant hollers to march back to the hut, I awake with a start, unable to find my glasses. "Sergeant, wait!"

He comes back and peers down at me with a slightly bemused, if annoyed, smile. "You can't find your glasses?" I might as well hang a placard in front of me that says, NERD. My glasses were hanging on the front of my body armor, and I join the march back to the waiting area. A couple hours later, I join a line of about 300 soldiers and marines to march back to the flight line and, miraculously, onto another C-17. I marvel at the sights and sounds from inside this Moby Dick–sized aircraft. Its rear tail is about three stories high, and each of its four engines are as a big as house trailer.

We crowd into passenger seats five abreast, but it's nowhere near as cramped as the C-130 that brought me to Baghdad. The C-17 is so huge that the pilots walk upstairs to the cockpit, and unlike commercial planes, all of the wiring and hydraulics are uncovered. When they crank up the engines, the aerial mammoth emits a deep moan.

Then the pilot hits the throttle and we are rolling along. At takeoff, the G-forces slam me back into my seat, and I marvel at the way the pilots perform evasive maneuvers—like an aircraft carrier turning on a dime. It twists and turns upward, and after a few minutes, a young airmen says over the p.a.: "We're out of Iraq." Nobody cheers, but inwardly, I feel a sense of relief.

I think back to my long wait to get out and one marine who was also waiting for a flight at Camp Fallujah. He was a skinny young man, with a high and tight crew cut, and so slight of build he didn't seem to fit into the muscle-bound corps. I eavesdropped as he sat on the floor, typing on a laptop computer, engrossed in his writing.

Another young marine noticed him writing in the hours before dawn.

"Are you working on a novel?" he asked.

Yeah, the writer explained. It's about a marine who goes through a wicked firefight and sees a buddy killed. He struggles with what he's seen in war and tries to reconcile his experiences with the principles of honor, duty, and country that led him to join the corps in the first place.

"You written much?"

About forty pages, the writer replied.

"How'd you get this idea?"

It came in a dream.

My ears strained to hear what inspired, or haunted, him to write from the war zone. Did Norman Mailer and Tim O'Brien and other great war novelists also sit in shacks on their way home from battle, trying to make sense of it all?

But the marine spoke too quietly for me to hear any more about his dream. Even for snoops like me, there seem to be some things we're just never meant to hear.

Notes

CHAPTER ONE: WAR? WHAT WAR?

1. "Media Coverage of the Campaign Rises, War Coverage Falls, During the Second Quarter of 2007," Project for Excellence in Journalism: Understanding News in the Information Age (journalism.org), August 20, 2007.
2. Howard Kurtz, "Martha Raddatz, Putting Herself in the Thick of Things," *Washington Post*, November 12, 2007, C1.

CHAPTER TWO: BRIGHT SHINING WAR

1. Bob Woodward, *Plan of Attack* (New York: Simon & Schuster, 2004), 37.
2. John J. Fialka, *Hotel Warriors: Covering the Gulf War* (Washington, DC: The Woodrow Wilson Center Press, 1991), 2.
3. Harold Evans, *War Stories: Reporting in the Time of Conflict from the Crimea to Iraq* (Boston: Bunker Hill Publishing, 2003), 57.
4. Ibid, 57.
5. Phillip Knightley, *The First Casualty: The War Correspondent as Hero and Myth-Maker from the Crimea to Iraq* (Baltimore, MD: The Johns Hopkins University Press, 2004), 15.
6. Ibid., 28.

CHAPTER THREE: ON THE WAR WAGON

1. Woodward, *Plan of Attack*, 92.
2. G. M. Gilbert, *Nuremberg Diary* (New York: Da Capo Press Inc., 1995), 41.
3. Joan Shorenstein Center on the Press, Politics, and Public Policy, *The Iraq War and the Press*, second panel, September 20, 2007
4. Rick Atkinson, *In the Company of Soldiers* (New York: Henry Holt and Co., 2004), 71.

CHAPTER FOUR: RED, WHITE, OR YELLOW?

1. Atkinson, *In the Company of Soldiers*, 165.
2. Ibid., 171–72.
3. Ibid., 167.
4. Ibid., 177.
5. Dusty Saunders, "Fox News Winning the War," *Rocky Mountain News*, 7 April 2003.
6. Larry Eichel, "Fox Leads Cable Ratings—Covering the War with an Optimistic, Patriotic View is Winning Viewers," *Philadelphia Inquirer*, 13 April 2003.
7. Ibid.
8. Greg Mitchell, "Devastating Moyers Probe of Press and Iraq Coming," *Editor and Publisher*, 19 April 2007.
9. Ibid.

244   RED, WHITE, OR YELLOW?

244   RED, WHITE, OR YELLOW?

12. Susan Page, "Prewar Predictions Coming Back to Bite," *USAToday*, 1 April 2003.

14. Peter Johnson, "Military Experts Draw Unfriendly Fire," *USA Today*, 3 April 2003.

16. W. A. Swanberg, *Citizen Hearst* (New York: Charles Scribner's Sons, 1961), 97.

17. Ibid., 107.

18. Ibid., 127.

CHAPTER FIVE: "A MOMENT OF REAL WAR"

1. Bing West and Maj. Gen. Ray L. Smith, *The March Up: Taking Baghdad with the 1st Marine Division* (New York: Bantam Dell, 2003), 2.

2. Michael Tharp, "War Dogs," master's thesis, California State University Fullerton, 2006, 9.

3. Knightly, *The First Casualty*, 357.

4. Ibid.

5. Ibid.

6. Ibid., 358.

7. Ibid.

8. Tharp, *War Dogs*, 9.

9. Atkinson, *In the Company of Soldiers*, 245.

10. Ibid., 167.

11. Ibid., 264.

12. Ibid., 268.

13. Ibid., 269.

14. Ibid., 287.

15. Ibid., 294.

16. Ibid., 296

17. Dana Milbank, "Curtains Ordered for Media Coverage of Returning Coffins," *Washington Post*, 21 October 2003.

CHAPTER SIX: GERALDO TO JESSICA: THE SHOW CONTINUES

1. Mohammed Odeh Al-Rehaief with Jeff Coplon, *Because Each Life is Precious: Why an Iraqi Man Risked Everything for Private Jessica Lynch* (New York: HarperCollins Publishers, 2003), 33.

2. Ibid.

3. Peter Baker, "Iraqi Man Risked All to Help Free American Soldier," *Washington Post*, 4 April, 2003.

4. Richard A. Serrano and Mark Fineman, "Army Describes What Went Wrong for Jessica Lynch's Unit," *Los Angeles Times*, 10 July 2003.

CHAPTER SEVEN: PATRIOT GAMES

1. Josh Rushing, *Mission Al Jazeera: Build a Bridge, Seek the Truth, Change the World* (New York: Palgrave Macmillan, 2007), 50.

2. Joshua Green, "The Rove Presidency," *The Atlantic*, September 2007.

3. Michael Wolff, "Live from Doha," *New York*, 7–14 April 2003.
4. Michael Wolff, "My Big Fat Question," *New York*, 21 April 2003.
5. Ibid.
6. Peter Spiegel, "A Hawk with Ruffled Feathers," *Financial Times*, 10 October 2003.
7. Ibid.
8. David Barstow, "Behind TV Analysts, Pentagon's Hidden Hand," *New York Times*, 24 April 2008.
9. Ralph Peters, *Beyond Baghdad: Postmodern War and Peace* (Mechanicsburg, PA: Stackpole Books, 2003), xxi.

CHAPTER EIGHT: THE POLITICAL THEATER OF WAR
1. Bob Woodward, *State of Denial* (New York: Simon & Schuster, 2006), 186.
2. Ibid.
3. Howard Kurtz, "For Media After Iraq, A Case of Shell Shock—Battle Assessment," *Washington Post*, 28 April 2003.
4. Ibid.
5. Thomas Ricks, "Reduction in U.S. Troops Eyed for '04—Gradual Exit Strategy Tied to Iraq's Stability," *Washington Post*, 19 October 2003.

CHAPTER NINE: WASHINGTON ON THE EUPHRATES
1. Rajiv Chandrasekaran, *Imperial Life in the Emerald City* (New York: Alfred A. Knopf, 2006), 10.
2. Ibid.
3. Joan Shorenstein Center on the Press, Politics, and Public Policy, *The Iraq War and the Press*, first panel, 20 September 2007.
4. Chandrasekaran, *Imperial Life in the Emerald City*, 68.
5. Shorenstein Center on the Press, first panel.
6. Ibid.
7. Farnaz Fassihi, "From Baghdad: A Wall Street Journal Reporter's E-Mail to Friends," *www.commondreams.org*, 30 September 2004.
8. Bing West, *No True Glory: A Frontline Account of the Battle for Fallujah* (New York: Bantam Books), 3.
9. Ibid., 321–22.
10. Seymour M. Hersch, "Torture At Abu Ghraib: American soldiers brutalized Iraqis. How far up does the responsibility go?" *The New Yorker*, 10 May 2004.
11. *The Military-Media Relationship 2005: How the Armed Forces, Journalists, and the Public View Coverage of Military Conflict* (Chicago: McCormick Tribune Foundation, 2005), 21.
12. Eric Schmitt, "Career of General in Charge During Abu Ghraib May End," *New York Times*, 5 January 2006.

CHAPTER TEN: "WAR IS ABOUT KILLING PEOPLE"
1. Stanley Karnow, *Vietnam: A History* (New York: Penguin Books, 1984), 561.
2. Ibid.
3. *Reporting Vietnam—Part One: American Journalism, 1959–1969* (New York: Library Classics of the United States, 1998), 58-1,582.

4. Col. Oliver North, "Vietnam and Iraq: Myth vs. Reality," www.foxnews.com, 27 October 2006.
5. Christopher Hitchens, "Fighting Words: Beating a Dead Parrot," www.slate.com, 31 January 2005.
6. "The Iraq War and the Press," Joan Shorenstein Center on the Press, Politics and Public Policy, second panel, 20 September 2007.
7. Ibid.
8. *The Military-Media Relationship 2005*, 24–26.
9. Robin Wright, "From the Desk of Donald Rumsfeld . . . In Sometimes-Brusque 'Snowflakes,' He Shared Worldview, Shaped Policy," *Washington Post*, 1 November 2007.
10. Howard Kurtz, "Ultimately, Newspapers Can't Move the Earth," *Washington Post*, 22 August 2004.

CHAPTER ELEVEN: THE BLOG OF WAR

1. Nicolas Lemann, "Right Hook," *The New Yorker*, 29 August 2005.
2. Ron Hutcheson, "Media Caught in the Crossfire Over Iraq War—the Left Accuses Journalists of Sanitizing Events, While the Right Says They Ignore Progress," *Philadelphia Inquirer*, 21 August 2005.
3. Jonathan Finer and Doug Struck, "Bloggers, Money Now Weapons in the Information War: U.S. Recruits Advocates to the Front, Pays Iraqi TV Stations for Coverage," *Washington Post*, 26 December 2005.
4. "Is the Conflict in Iraq 'Civil War'?" Compiled by Annie Schleicher for *NewsHour Extra*, 29 November 2006.
5. Peter Hardin, "Webb: Iraq Situation 'An Occupation'?" *Richmond Times-Dispatch*, 3 May 2007.
6. Rick Maze, "No More GWOT, House Committee Decrees," www.militarytimes.com, 3 April 2007.

CHAPTER TWELVE: AS HE LAY DYING

1. Damien Cave and James Glanz, "In a New Joint U.S.-Iraqi Patrol, the Americans Go First," *New York Times*, 25 January 2007.
2. Damien Cave, "Man Down': When One Bullet Alters Everything," *New York Times*, 29 January 2007.
3. Michael Hedges and James Pinkerton, "Images of Dying Soldier Renew War Coverage Debate," *Houston Chronicle*, 31 January 2007.

CHAPTER THIRTEEN: "GOING TO BAGHDAD! WOOHOO!"

1. Cesar G. Soriano, "General: Attack May Light Fuse," *USA Today*, 14 June 2007.
2. Paul E. Steiger, "Read All About It: How newspapers got into such a fix, and where they go from here," *Wall Street Journal*, 29 December 2007.

CHAPTER FIFTEEN: NEXT STOP: THE GREEN ZONE

1. Tom Wolfe, *Radical Chic & Mau Mauing the Flak Catchers* (New York: Farrar, Straus & Giroux, Inc. 1971), 132.

Selected Bibliography

Al-Rehaief, Mohammed Odeh, with Jeff Coplon. *Because Each Life Is Precious: Why an Iraqi Man Risked Everything for Private Jessica Lynch.* New York: Harper-Collins Publishers Inc., 2003.

Atkinson, Rick. *In the Company of Soldiers.* New York: Henry Holt and Co., 2004.

Cameron, Garry M. *Last to Know, First to Go: The Marine Corps Combat Correspondents.* Capistrano Beach, CA: Charger Books, 1988.

Chambers, John Whiteclay. *The Oxford Guide to American Military History.* New York: Oxford University Press, 1999.

Chandrasekaran, Rajiv. *Imperial Life in the Emerald City.* New York: Alfred A. Knopf, 2006.

Evans, Harold. *War Stories: Reporting in the Time of Conflict from the Crimea to Iraq.* Boston: Bunker Hill Publishing, 2003.

Fialka, John J. *Hotel Warriors: Covering the Gulf War.* Baltimore, MD: The Johns Hopkins University Press, 1991.

Gilbert, G. M. *Nuremberg Diary.* New York: Da Capo Press Inc., 1995.

Gordon, Michael R., and Bernard E. Trainor. *Cobra II: The Inside Story of the Invasion and Occupation of Iraq.* New York: Vintage Books, 2006.

Karnow, Stanley. *Vietnam: A History.* New York: Penguin Books, 1984.

Knightley, Philip. *The First Casualty: The War Correspondent as Hero and Myth-Maker from the Crimea to Iraq.* Baltimore, MD: The Johns Hopkins University Press, 2004.

McCormick Tribune Foundation. *The Military-Media Relationship 2005: How the Armed Forces, Journalists and the Public View coverage of Military Conflict.* Chicago: McCormick Tribune Foundation, 2005.

Orwell, George. *A Collection of Essays.* New York: Anchor Books: 1954.

Peters, Ralph. *Beyond Baghdad: Postmodern War and Peace.* Mechanicsburg, PA: Stackpole Books, 2003.

Reporting Vietnam. Pt. 1: *American Journalism, 1959–1969.* New York: Library Classics of the United States, 1998.

Ricks, Thomas E. *Fiasco: The American Military Adventure in Iraq.* New York: The Penguin Press, 2006.

Rushing, Josh. *Mission Al Jazeera: Build a Bridge, Seek the Truth, Change the World.* New York: Palgrave Macmillan, 2007.

Sweeney, Michael S. *The Military and the Press: An Uneasy Truce.* Evanston, IL: Northwestern University Press, 2006.

Swanberg, W. A. *Citizen Hearst: A Biography of William Randolph Hearst.* New York: Charles Scribner's Sons, 1961.

West, Bing. *No True Glory: A Frontline Account of the Battle for Fallujah.* New York: Bantam Books, 2005.

Woodward, Bob. *Plan of Attack.* New York: Simon & Schuster, 2004.

Woodward, Bob. *State of Denial.* New York: Simon & Schuster, 2006.

Wolfe, Tom. *Radical Chic & Mau-Mauing the Flak Catchers.* New York: Bantam, 1971.

Acknowledgments

This book would never have been written without the encouragement, advice, and understanding of scores of people in the military and the media and in my life. The initial idea to write about the war coverage came from Christopher Evans, history editor at Stackpole Books. Chris's steady guidance and good humor throughout have helped me survive the inevitable ups and downs of research and writing. His able assistant, David Reisch, helped me stay on track and handle the many details that make up this work, including sorting through the pile of photographs I brought back from Iraq.

Military writer David Danelo, also a Stackpole author, showed great wisdom in how he encouraged me to get out into the field to experience embedded reporting.

U.S. Army Maj. Armando Hernandez of the Combined Press Information Center in Baghdad helped me traverse the military's labyrinth of rules and regulations for embedding. U.S. Marine Maj. Cliff Gilmore provided the connection to meet the practitioner of military public affairs profiled here, his friend Maj. Jeff Pool.

I am deeply indebted to Jeff Pool, who was public-affairs director for Multinational Force West in Fallujah, along with his bright staff, who exhibited a high degree of professionalism and humor. Lts. Shawn Mercer and Roger Hollenbeck, along with Cpl. Chris Stankiewicz, were particularly helpful and patient with the intruder in their midst.

U.S. Marine Brig. Gen. John Allen took time out to explain the subtleties of the culture of Anbar Province, including the correct way of eating lamb and goat with Sunni sheiks. General Allen also allowed me to accompany him to Haditha for a fascinating summit between local and provincial leaders. Maj. Gen. W. E. Gaskin also provided an informative interview at Camp Fallujah.

Damien Cave, a reporter at the *New York Times*'s Baghdad bureau, and freelance photographer Bob Nickelsberg patiently discussed their difficult and dangerous coverage of the "surge" of American forces in early 2007. Their insights helped me better explain the tough choices facing journalists under fire, both in the field and back home. Michael Hedges, managing editor of *The Examiner* in Washington, provided his own insights into the life of a combat correspondent.

Longtime friend Rick Atkinson of the *Washington Post* was generous with his time describing his weeks with Gen. David Petraeus and the 101st Airborne Division, which he later documented so well in his combat memoir, *In the Company of Soldiers*. Rex Bowman of the *Richmond Times-Dispatch* gave me a gripping account of his embedded experience with the Marines.

I was helped immeasurably by the reporting and analysis in the *Washington Post*—especially its media critic, Howard Kurtz—and by the *New York Times*, *USA Today*, and other major newspapers. *Bill Moyers Journal*'s "Buying the War" provided a helpful summary of the widespread failure of the mainstream media.

Jamie McIntyre, CNN's senior Pentagon correspondent, gave me an inside look at his coverage of Donald Rumsfeld and the early days of the war. Other veteran journalists and commentators, from Jim Lehrer of PBS to Oliver North of Fox, also shared their own unique perspectives. This group included Josh Rushing, the former Marine Corps spokesman who became a commentator for *Al Jazeera*.

Former Marine Corps Commandant Gen. James L. Jones, my first cousin, provided his own overview of the recent history of military-media relations.

No one exploring a topic this broad and complex can function without assistance from resourceful friends such as Kathy Albers, research librarian at the *Richmond Times-Dispatch*, and reporter Linda Dunham, whose bibliographic skills are nonpareil.

U.S. Army PFC Matthew MacLean, whom I met on the way to Baghdad, remains a long-distance correspondent who provides one soldier's perspective from the war zone. Bill Bergman, president of The Bergman Group in Richmond, Virginia, gave me a refuge to keep writing.

Finally, I would like to thank my three children—Lauren, Chief, and Mary—who supported me every day and kept my spirits up. And to my biggest encourager and editor, my wife, Deborah, I would like to express my deepest thanks and love.

Index